LOSER TAKE ALL

ELECTION FRAUD AND THE SUBVERSION OF DEMOCRACY, 2000-2008

★

EDITED BY MARK CRISPIN MILLER

IG PUBLISHING

Brooklyn, New York

Please direct inquires to:

Ig Publishing
178 Clinton Avenue
Brooklyn, NY 11205

"The News Media and Theft of the 2000 Election" adapted from David W.
Moore, *How to Steal An Election: The Inside Story of How George Bush's Brother
and FOX Network Miscalled the 2000 Election and Changed the Course of History*
(Nation Books, 2006), printed with permission of Perseus Books Group.

Diebold and Max Cleland's "Loss" in Georgia by Robert F. Kennedy, Jr.
Originally published in *Rolling Stone*, September 2006 as "Will the Next
Election Be Hacked." Reprinted with permission of the author.

Library of Congress Cataloging-in-Publication Data

Miller, Mark Crispin.
  Loser take all : election fraud and the subversion of democracy, 2000-2008 /
edited
by Mark Crispin Miller.
     p. cm.
  ISBN-13: 978-0-9788431-4-4
  ISBN-10: 0-9788431-4-2
  1. Elections--Corrupt practices--United States--History--21st century. I.
Title.
  JK1994.M63 2008
  324.973'0931--dc22
                              2008005891

CONTENTS

Introduction: Common Sense
Mark Crispin Miller
1

INTRODUCTION:
COMMON SENSE

★

MARK CRISPIN MILLER

For years, it was an open secret that the Bush administration had its own ideas about the rule of law, and, in particular, a fierce reactionary grudge against the U.S. Constitution. What made such high extremism an open secret was the deferential silence of the whole Establishment: i.e., the press, the Democratic Party (with very few exceptions), and those odd Republicans—moderates, libertarians and non-apocalyptic evangelicals—who kept their qualms about Bush/Cheney to themselves. As long as Big Money liked what Bush et al. were doing, the Establishment obligingly ignored his un-American activities, which, meanwhile, preoccupied the blogosphere, indie radio (as well as certain shows on Air America) and other lowly, heated forums, as well as countless homes and other private haunts.

Since 2005, however, some within "the liberal media," and certain leading members of both parties, have increasingly taken aim at Bush & Co.'s radical betrayals of our founding revolution. By and large, such censure has been far too mild, and also too selective, as this government's belated critics mostly rail at just one scandal at a time (ignoring others just as bad, or worse), and then move on as if it hadn't happened; nor do they dare "connect the dots" between the scandals, so as to build the sort of large and devastating case that Tom

Paine would certainly have made if he were here today.* Moreover, much of this late criticism has dealt less with Bush & Co.'s defiance of the Constitution than with his team's alleged "incompetence," as in Baghdad post-invasion, and New Orleans pre- and post-Katrina. Such complaint suggests that Bush's problem, and therefore America's, is merely technical and managerial, not civic and, in the most important sense, political.

And yet, however insufficiently, this random and diffuse response has helped to keep us, or some of us, alert to most of Bush & Co.'s major strikes against the Constitution. Dick Cheney's overt drive to turn the U.S. president into an emperor, above the law, ultimately moved the press and Senate—especially the Republicans—to speak up on behalf of checks and balances, which Bush has trashed in every way, on every front, conducting foreign *and* domestic policy without consulting Congress, and through his unprecedented use of signing statements (1100 at last count, "almost twice as many as all previous presidents put together," as *Raw Story* has observed).[1] Less audibly, the administration's vast abuses of our civil liberties have roused Establishment protest, with (maverick) figures such as Senator Arlen Specter defending the essential right of habeas corpus, and many august voices (briefly) speaking out against Bush/Cheney's wholesale violation of the Fourth Amendment, through mass surveillance of our phone calls and emails, our libraries and schools, and on and on.[2]

Bush/Cheney's routine use of torture on its "detainees" abroad, ostensibly to garner vital information for the "war on terror," has also been condemned by leading journalists and certain politicians, not just because such methods lead to false "confessions," but because they barbarously

---

* There have, of course, been notable exceptions, such as Senator Robert Byrd and, in the House, John Conyers and Ron Paul; and, in the media (although not really of it), Bill Moyers at PBS, Paul Krugman and Bob Herbert at *The New York Times,* and the rare Keith Olbermann at MSNBC—as well as Stephen Colbert, who makes his patriotic case satirically on Comedy Central and elsewhere.

violate the Constitution's ban on "cruel and unusual punishment" (as is the growing use of tasers by U.S. police—a practice that has spiked since 9/11).[3] And there has even been some mainstream outcry over Bush & Co.'s encouragement of theocratic efforts by the so-called Christian right, in blatant opposition to the Establishment Clause of the First Amendment. As early as January, 2003, *USA Today* ran a news analysis entitled "Bush's agenda walks the church-state line," and since then other voices have been raised against the Christianist crusades to "save" Teri Schiavo, force creationism (or "Intelligent Design") into public school curricula, mandate abstinence-based sex education (even though it doesn't work), and, worst of all, transform our military bases and academies into hives of violent evangelism.[4]

Although largely weak and intermittent in itself, this late barrage of mainstream protest and/or critical reporting has been powerfully augmented by a lot of first-rate books and movies—genuinely patriotic works that pull no punches in decrying Bush & Co.'s assault on our republican traditions. Such necessary works have been too numerous for me to name them here, and so a very few examples must suffice. The scourge of torture by the US government has been vividly exposed in movies like *Rendition*, the documentary *Taxi to the Dark Side*, and on episodes of "Law & Order" and "The West Wing" (a show that nailed many of Bush/Cheney's crimes against the Constitution). Several cogent books have probed the U.S. theocratic movement (which, despite its recent headlessness, is far from dead): Michelle Goldberg's *Kingdom Coming*, Kevin Phillips's *American Theocracy*, Damon Linker's *The Theocons*, and, on the specific danger of a Christianist paramilitary, Jeremy Scahill's *Blackwater: The Rise of the World's Most Powerful Mercenary Army*. Other books have carefully, yet bluntly, noted the explicit fascist threat posed by the Bush regime: Naomi Wolf's *The End of America*, Joe Conason's *It Can Happen Here*, John Dean's *Conservatives Without Conscience* and *Broken Government*, Chris Hedges's *American Fascists*, and Al Gore's *The Assault on Reason*. Such bold works have resonated through TV and radio, making clear that it *can* happen here (just as the Framers understood), and that, in fact, it started happening some time ago.

• • •

Of course, the guardians of the Establishment reflexively laugh off the thought that fascism could ever come to the United States. For it *can't* happen here, as this is a democracy, and, at that, the greatest one the world has ever known, far tidier and more sophisticated than the messy, backward versions that keep blowing up in such combustible locales as Mexico and Pakistan and Kenya. And so, whatever the excesses of this White House, they cannot possibly amount to any sort of conscious, systematic drive against democracy, because democracy in these United States is perfect. Bush/Cheney, therefore, may claim that their word is law, and that their authority derives from God, and that they can make whatever wars they like, and for as long as they might think it takes, and jail and torture anyone they want to, and keep us all under complete and permanent surveillance; and yet such regal claims, however troubling each may be, certainly do not add up to a negation of American democracy, and it's insane to argue that they do.

That rosy view accounts for the Establishment's peculiar blindness toward one major aspect of Bush/Cheney's rule. According to "the liberal media" and both the parties, there is, anomalously, one big bright spot on the U.S. civic landscape: our national elections. In this dark new millennium, while every other institution of American democracy has been corrupted, or disabled, by fraud, bribery, cronyism, covert propaganda, police brutality and/or extreme judicial activism, those biennial contests have all been just as honest as the day is long. Sure, there have been glitches in a few of those machines (computers *can* be unpredictable), and some administrative foul-ups (those old geezers at the polling places *can* be dim), and, no doubt, *some* (minor) mischief "on both sides." But, according to the press, there is no evidence of any big bad deeds that might have changed the vote-counts in 2000 or afterward.

First of all, Bush beat Al Gore in Florida back in 2000, and so became our 43rd American president. True, the vote-counts there were halted, maybe wrongly, by the Supreme Court, whose *Bush v. Gore* is, no doubt, oddly reasoned. But all those votes were ultimately counted, and they added up to a decisive, although razor-thin, advantage for the governor—primarily, of course, because Ralph Nader had leached scores of crucial votes away from Gore, particularly in South Florida. Thus the Democrats were beaten by a cranky independent "spoiler," and also by our creaky old two-tier election system, since Gore, who won more votes than Bush, finally lost in the Electoral College. Throughout the thirty-six day post-election brawl, moreover, the Democrats were also outmaneuvered on the ground by Bush's quicker-witted operatives, who seized each moment's opportunity while Gore's men slept (in Washington, flying in and out of Florida as if attempting multiple one-day vacations there).

Then came November 5, 2002—and Bush/Cheney's party triumphed once again, reclaiming control of the Senate after having lost it in May of 2001, when Senator Jim Jeffords of Vermont left the GOP in protest over its hard rightist line. The party now enjoyed a comfortable margin in the Senate (while gaining no seats in the House), thanks to unexpected wins in Georgia, where Saxby Chambliss beat Max Cleland; Colorado, where Wayne Allard beat Tom Strickland; New Hampshire, where John Sununu beat Jeanne Shaheen; and Minnesota, where Norm Coleman beat Walter Mondale. (Mondale was a proxy for the popular Paul Wellstone, who had died when his campaign plane crashed on October 25.) As all four wins surprised the pollsters, who had mostly put the Democrats ahead by several points, the press exultantly ascribed that sweep to the electoral wizardry of Bush and, especially, Karl Rove—who had "aced their midterms," as *Time* jubilantly put it.[*5]

---

[*] The results were odd in other ways. It is unusual, first of all, for the party of a President to make Congressional gains in off-year elections. Also, in late November, Harris noted that the party's senatorial advance had somehow left the standing of all sides anomalously unaffected:

> This survey also finds, rather surprisingly, that the ratings of the president, of his senior cabinet members and of the two parties in Congress are virtually unchanged since before the November elections. This—like Sherlock Holmes' famous "dog that did not bark"—is not what would

Rove's brilliant tactics awed the press. "His name was not on any ballot," wrote Elizabeth Bumiller and David Sanger in "The Strategist," a rapt post-mortem in *The New York Times*, "but Karl Rove, the West Wing mastermind who has plotted for years to bring George W. Bush and the Republican Party to dominance, emerged as one of the biggest winners in the midterm elections of 2002."[6] Rove scored by sending Bush out on "a 10,000-mile, 17-city, 15-state blitz" the last few days of the campaign; by zapping Minnesota with a livid propaganda drive attacking Wellstone's mourners for their booing of Trent Lott at the late senator's memorial; by hitting Georgia with attack ads that portrayed Max Cleland as a traitor for opposing the creation of the Department of Homeland Security (the tactic that put Saxby Chambliss in the Senate); and countless other sly strokes of electioneering genius.

Two years later, on November 2, 2004, Bush/Cheney triumphed yet again, winning re-election notwithstanding their high disapproval ratings. This time, moreover, Bush "aced" the popular election, beating Kerry by 3 million votes, and garnering over 11 million more votes than he'd won four years before. He also won, of course, in the Electoral College, thanks to his dramatic showing in Ohio, where he squeaked by with a margin of 118,000 votes. The victory in Ohio, and Bush/Cheney's big jump nationwide, were made possible, according to the dominant Establishment narrative, by the unprecedented turnout of the Christian right. The voters in Ohio, and elsewhere, were moved primarily by "moral values"—above all, hatred of gay marriage—and, after that, the fear of terrorism. That huge wave of "faith-based" ballots gave the re-elected president a mandate for his further plans: "political capital," as

---

have been expected. Normally a resounding election victory, such as the gains made by the Republicans this year, would lift the winners. But virtually nothing has changed since October.

"Majorities of Voters in Mid-Term Elections Were Ticket Splitters," *The Harris Poll*, #62 (11/21/02), http://www.harrisinteractive.com/harris_poll/index.asp?PID=341.

he put it two days after the election. Although there were some charges of Republican malfeasance in Ohio, they turned out to be mere wishful speculation by sore losers and the usual mad hatters, the Establishment claimed. Much was made, for instance, of the discrepancy between the vote-count in Ohio and the exit polls conducted there, but there was finally nothing to it, as those exit polls were wrong.

In any case, the theory of Republican election fraud was mooted by the Democratic comeback in the midterm races of 2006. Certainly, if Bush's party had the power to fix elections, the Democrats would not have knocked off six pro-Bush incumbent senators—including top guns like George Allen in Virginia, and Rick Santorum in Pennsylvania—and picked up an amazing twenty-nine seats in the House. It was, of course, the Democrats who gave the GOP that "thumpin'" (as Bush colorfully referred to it). The press hailed Rahm Emanuel and Chuck Schumer as the canny "architects" of that great victory, lionizing them as it had lionized the now defunct Karl Rove. Although Rove himself was still surprisingly upbeat ("The Republican philosophy is alive and well and likely to reemerge in the majority in 2008," he told *The Washington Post*), the press was near unanimous in claiming that Bush/Cheney's day was done.[7] "The realists" were now in charge (noted *Time*'s Joe Klein), as the Democrats were "now equal partners in power" (noted *Newsweek*'s Eleanor Clift).[8] Standing in the offices of the Democratic Congressional Campaign Committee, "watching young aides with markers erase and replace the latest election numbers on a white board," *The New York Times*'s Matt Bai observed that they were "effectively wiping away what remained of Bush's influence in Washington."[9]

Thus, in every national election from 2000 on, "the system worked." Such is the tale told by the media, and retold time and time again by both Republicans and Democrats—and also, with very few exceptions, by the left. That Bush was duly re-elected has been argued, often hotly, by *The Nation*, *Mother Jones*, Salon, TomPaine.com and Michael Moore, among others. The tale has even been confirmed, if tacitly, by all those trenchant critics of Bush/Cheney's radical crusade against the Constitution: John

Dean, Chris Hedges, Joe Conason, the excellent Naomi Wolf—and, startlingly, Al Gore, who seems to be assured that the Republicans have played it fair and square in our elections, notwithstanding the ferocity of their "assault on reason" (and their treatment of himself and, more important, those who tried to vote for him). Such patriots either say nothing on the subject of elections, or gloomily concede that Bush and Cheney were indeed the people's choice.

In short, *everyone* (apparently) subscribes to the official story. Thus that comfy tale now has, for many good Americans, the ring of truth—a fact that is at once quite understandable and deeply terrifying. For that familiar tale is simply false, its every last assertion either wrong, exaggerated, or irrelevant. And if this counter-claim itself sounds like a Big Lie or a wild delusion, it is not because there is no evidence to back it up. As the essays in this book make very clear (and as many other writings have already done), there is a rising flood of solid evidence that Bush/Cheney have subverted our elections (with the collusion—surely passive—of the Democrats). Rather, the counter-claim sounds false, and the official tale believable, because the truth is not just inconvenient for a lot of powerful interests, but also just too hard for us, or some of us, to bear.

Certainly the truth has scared away the press, whose members have consistently behaved as if it isn't so, like upscale diners too polite to comment on the screams and gunshots coming from the kitchen. Take the notion that Gore "lost" in Florida. In fact, as David W. Moore and Lance DeHaven-Smith remind us here, Gore *won* in Florida—a finding made, at great expense, by the National Opinion Research Center (at the University of Chicago), whose analysts meticulously *counted every vote.*[10] (From its own study, the *Miami Herald* also found that Gore had won.) And yet, when NORC released its study two months after 9/11, the media reported it—or spun it—as official confirmation that *Bush* won: a line that both absolved the Bush Republicans and mooted the Supreme Court's interference.

"Study of Disputed Florida Ballots Finds Justices Did not Cast the Deciding Vote," proclaimed the *New York Times.*[11] "Study: Recounts

8

Would have Favored Bush," announced the *Washington Post*.[12] "In Election Review, Bush Wins Without Supreme Court Help," declared the *Wall Street Journal*.[13] "Bush Still Had Votes to Win in a Recount, Study Finds," asserted the *Los Angeles Times*.[14] "Florida Recount Study: Bush Still Wins," claimed CNN.com.[15] Even the non-corporate press joined in the celebration, as the *St Petersburg Times* ran the terse headline, "Recount: Bush."[16] Thus the press *itself* found that Bush won, despite the very evidence that they were now "reporting," while burying, deep down in their articles, the awful truth that Gore had won in Florida, and therefore was the rightful president of the United States.

Perhaps that journalistic fiction was (unconsciously) dictated by the "war on terror," which Bush could not have waged so brilliantly if We the People thought that he was not our president. However, such a strategy cannot explain why journalists continue to assert that Gore lost Florida. The myth of his defeat is weirdly incontestable. Writing in *The New York Times*, Walter Gibbs and Sarah Lyall recall Gore's "loss in the muddled 2000 presidential election," and *The Wall Street Journal*'s Jackie Calmes claims that Gore "lost in the Electoral College after a U.S. Supreme Court ruling," while *The Washington Post*'s Peter Baker offers this heroic retrospective: "The winner of that struggle went on to capture the White House and to become a wartime leader now heading toward the final year of a struggling presidency. The loser went on to reinvent himself from cautious politician to hero of the activist left now honored as a man of peace."[17] Some journalists have gone further in revising history. According to *The Los Angeles Times*'s Michael Finnegan, Gore "lost the presidency in the Electoral College after the lengthy and hotly contested Florida recount—which went all the way to the Supreme Court—determined that Bush had won the state by fewer than 600 votes." That's news indeed, since the only recount of the votes occurred months after *Bush v. Gore*, and it "determined" that Bush lost.

Contrary to the official tale, Bush/Cheney's "victory" in December of 2000 was no deft improvisation, but, as Lance DeHaven-Smith makes clear, the upshot of a long conspiracy—there is no other word for it—to slash the Democratic vote before the fact, through covert and illegal means; Jeb Bush and Katharine Harris were its fierce co-managers, whose job it was to cut, through varied means, the number of those votes that finally would be there to count (or not). That plot was thoroughly exposed in formal hearings by the U.S. Civil Rights Commission— whose findings were ignored completely by the press. (The BBC's Greg Palast was the only journalist who nailed Bush/Harris's collusion with Bush/Cheney.) While Jeb Bush largely ran that operation, furthermore, he also personally called the contest for his older brother on November 7, 2000—a revelation made by David W. Moore, who, as a top pollster, was right there in the trenches on Election Night, and saw exactly how Jeb's mere say-so, bolstered by no data whatsoever, led FOX News, the other networks, *and* the Voter News Service (the statisticians covering the race) to claim officially—and groundlessly—that Bush had won.

Eager not to look too deeply into that election, the press ignored the disenfranchisement of tens of thousands of Floridians, and there-fore focused only on those ballots that the Bush machine had not pre-empted, altered or destroyed. Thus the journalists neglected the real story, while playing up the superficial drama of Ralph Nader's role as "spoiler"—a story as simplistic as it is irrelevant, however many Demo-crats still can't get over it; for Team Bush would have "won" that contest if Ralph Nader never had been born, as Jeb's machine kept coming up with still more ballots for his brother, and would have kept discovering them until the job was done. (There is scant evidence, moreover, that Nader's votes would otherwise have gone to Gore.) In short, Nader's candidacy served the press both as a mere distraction from the Bush machine's malfeasance, and—more important—as a handy *rationale* for Gore's "defeat."

After Florida, the Bush Republicans continued stealing our elections, as the press (and Democrats) did nothing, other than repeat the guilty party's cover story. Take that unexpected sweep of victories in 2002, when Bush and Rove "aced their midterms." As Robert F. Kennedy, Jr. points out here, there is good reason to suspect the outcome of two Democratic re-electoral bids in Georgia, where Senator Max Cleland

and Governor Roy Barnes were both startlingly defeated. Those upsets, and others felling Georgia Democrats, followed the stealthy and illegal application of an unauthorized software patch to some 5,000 Diebold e-voting machines in two heavily Democratic counties. That Diebold was effectively in charge of Georgia's voting system went unmentioned by (and was no doubt unknown to) reporters, who offered two reasons for the turnarounds. That there was not a shred of evidence for either claim did not detract from their utility: Cleland was done in by those attack ads subtly charging him with treason (although the popular war hero—a triple amputee—had led by five points just before Election Day, then lost by seven points); and Barnes went down still more dramatically—eleven points ahead before Election Day, he lost by five—because he'd changed the state's beloved Confederate flag, thereby infuriating countless Georgians (a statewide bitterness "so private," marveled *The New York Times*, "that no polls picked it up").[18]

That year, Diebold's wares were also used to count the votes in Colorado, where Wayne Allard, down by nine points against Tom Strickland, won by five; and in New Hampshire, where John Sununu, down by one point against Jeanne Shaheen, won by five points. (Sununu was helped also by the RNC's phone-jamming operation down in Manchester and other cities, where party agents blocked the Democrats' get-out-the-vote drive with 800 hang-ups—a venture evidently paid for by Jack Abramoff, with funds defrauded from his Choctaw clients.) While Diebold's product was not used in Minnesota, there are also questions about Norm Coleman's victory there, as he was trailing Walter Mondale by five points prior to Election Day, then won by 2.2 points (a jump too big, perhaps, to have been caused by Trent Lott's putative ordeal at Paul Wellstone's memorial).*

---

* Of course, such pre-election polls per se do not prove anything, as pollsters err and voters change their minds. The strongest evidence lies in the "unadjusted" exit polls that come out on Election Day. It was, therefore, unusually difficult to analyze the vote-counts in the 2002 elections, as there were no exit poll results released that year.

Thus Karl Rove's reputation as the "mastermind" of all those wins was based on a naïve conception of his actual modus operandi. While the press portrayed him merely as a genius at hardball campaigning—smearing, spinning, getting out the vote—Rove's doings were far darker than that image would suggest. As Larisa Alexandrovna tells us, Rove clearly "masterminded" the destruction of Don Siegelman, Alabama's governor until his re-electoral "defeat" in 2002—a loss based on election fraud in Baldwin County, as Jim Gundlach demonstrates in his analysis. For speaking out about that race and other sticky subjects, Siegelman was soon railroaded by the GOP in Alabama, and, on June 27, 2007, sent to federal prison on trumped-up charges, gagged by the judge who put him there, and, on a technicality, unable to appeal his conviction.

Siegelman's ordeal, as of this writing, has made little news beyond the Alabama press; MSNBC's Dan Abrams did a strong hour on the case, and there was a passing reference to it in a *New York Times* editorial on December 26, 2007. Neither mentioned the election, though.

Then there was Bush/Cheney's "re-election" in 2004—which, in fact, was not effected by the Christian right, as there were far too few of them to pull it off. Voters, furthermore, were not especially concerned with "moral values"—a major issue in the minds of only 9 percent of the electorate—nor, certainly, did "we" come out to vote against gay marriage, which thus excited only 3 percent. Nor did fear of terrorism drive a lot of people to the polls, as only 9 percent cited that stimulus. (These figures come from Pew's final post-election poll.) The issues uppermost on voters' minds were, above all, the war in Iraq, and then jobs and the economy—not the most propitious topics for Bush/Cheney, who, moreover, went into the race with disapproval ratings in the mid- to high Forties: higher than LBJ's in 1968, and higher than Jimmy Carter's in 1980.

As these essays make crystal clear, Bush/Cheney's "re-election" was a masterpiece of fraud—*not* committed only in Ohio, furthermore, but nationwide. In "The Urban Legend," Michael Collins demonstrates that Bush/Cheney lost support among both rural and small-town voters—the critical components of his base—and therefore relied on an imaginary outpouring of urban whites, while millions of real votes were, and still are, unaccounted for. Although Team Bush used every kind of tactic to effect that "victory," e-voting was their primary instrument of fraud. In his essay on the vote in Pima County, Arizona—a state with an extraordinary legacy of rigged elections—Dave Griscom, on the basis of his diligent research with election reform activist John Brakey, carefully analyzes the exquisite method—"hack and stack"—that party operatives employed to make a "blue" precinct look "red," and thereby neutralize the votes of the large Spanish population: 32.5% in Pima County, 29.2% statewide.*

From Brad Friedman and Michael Richardson we get the harrowing pre-history of the 2004 election in Nevada, whose voting system had long since been hijacked by Secretary of State Dean Heller, a party operative (and now a House Republican) colluding with like-minded players at the National Association of State Elections Directors (NASED). That partisan cabal induced Nevada to use the new Sequoia Edge II e-voting machines equipped with VeriVote Printers: the first use of the "voter-verified paper trail" (or VVPAT, about which see below). Although loudly advertised as "fail-proof," the system had failed test after test, and was in fact a hacker's dream; and that vaunted "paper trail" was ineffectual. As activist Patricia Axelrod has charged, the system clearly served Bush/Cheney's "re-election" by screwing up repeatedly in Democratic districts only, thereby helping Bush to "win" by under 22,000 votes (out of 820,000 cast). (More important, the selling of the VVPAT entailed the co-optation of the Election Assistance Commission, which finally turned a blind eye to the system's proven flaws.)

And then there was, of course, Ohio, where Bush/Cheney had re-

---

* Brakey's efforts ultimately led to a landmark lawsuit on behalf of electoral transparency, as Pima County long refused to make its databases publicly available.

portedly prevailed by some 118,000 votes—and where Kerry/Edwards *actually* prevailed by 350,000 votes (at least), or would have, if all would-be voters could have voted, and if all votes were counted. (Such is the modest estimate of Robert F. Kennedy, Jr., who surveyed the evidence in *Rolling Stone*.) As the vast fraud in the Buckeye State was not unique, however, neither did it stop with the subversion of the recount in 2004. Here Bob Fitrakis tells us all that's happened in Ohio, and much that's finally come to light, *since* that infamous election. Not all the news is bad. In March, 2007, two election workers were convicted for trying to rig the recount in Cuyahoga County. Otherwise, the post-election story is unpromising: a referendum to prevent election fraud "defeated" *by* election fraud; the wholesale destruction of millions of ballots from the 2004 election, in defiance of a court order; the passage of a Russian-style "reform" bill (HB3) that, among other things, ends the oversight of e-voting machinery, allows partisans to challenge (i.e., halt) voter registration drives, quintuples the cost of recounts, and *outlaws* challenges to presidential vote counts; and so on. Such steps were clearly meant not just to hide the traces of Ohio's prior crimes against democracy, but, more important, to *prevent* democracy in elections yet to come, primarily by "legal" means.

In other words, what happened in Ohio was not a fluke, but one step in a larger process of mass disenfranchisement: a *national* process, as was obvious in the 2004 election, although the Establishment refused to notice it. Ignoring the preponderance of evidence, the press seized only on the exit polls that had foretold a Kerry win, and arbitrarily shrugged them off as "flawed"—as if the official count were, a priori, unimpeachable. In fact, the press's arguments, or talking points, against the exit polls were highly dubious, as Steve Freeman and Joel Bleifuss have made clear.[19] Even if we overlook those polls, however, the evidence of fraud was overwhelming. Americans reported by the tens of thousands that their votes had been flipped electronically; or that their polling places had too few machines and, therefore, lines so long that voting was impossible; or that they'd been told that they couldn't vote because they hadn't registered (although they had registered) or because they had committed felonies (although they had not); or that their polling sites were closed, or had been moved elsewhere; or that the few machines on hand had broken down, or wouldn't boot up, or, if they used paper, had run out of paper; and so on. With very few exceptions (five or six Republicans claimed that their Bush votes had been flipped to Kerry), *all those voting problems hurt the Democrats*—sufficient proof that the election had been rigged (unless, of course, God said, "Let there be Bush"—and, lo! there was a vast coincidence).

On the 2006 election, the media got the story partly right, yet fundamentally wrong.[20] On the one hand, it was true that the electorate had had it up to here with Bush & Co. But it was *not* true that such disenchantment was so recent, Bush having lost Republican support before his "re-election," as Michael Collins shows us. (By Election Day, 2004, sixty newspapers that had endorsed Bush/Cheney in 2000 were now backing either Kerry/Edwards or None of the Above.)[21] The press, moreover, understated the intensity and sweep of that reaction—which would, in fact, have wrecked the GOP if that fringe party had not rigged so many races. In short, it was, or should have been, not just "a thumpin'" but a rout. Although the Democrats, in other words, had every right to celebrate their wins, that timid party also should have fought for all those further wins that were illicitly denied them; for the evidence suggests that they had actually done better than they think, especially in the House.

In Florida, for instance, four Democratic challengers had solid evidence that their defeats were illegitimate. In Sarasota, Christine Jennings "lost" by fewer than 400 votes to incumbent Vern Buchanan, while there were more than 18,000 undervotes mysteriously cast on the machines deployed in Democratic districts only. In Orlando, Clint Curtis lost by sixteen points to Republican Tom Feeney, although they had been running neck and neck until Election Day. Curtis quickly ran a canvassing campaign throughout his district, collecting signed, sworn affidavits from individual voters, and found that the official count had cheated him by 7-11 percent, which would have changed the outcome of the race. With Curtis's help, candidates John Russell and Frank Gonzalez also canvassed their respective districts, and also found that the official count had been inflated to beef up the GOP. Nationally, Democratic candidates for Congress were disabled by apparent fraud that surely would have been exposed if they had been Republicans: Heather Wilson in New Mexico, Angie Paccione in Colorado, Lois Murphy in Pennsylvania, Francine Busby in California, and, in Ohio, Mary Jo Kilroy and Victoria Wulsin, among others—all defeated narrowly and/or under strange circumstances. There were also major problems with the Senate race in Tennessee, where Harold Ford lost by some 50,000 votes (out of 1,800,000) to Republican Bob Corker, in part because of vote suppression tactics and apparent fraud throughout Memphis and Nashville, two Democratic strongholds.

One of those candidates who was robbed of her apparent victory was Tammy Duckworth, who ran against Republican Peter Roskam for the House seat of GOP warhorse Henry Hyde, retiring after thirty-two years as the U.S. Congressman for Illinois's 6th district. Here Jean Kaczmarek tells of her surreal experience monitoring that race in DuPage County—a Republican stronghold even more corrupt than the old Democratic fiefdom in nearby Cook County. (DuPage County is one of the nation's worst places to vote, according to Bev Harris.) As Kaczmarek vividly observes, that coup was enabled by the county's long subversion of the democratic process—a sordid prior history of cronyism, public records trashed, registrations purged, etc.—and carried out through sundry criminal practices, including the manipulation of the Diebold e-voting machines (in ways recalling what went down in Pima County, Arizona back in 2004).

While fraud was rampant in 2006, however, it is fair to ask exactly how the Democrats could possibly have taken *any* races, if the GOP exerted such control. In "Landslide Denied," Jonathan Simon and Bruce O'Dell answer that key question, and thereby help us understand where we are now. Through close comparative study of the exit polls—i.e., the "weighted" polls that came out on Election Night, and the "adjusted" numbers that came out the following morning—Simon and O'Dell discovered that the party gave itself a 3.9 percent advantage nationwide (but not in Maryland or Pennsylvania, two states where the GOP was poised to charge the *Democrats* with systematic fraud). This would have been accomplished easily by programming the memory cards in the e-voting system. As those machines, by now, were often vigilantly monitored by election reform activists, the party would have had to make that covert change as long as possible before Election Day. The Republicans, moreover, could not give themselves a boost of more than 4 percent, or else their "victory" margins might exceed the margin of error, and raise eyebrows. Thus they had assured themselves a lead that, while it looked good at the time, was finally not enough to make them win. That fake lead was neutralized by two developments beyond the party's reach: a mammoth turnout on Election Day, by millions keen on voting, and newly vigilant against all moves to thwart them; and, no less, a late barrage of devastating news, anomalously played up by the corporate press—Mark Foley's appetite for boys; the CIA's leaked finding that the Iraq war was now "the 'cause celebre' for jihadists" everywhere; Bob Woodward's *State of Denial* (in which, surprisingly, the Great Stenographer depicted Bush-at-War as out to lunch); and the outing of Ted Haggard. Thus the party's "thumpin'" was an odd joint venture by the anti-Bush electorate and the Establishment itself, which clearly had perceived that Bush & Co. was not so good for business.

Meanwhile, the press, fixated on celebrity, gave all the credit to Emanuel and Schumer, who were too busy basking in that adulation (for them, admittedly, a rare experience) to note those races that their party *should* have won. Whereas the Republicans would fight like feral dogs for every seat that they could possibly (or impossibly) lay claim to, the Democrats refused to fight at all. Indeed, the party pressed its obviously cheated candidates to grin and bear it. Those who kept on fighting, amassing evidence of GOP subversion, ultimately hit the wall. Although certain party elders huffed and puffed about the plight of Christine Jennings, they discreetly sold her out; and when Clint Curtis brought his *proof* of fraud to the House Administration Committee, they refused unanimously even to inspect his evidence, much less investigate.

• • •

Thus the Democrats have kept their eyes wide shut to BushCo's civic crime wave ever since it started in 2000. Certainly election fraud per se is nothing new in the United States, both parties having always used illicit methods to seize power, or—more often—keep it. The fraud in this millennium, however, has been something else entirely: a drive against democracy itself, conducted on a scale, and with a technological sophistication, far beyond the wildest dreams of Boss Tweed, old Joe Kennedy or Mayor Daley. Small wonder, then, that Democrats have wanted not to know about it. When Robert Hagan, a Democratic state senator in Youngstown, Ohio, tried to vote for Kerry in 2004, the machine repeatedly flipped his vote to Bush. He informed the Kerry/Edwards campaign. "Leave it alone," they told him. "Don't talk about it. It's not something we want to get out." Then there was my own experience with Kerry, who, in October of 2005, agreed that the election had been stolen, and wondered heatedly at the inaction of his fellow Democrats in Washington. The week before, he said, he had tried to get Chris Dodd to focus on the dangers of electronic voting—and Dodd had bluntly shut him down. "'We looked into it,' he said. 'There's nothing to it!'" Kerry looked at me, amazed: "They're in denial," he said to me, wide-eyed. And yet he too was in denial; for when I spoke about our conversation publicly, a few days later (on Amy Goodman's radio show *Democracy Now!*), his office quickly and categorically denied that he and I had ever talked at all.

Some argued that the senator retreated so that nobody could call him a "sore loser"—a charge that he did mention when we spoke. That explanation is inadequate, however; for if Kerry *actually believed* that the election had been stolen, and fully grasped the implications of that fact, he surely wouldn't care if people called him names for speaking out about it. What silenced him was finally not the fear of loud derision by Rove's troops and/or the corporate press, but the sheer enormity of what had happened. Like Al Gore before him, and like Hillary Clinton, Harry Reid, Nancy Pelosi, Barack Obama, Howard Dean and nearly every other leading Democrat, Kerry cannot go where the appalling truth would have to take him.

Such deep paralysis is complicated. First of all, the hard truth is a violent affront to our most cherished notions of America; and so it's far more comfortable to say, or act as if, it's not the truth—a sort of blindness that afflicts not just the families of alcoholics and the wives of batterers but the citizens of "democratic" nations that are gradually succumbing to the iron fist. And, for those citizens with much to lose, there also are strong social and material concerns. As a longtime Washingtonian and party elder (and a billionaire at that), John Kerry simply isn't built to throw himself into the democratic struggle that this crisis now requires; and neither are most other "Democrats," who care far more about their turf and standing in the party—and, therefore, the party's giant donors—than they do about American democracy. Nor, certainly, are those huge donors interested in seeing We the People in control of the United States: on the contrary. It is *their* consensus, and not ours, that now compels the Democratic Party—and the media, whose centrist stars have also long refused to see what's right before their eyes, because doing so would screw up their careers.

There are, of course, exceptions to the rule, throughout the party and the press—stray idealists who revere this nation's founding principles, and who, therefore, would surely stand up for democracy, despite the pressures from on high. By and large, however, those idealists also cannot see what's really happening because it hurts too much to think that it's been happening here.

And so, on the eve of yet another presidential race, this nation is no longer inching toward democracy, but lurching in the very opposite direction. Although this backward movement started well before Election Day 2000 (with the glimmerings of "Morning of America"), we didn't feel the first big jolt until the post-election crisis of 2000, when the Republicans went brownshirt right before our eyes. There was the mob that stopped the vote-count in Miami-Dade—and, *The New York Times* reported, "trampled, punched or kicked" whoever tried to block its way, while shouting that a thousand angry Cubans would soon be there to help make the point.[22] Although posing as a mere spontaneous assembly of plain citizens ("a bourgeois riot," as *The Wall Street Journal's*

Paul Gigot approvingly described it), that seeming rabble was a corps of party operatives, dispatched by GOP congressman John Sweeney with the help of Tom DeLay.[23] The action worked, as Miami-Dade's canvassing board called off their plan to count the undervotes.

Elsewhere there were other strokes of pseudo-popular "resistance." "Republican supporters waving 'Sore-Loserman' placards, some of them bussed in from outside Florida, jostled and heckled reporters and officials in both Broward and Palm Beach County," *The Guardian* (UK) reported on November 25, 2000. "A brick inscribed 'We would not tolerate an illegal government' was thrown through the windows of Democratic Party offices in Broward County, where one of the recounts resumed yesterday." Meanwhile, up in Washington, a livid horde of party activists laid siege to the Vice Presidential mansion, screaming "Get out of Cheney's house!" all day and through the night, while Al Gore and his family hid inside. It was "an organized effort," Karenna Gore said later. "Some of them were anti-abortion groups, and some of them were pro-gun groups, and some of them—they all had different signs." Among them too was Doro Bush, George W.'s sister, whose moment with the goon squad much amused their mother, Barbara. "'That's Doro!' Mrs. Bush hoots when telling about it. 'She felt better' after yelling at the Gores' house for a while, Mrs. Bush says," *Newsweek* reported later.

Here was an openly fascistic drive against the democratic process: a fact that both "the liberal media" and the Democrats were eager not to see. Beyond some volleys of indignant punditry, the shutdown in Miami-Dade had no consequences—even though the perpetrators' names and faces were all public knowledge—and it quickly slipped right down the memory hole. The U.S. media also largely failed to note those packed busloads of seething true believers in the other counties, and downplayed, or ignored, the mob's harassment of Gore's family in our nation's capital. In November of 2002, Barbara Walters interviewed the Gores for *20/20*, and had them speak at length of their ordeal. ABC then cut that whole exchange, and so the program aired without it.

• • •

As shocking as it was, the Republican Party's thuggery in Florida was actually the least important aspect of Bush/Cheney's opening move against American democracy. Above all, there was *Bush v. Gore*, which, as Paul Lehto argues, was far more than a simple (albeit tortuous) intrusion into just that one election. Despite its claim that it is "not a precedent," that decision radically expanded the Supreme Court's power to *nullify* elections generally—a power that we cannot appeal, exerted by a body that cannot be voted out. Although it strikes a death blow at republican democracy (and, moreover, was the ultimate expression of "judicial activism"), *Bush v. Gore* roused little protest from conservatives *or* liberals, and was soon forgotten by the press and Democrats alike; John Roberts replaced William Rehnquist, and Samuel Alito replaced Sandra Day O'Connor, so that the Court's strong anti-democratic bloc remained intact, ready to resume its drive against our voting rights.

Hearing arguments, in January of 2008, about Indiana's voter ID law—the strictest in the nation—those justices shrugged off the fact that voters lacking photo ID's must then travel to the county seat to get their provisional ballots counted. "County seats aren't very far for people in Indiana," offered Roberts, unaware, perhaps, that such a journey could require a long and costly bus ride for the poor. And Roberts et al. waved away the fact that, throughout Indiana's history, there actually were no known cases of the sort of "voter fraud" that this new law was allegedly intended to prevent: "It's a type of fraud that, because it's fraud, it's hard to detect," reasoned the Chief Justice, apparently invoking Donald Rumsfeld's thought concerning Saddam's huge imaginary arsenal of nukes and poison gas, that "absence of evidence is not evidence of absence." The Court's decision is, as of this writing, due in June of 2008. If they uphold it (an upset is always possible), the cause of voting rights will have been set back fifty years.

While marking the Supreme Court's right to nullify our votes, Bush/Cheney's "victory" was also used to propagate a new distrust of paper ballots counted openly by hand. Having watched the tragicomedy of all those frazzled bureaucrats attempting to decode the Mystery of the Chads, we were informed repeatedly that *paper* was the problem there: a calculated misconception that, as Nancy Tobi argues, helped to make the case for *paperless computerized machines* to count our votes. (They are known technically as DRE machines, for "Direct Recording Electronic.") Thus Americans were sold on the profoundly un-American idea of *secret vote counts*—for computers tabulate invisibly (and no more honestly than their programmers command). From there it was a simple step to call for privatizing our elections, as *both* parties did with equal fervor, although only one of them would benefit. Eager not to see the coup that they were helping to prepare against themselves (and all the rest of us), the Democrats—allied with liberal groups like Common Cause and People for the American Way—pushed staunchly for "election reform" as Bush & Co. had defined it, which meant dumping all that messy paper, and/or those senescent volunteers, in favor of computer systems made and serviced by private companies. Thus the Democrats and liberal groups supported former Representative Bob Ney's Help America Vote Act (HAVA), which mandated the eventual use of e-voting technology in every state.

And so U.S. elections—as intended—soon became opaque, incomprehensible and (obviously) stacked, like corporate healthcare or your contract with Verizon. In hesitant response to this catastrophe, the Democrats and others have, as Tobi notes, consistently supported *technological* solutions, as if all such tricky and hermetic gadgetry were not itself the problem. First there was the voter-verified "paper trail" (VVPAT)—which, as Richardson and Friedman tell us here, had its inglorious beginnings in Nevada. Proposed for national use by Representative Rush Holt (D-NJ), and fiercely championed by the same left/liberal groups that had backed HAVA, the plan was to place printers in all paperless machines, and show each voter a hard copy of his ballot, which s/he would theoretically approve before it disappeared into the mechanism. That paper slip is *not* a ballot (although it was advertised as such), but a sort of marker that officials might or might not count eventually, if there should be an audit. (Most such "ballots" never would be counted, as the auditors take just a sample.) Thus the "paper trail" does not prevent election fraud, as any hacker can, in seconds, program the machine to print your document one way, and count your "vote" the other way—or even to misprint your "ballot," since most voters either don't look at their "paper trails" or can't decipher them, as they are often purposely illegible. (The lettering on Diebold's is so tiny that you need a magnifying glass to read it.) Unsurprisingly, VVPATS have been used in several of our most suspicious recent races: New Mexico in 2004 (where Bush "won" by 7,047 votes, while there were over 17,000 undervotes recorded on the DRE machines in Democratic precincts), and, in that same year, Washington's Snohomish County (where GOP gubernatorial candidate Dino Rossi stole some 3,000 votes); and in 2006, Florida's 13th district, where those 18,000 undervotes helped Christine Jennings "lose" to Vern Buchanan; and so on.

After the push for "paper trails" (which foundered when Holt's bill, HR 811, failed in the fall of 2007), the Democrats et al. decided on a different technological solution: optical scanners, which count up paper ballots, and report the totals, electronically. Surely that choice represents a major theoretical improvement over DRE machines, which "count" *no* ballots, only abstract "votes," while op-scans do leave *paper ballots* in their wake, which human beings may then recount in public, theoretically. Op-scans have become the voting medium of choice for the reformers generally, from Rush Holt, MoveOn and Common Cause, to the Secretaries of State in California, Florida, Ohio, Maryland and Colorado (among other states), to *The New York Times*, *The Washington Post*, *Roll Call* and Lou Dobbs.

While it is obviously better to have paper ballots than mere electronic signals, the scanners have been oversold. They are, at best, as quirky as the DRE machines. In the 2006 election, for example, op-scans broke down, froze or crashed at polling sites in Athens County, Ohio; Montrose County, Colorado (as well as Denver); Greenville County, South Carolina; Bannock County, Idaho; Mendocino County, California; Flathead County, Montana; Pawtucket, Rhode Island; Waterville, Maine; and thirteen counties in Kentucky. Those gadgets are, however, not just prone to random glitches, but susceptible to fraud. They were clearly hacked in Arizona in 2004, as Dave Griscom argues here, and have performed suspiciously in other doubtful races, including the notorious primary and general congressional elections in San Diego in 2006—both "won" by Republican Brian Bilbray, after the machines had been illegally kept for days in certain private homes—and the Democratic primary in New Hampshire in 2008, which Hillary Clinton won according to the op-scans only, while Barack Obama won the precincts where they counted votes by hand. (The media, as ever, rushed out many baseless explanations for her victory, which contradicted every poll.)

Such events would not surprise the experts. In October of 2006, Avi Rubin, a computer scientist at Johns Hopkins (and a longtime advocate of electronic voting) fretfully reported a new study published by researchers at the University of Connecticut, who had found that Diebold's Accuvote AV-OS, an op-scan machine, was easy pickings for malicious hackers. "The authors show," wrote Rubin,

> that even if the memory card is sealed and pre-election testing is performed, one can carry out a devastating array of attacks against an election using only off-the-shelf equipment and without having ever to access the [memory] card physically or opening the AV-OS system box.

Such "attacks," Rubin continued,

> are cleverly designed to make a compromised machine appear to work correctly when the system's audit reports are evaluated or when the machine is subjected to pre-election testing. Besides manipulation of the voting machine totals and reports, the authors explain how any voter can vote an arbitrary numbers of times using (get this) Post-it notes, if the voter is left unattended.[24]

Certainly the makers of so porous a contraption have no interest in the preservation of democracy. Their interest lies, demonstrably, not with the people but with Karl Rove's party—a fact that Rush Holt, MoveOn, Common Cause et al. refuse to face, and that the U.S. press will not report. The largest companies behind those op-scans—Diebold, ES&S and Hart InterCivic—all enjoy extremely close relations with the GOP. In 2004, Wally O'Dell, CEO of Diebold (headquartered in Canton, Ohio), created a small furor when he sent a fundraising letter out to prominent Ohio Republicans, stating that he was "committed to helping Ohio deliver its electoral votes to the president next year." For four years, Nebraska Republican Chuck Hagel served as CEO of ES&S (headquartered in Omaha), departing that position in 1996 to mount his own run for the Senate. (In that race and the next one, ES&S machines were used to count the votes, with Hagel winning both times by surprisingly high margins.) Among Hart InterCivic's top investors is Stratford Capital, the investment firm of Tom Hicks, a longtime friend and backer of George W. Bush.

The problem here is not that those hermetic firms are managed by and for Republicans per se. This nation would be in no better shape if Diebold and the others serviced only Democrats (and there are Democrats, like Steny Hoyer, who also serve the likes of Diebold.). The problem, rather, is that *any* private companies, or *any* closed technology, should be allowed to play a role in our elections. Our votes should all be counted in the open, and in a way that every citizen can see and understand. Any other course, however more "efficient" it may sound, will certainly empower the seething adversaries of democracy, who will do—have done—anything and everything to thwart the will of the majority.

Meanwhile, those still advocating purely technical solutions have refused to see that this is even possible. Thus their plans pose no real threat to the crusade against American democracy, which has moved well beyond the point where any anodyne "reforms" could knock it out or even slow it down. Throughout the states, the GOP has disenfranchised voters with a brazenness that harks back to the days before the march on Selma. "To date, the Kansas GOP has identified and caged more voters in the last 11 months than the previous two years [*sic*]!"

Thus Kris Kobach, chairman of the Kansas party, crowed in a circular sent out in December of 2007. In Ohio—where, as Bob Fitrakis tells us, the party apparatus illegally trashed countless ballots from the 2004 election—Republican election personnel have openly defied the Secretary of State, shrugging off her orders even to fill out a survey on their voting systems. Outraged by her drive to dump the DRE machines (and replace them with op-scans), party chair Bob Bennett bitterly charged *her* with the subversion of democracy: "Jennifer Brunner wants to run the elections system in this state like a dictator," he fumed in January, 2008. "I think she'll find out pretty quickly that she needs these people a lot more than they need her."[25]

Elsewhere the Republicans have been less confrontational, albeit just as ardent, in limiting the franchise, by passing laws that hinder registration drives, ease "challenges" by partisans, make would-be voters bring state-issued ID's to the polls, and so on. While such obstructive laws are nothing new, this unelected government has radically reversed the course of federal activism in the realm of voting rights, so that the anti-democratic movement nationwide now has a very powerful friend in Washington. While the Roberts Court aggressively rolls back the Warren Court's remarkable expansion of the franchise, Bush/Cheney's Department of Justice too has given up protection of the people's right to vote, and, to put it bluntly, joined the Klan. As Steve Rosenfeld shows here, this DOJ is working not to make sure that Americans can vote, but to ensure that Democrats *can't* vote—an effort driven by the cynical pretense, and/or the mad belief, that such suppression is necessitated by the threat of (Democratic) "voter fraud." To the true believers at the helm, it makes no difference that there is, in fact, no evidence of widespread "voter fraud," which is (and has been for some time) a serviceable figment of the paranoid imagination. As Rosenfeld points out, Bush/Cheney's EAC suppressed, and then rewrote, its own report on "voter fraud," so as to make it serve the interests of the GOP.

The Party's strategy, in short, is far more radical than most reformers seem to understand; for its aim is ultimately not to steal our votes, or change them, or delete them—a sort of fraud that could become detectable—but to *pre-empt* them. As Rosenfeld reported in December of 2007, the DOJ "is seeking to apply the principle of 'pre-emption,' or acting now to offset future threats—as the Bush Administration argued before invading Iraq—to voting rights. When applied to elections, the Department said there does not need to be evidence of actual voter fraud, or individuals impersonating other voters, before states can pass new laws to police that possibility."

Thus are the Bush Republicans now poised to take us all back to the days of poll taxes, white primaries, literacy tests and burning crosses—although, of course, the fire this time will be quite different. For one thing, the suppression of the vote will, by and large, be much less violent than it was decades ago: "The best way to stop niggers from voting is to visit them the night before the election," Senator Theodore Bilbo of Mississippi remarked back in the 1940s, with a frankness that today's Republicans can only envy. In their new millennium, the methods used to block the vote would not be that ham-fisted (although some "challengers" might go too far, and there will always be a few policemen at some polling places). And there will be another difference, if the party should prevail; for this time they would take us *all* back to the days when "the best way" to block the vote was to pre-empt it. For if the party has its way, and We the People, having never voted for it, cannot ever vote them out, we will then *all* be that party's slaves—even those of us who have white skin, and make good money. So that that is not our fate (and instead of waiting for the other party to respond), we had better face the facts, and then resume our founding Revolution, and make it happen at long last.

NOTES

1. Mike Aivaz and Muriel Kane, "MSNBC: 'How Bush became a government unto himself.,"*Raw Story*, December 12, 2007, http://rawstory.com/news/2007/MSNBC_probes_How_many_laws_has_1212.html

2. Jeffrey Tobin, "Killing Habeas Corpus: Arlen Specter's About Face," *The New Yorker*, December 4, 2006, http://www.newyorker.com/archive/2006/12/04/061204fa_fact

3. Newsmax.com, "John McCain: Torture Worked on Me," November 29, 2005, http://archive.newsmax.com/archives/ic/2005/11/29/100012.shtml

4. Jill Lawrence, "Bush's Agenda Walks the Church-State Line," *USA Today*, January 29, 2003, http://www.usatoday.com/news/washington/2003-01-29-bush-religion_x.htm

5. *Time*, "How They Aced Their Midterms," November 18, 2002, Cover, http://www.time.com/time/covers/0,16641,1101021118,00.html

6. Elisabeth Bumiller and David E. Sanger, "The 2002 Elections: The Strategist; Republicans Say Rove Was Mastermind Of Big Victory," *New York Times*, November 7, 2002, http://query.nytimes.com/gst/fullpage.html?res=9C0DE1DF1F3EF934A35752C1A9649C8B63

7. Peter Baker, "Rove Remains Steadfast In the Face of Criticism," *Washington Post*, November 12, 2006, http://www.washingtonpost.com/wp-dyn/content/article/2006/11/11/AR2006111101103.html

8. Joe Klein, "The Realists Take Charge," *Time*, November 12, 2006, http://www.time.com/time/magazine/article/0,9171,1558293,00.html; Eleanor Clift, "The Slapdown of Polarization," *Newsweek*, November 10, 2006, http://www.newsweek.com/id/44477

9. Matt Bai, "The Last 20th-Century Election?," *New York Times Magazine*, November 19, 2006, http://www.nytimes.com/2006/11/19/magazine/19wwln_lede.html

10. Julian Pecquet, "Al Gore really did beat George W. Bush in 2000. Six years on, this is still a problem?," *Research in Review Magazine*, Fall/Winter 2005, http://www.rinr.fsu.edu/winter2005/features/battlefield.html; John K. Wilson, "Gore Wins!," Chicago Media Watch, http://www.chicagomediawatch.org/01_4_gore.shtml

11. Ford Fessenden and John M. Broder, "Study of Disputed Florida Ballots Finds Justices Did Not Cast the Deciding Vote," *New York Times*, November 12, 2001, http://www.nytimes.com/2001/11/12/politics/12VOTE.html?ex=1201496400&en=b82b9a96d775d918&ei=5070

12. Dan Keating and Dan Balz, "Florida Recounts Would Have Favored Bush: But Study Finds Gore Might Have Won Statewide Tally of All Uncounted Ballots," *Washington Post*, November 12, 2001, http://www.washingtonpost.com/wp-dyn/articles/A12623-2001Nov11.html

13. Jackie Calmes and Edward P. Foldessy, "In Election Review, Bush Wins Without Supreme Court Help," *Wall Street Journal*, November 12, 2001.

14. Doyle McManus, Bob Drogin and Richard O'Reilly, "Bush Still Had Votes to Win in a Recount, Study Finds," *Los Angeles Times*, November 12, 2001.

15. CNN.com, "Florida Recount Study: Bush Still Wins," 2001, http://www.

cnn.com/SPECIALS/2001/florida.ballots/stories/main.html

16. Tim Nickens, "Recount: Bush," *St. Petersburg Times*, November 12, 2001, http://www.sptimes.com/News/111201/Lostvotes/Recount__Bush.shtml

17. Walter Gibbs and Sarah Lyall, "Gore Shares Peace Prize for Climate Change Work," *New York Times*, October 13, 2007, http://query.nytimes.com/gst/fullpage.html?res=9A07EFDC1430F930A25753C1A9619C8B63&partner=rssnyt&emc=rss; Jackie Calmes, "Al Gore Might Yet Join 2008 Contenders," *Wall Street Journal*, May 8, 2006, http://online.wsj.com/public/article/SB114704312621046146-lkhKNtLxXyeMs8Oo1vlKOzOKlb0_20070507.html; Peter Baker, "Feats Divide Pair Linked by Election," *Washington Post*, October 13, 2007, http://www.washingtonpost.com/wp-dyn/content/article/2007/10/12/AR2007101202296.html

18. Jeffrey Gettleman, "The 2002 Elections: Georgia; An Old Battle Flag Helps Bring Down A Governor," *New York Times*, November 7, 2002, http://query.nytimes.com/gst/fullpage.html?res=9C0CEEDF1F3EF934A35752C1A9649C8B63

19. Steve Freeman and Joel Bleifuss, *Was the 2004 Presidential Election Stolen? Exit Polls, Election Fraud, and the Official Count* (New York: SevenStories Press, 2006).

20. For a full acount of the apparent fraud in the 2006 elections, see Mark Crispin Miller, *Fooled Again: The Real Case for Electoral Reform*, exp. ed. (New York: Basic Books, 2005), pp. 368ff.

21. Greg Mitchell, 'Daily Endorsement Tally: Kerry Wins, Without Recount,' *Editor & Publisher*, November 5, 2004. For further evidence that Republicans had turned against Bush/Cheney prior to Election Day, 2004, see Miller, *Fooled Again*, pp. 7-18.

22. *New York Times*, "Contesting The Vote; Excerpts From Vice President's Legal Challenge to the Results in Florida," November 28, 2000, http://query.nytimes.com/gst/fullpage.html?res=9D0CE3D8173DF93BA15752C1A9669C8B63&sec=&spon=&pagewanted=2

23. Paul Gigot, "Miami Heat: A burgher rebellion in Dade County," *Wall Street Journal*, November 24, 2000, http://opinionjournal.com/columnists/pgigot/?id=65000673

24. Avi Rubin's Blog, "UConn VoTeR center report: Diebold AV-OS is vulnerable to serious attacks," October 31, 2006, http://avi-rubin.blogspot.com/2006/10/uconn-voter-center-report-diebold-av-os.html

25. Mark Rollenhagen, "Bennett v. Brunner: The Sequel," Openers: The Plain Dealer Politics Blog, January 24, 2008, http://blog.cleveland.com/openers/2008/01/bennett_v_brunner_the_sequel.html

2000

★

The myth that Bush won Florida depends on our forgetting, or not knowing, the true circumstances of his "victory" there. When, late on Election Night, he was abruptly—and, as it turned out, decisively—declared the winner, having pulled ahead of Gore, there was in fact no scientific basis for that claim. Bush's win was (dubiously) called by FOX News, and quickly seconded by NBC and then the other networks, entirely on the basis of his brother Jeb's assertion that he'd won. That call was then confirmed by the consortium of pollsters hired to track the data. According to Warren Mitofsky, the man in charge, that confirmation had been based on the polling data then available. This was not the case, however—a revelation made here by David W. Moore, a seasoned and respected statistician who was right there watching it all happen.

Contrary to Establishment mythology, Bush did not win because Ralph Nader had snatched votes from Gore. As Lance DeHaven-Smith reminds us here, Bush "won" Florida through the deliberate preemption, long before Election Day, of tens of thousands of Democratic votes. In his essay, DeHaven-Smith outlines the partisan conspiracy to disenfranchise those citizens, slant the count of military voters overseas, block a proper recount, and invite the intervention of the Supreme Court.

BECAUSE JEB SAID SO: WHAT REALLY HAPPENED ON ELECTION NIGHT IN FLORIDA

★

DAVID W. MOORE

"In my heart, I do believe that democracy was harmed by my network and others on Nov. 7, 2000."
—Roger Ailes, chairman and chief executive of
FOX News Network, February 14, 2001

The presidential election of 2000 was stolen from Al Gore. This is an historical observation, not a partisan charge. The observation is no more partisan than acknowledging that supporters of Lyndon Baines Johnson helped steal the 1948 Democratic senatorial primary in Texas from Coke Stevenson, allowing LBJ to be elected as a U.S. Senator. There have been many other cases of stolen elections in American history, though typically evidence of such thefts takes decades to emerge.[1] In the present case, investigations in the past several years have revealed a series of events that provide evidence of theft beyond a reasonable doubt.

Let me clarify. Al Gore won the national popular vote for president of the United States by about half a million votes, though officially he lost the election because he did not receive a majority of the electoral votes. Had he been declared the winner in Florida, he would have won both the electoral and popular vote. Officially, Gore lost Florida to George W. Bush by 537 votes. In fact, the evidence shows that more people in Florida voted for Gore than for Bush by a margin of at least several thousand votes. Many of those votes were not counted because of ballot designs, especially in Palm Beach (the infamous "butterfly" ballot) and Duval counties, but these un-counted votes do not constitute theft by themselves. Some of these votes were left un-counted not because of partisan mischief, but because of genuine mistakes for which the law provided no clear remedy. But there were other uncounted votes that could have been counted, for which the law did provide a remedy, but which the U.S. Supreme Court denied.

The theft of the Florida election, and thus the presidency, resulted from illegal actions taken before the election by high Florida officials, including Governor Jeb Bush and Secretary of State Katherine Harris, to deprive qualified Florida citizens from exercising their right to vote—costing Gore tens of thousands of votes.[2] The theft also resulted from the illegally partisan actions of Florida and other officials after the election to prevent a fair hand-recount in the state as provided by law, and to count probable ballots for Bush that had been cast after Election Day.[3] The theft was ultimately assured when the U.S. Supreme Court decided to halt the Florida recount and essentially award the presidency to Bush, a decision that is widely seen among legal experts as unprincipled and without legal justification.[4]

In the midst of all the illegal activities both before and after the election were the television networks' erroneous projections of Bush as the next president of the United States at about a quarter past two in the morning, Eastern Time, on election night. There was nothing illegal about those projections. Yet, in one of those rare twists of fate, it's quite possible that had the networks not made the projections—or at least had not *all* the networks jumped on the Bush bandwagon—the efforts to steal the election would not have succeeded. The projections led to Gore's conceding the election to Bush, then retracting the concession a couple of hours later as the vote count revealed the election to be a toss-up. But the damage had been done. For the next thirty-six days after the election, the conservative media continually lambasted Gore for being a sore loser and trying to "steal" the election, while even the mainstream media treated the attempts at a recount as though it were a bizarre circus rather than a serious attempt to determine the intent of voters in Florida. Had the networks not made the projection and given the illusion that Bush had won, a very different political environment would have greeted the two candidates after the election, one that would have been more propitious for Gore's efforts to obtain a statewide hand recount of all the votes—and quite likely victory.

Regardless of whether Gore would have prevailed even with the improved environment, the networks' miscall by itself is worth examining. It turns out that the projections of Bush as the Florida winner were caused not so much by erroneous data, as all the networks claimed after the election, but by the respective networks' succumbing to competitive pressures to beat the other networks to make the call, even though the data demanded caution. Most ironically of all, the network calls were triggered not by statistical analyses showing that Bush would emerge the winner, but by Bush's brother urging his cousin at FOX network to make the call—even as Bush's lead in the statewide vote count was rapidly declining.

ELECTION NIGHT 2000 MISCALLS

"Jebbie says we got it! Jebbie says we got it!"

Those were the words uttered by John Ellis at a quarter after two in the morning following Election Night 2000, moments before FOX projected George W. Bush the winner over Al Gore in Florida, and thus the next president of the United States. Ellis was the head of FOX's decision team, responsible for projecting the winners in all the statewide contests on Election Night, as well as being the cousin of George W. and Jeb Bush. (Ellis' mother, Nancy Ellis, is the sister of former President George H. W. Bush.) For much of the previous evening and early morning, Ellis had been on the phone with his cousins, who were both at the same location in Austin, Texas. "It was just the three of us guys handing the phone back and forth," he told the *New Yorker* the following week, "me with the numbers, one of them a governor, the other the president-elect. Now, that was cool."[5]

The catalyst for projecting his cousin as the winner in Florida, Ellis wrote in the December 2000 issue of *Inside* Magazine, was his calculation of a "need/get" ratio—the percentage of the outstanding vote that Gore needed to catch up to Bush versus the percentage of the vote that Gore would actually get.[6] "At five minutes before two," Ellis wrote, "it became clear to me that Gore could not win. I called George W. and asked him what he thought." Bush turned the question around and asked Ellis what he thought. "I think you've got it," Ellis said. After discussing the need/get ratio with George W. for a little while, they signed off. A few minutes later, according to Ellis, after the need/get ratio showed that the gap between what Gore needed and what he would get was eight percentage points, "we called Florida for Bush."

That account is substantially different from what actually happened, according to the statistician who sat next to Ellis during the afternoon, evening, and next morning of FOX's 2000 presidential election coverage. Cynthia Talkov was, according to Ellis, his "statistical wizard," the one person on the FOX decision team who "knew the [voter projection] system inside out, knew the details and pitfalls of each and every estimator on our screens. . . ." But she never saw Ellis making any calculations for a need/get ratio, nor was there such a ratio displayed on the screens.[7] Instead, he was chatting with one or the other of his cousins on the phone when suddenly he stood up and announced, "Jebbie says we got it! Jebbie says we got it!" Almost immediately, the decision team projected Bush the winner, with the announcement made by FOX moments later. For all practical purposes, Jeb Bush had just called the election for his brother.

The official records show that FOX made that announcement at 2:16 in the morning. Within four minutes, NBC, CBS, CNN, and ABC followed suit, all now proclaiming Bush as the next president of the United States. Lying on the floor in his campaign's staff room on the seventh floor of the Loews hotel in Nashville, his chin propped up in his hands, Gore absorbed the news with his staff members in shocked silence. Moments later, lumbering to his feet, he said, "I want to concede.

I want to be gracious about this."[8] Ten minutes later, he called Bush to offer his concession and good wishes, and then he and his entourage set out for Nashville's War Memorial Plaza where he would make the concession public.

As it turned out, of course, the projection by all the networks was wrong. When they made the call, Bush had not won in Florida. In fact, it would take more than a month before Bush was finally declared the winner, though a post-election analysis of the Florida vote shows that more people in that state voted for Gore than Bush. After reviewing the results of that study, conducted by the National Opinion Research Center at the University of Chicago,[9] CBS News and the *Associated Press* both concluded, "Under any standard that tabulated all disputed votes statewide, Gore erased Bush's advantage and emerged with a tiny lead that ranged from 42 to 171 votes."[10] *The Washington Post* echoed that conclusion: ". . . the efforts of a consortium of news organizations to revisit the election controversy yielded a simple, even sensational, revelation: If there had been some way last fall to recount every vote—undervotes and overvotes alike, in all 67 Florida counties—former vice president Al Gore likely would be in the White House." The author went on to write, "The results plainly suggest that more Floridians intended to cast votes for him [Gore] than Bush, and that under most standards for counting ballots by hand he would have won in a statewide recount."[11]

Within two hours after declaring Bush the winner, the networks had all retracted their projections. In the meantime, as Bush's lead dwindled, Gore changed his mind about a public concession, and called an irritated George Bush to give him the news. When the Texas governor responded by saying that his "little brother" had assured him he had won the state, Gore said, "Let me explain something. Your little brother is not the ultimate authority on this."[12] Little did Gore realize at the time how influential "little brother" Jeb Bush had been in the networks' erroneous projections, and thus Gore's near-public concession.

It is difficult to overestimate the impact of the erroneous network call on the post-election political environment. It created havoc for Gore, giving rise to charges that he was a "sore loser" and undermining the legitimacy of his efforts to obtain a hand recount of the votes in Florida. Even some conservatives acknowledged the problem. Reed Irvine and Cliff Kincaid of Accuracy in Media noted, "The result of this [network projection for Bush] was that the Bush campaign and his supporters believed that they had won, and it was now being stolen away."[13] That clearly was the view of FOX's conservative commentator, Sean Hannity, who asserted repeatedly during the network's post-election coverage that "the vice president because of his blind ambition has brought us to the brink of a constitutional crisis." Hannity also charged the Democrats who were pressing for a vote recount in Florida with trying "to steal the election."[14]

Irvine and Kincaid went on to cite Steve Luxenberg of *The Washington Post*, who wrote, "The networks' call had a huge psychological effect on the electorate and the candidates, with political and historical ramifications. Voters might have shrugged off a long count in Florida as an acceptable delay in a contested election. But a 'reversal' fed the notion of a tainted result, contributed to the overheated rhetoric on both sides . . . and helped fuel the sense of a country in crisis."[15] The perception of a "reversal"—that Bush was the winner, but now Gore was trying to overturn the results—was caused by the erroneous network projections that left millions of people going to bed on election night believing that the Texas governor was the next president, and millions of other people waking up the next morning to read their newspapers which contained the same misinformation. Among the newspapers with such headlines were the *Boston Globe, USA Today, New York Post, San Francisco Chronicle, Philadelphia Inquirer, Washington Times, Sacramento Bee, St. Louis Post-Dispatch, Austin (Texas) American-Statesman*—along with at least three Florida newspapers, the *Miami Herald, Orlando Sentinel,* and *Tallahassee Democrat.*[16]

The miscall and the hostile environment that it created for Gore no doubt also affected the vice president's recount strategy in Florida, and perhaps even the Supreme Court decision that effectively handed the election to Bush. Among Gore's advisors, a major concern was to avoid reinforcing the perception of Gore as a sore loser, an image the Republicans were actively trying to foster.[17] Many in the news media treated Gore's efforts to get a hand recount as a losing battle that should not be fought. As Todd Gitlin wrote in the *Los Angeles Times,* even NBC's Tim Russert, a Democrat who had worked at different times for New York Senator Patrick Moynihan and New York Governor Mario Cuomo, was "telling viewers no fewer than three times on November 8 [the day after the election] that the way things were going in Florida . . . it was time for Al Gore to play statesman and concede." Gitlin added, "Not one barking head ever suggested that Bush concede under any conditions whatever."[18]

A logical strategy urged on Gore by some of his advisors was to ask for a recount in each of the sixty-seven Florida counties. He eventually proposed this idea to Bush, but did not initiate action immediately on his own. When Bush got the proposal, he dismissed it out of hand. Had there been a full statewide hand recount, the media consortium recount showed, Gore almost surely would have won. Instead, his team tried to identify the counties where Gore might be able to pick up enough votes quickly to justify his fight in Florida, all the while fighting the image of his being an obstructionist to the will of the people. But the media consortium also showed that if a limited hand recount had been authorized as Gore's legal team initially requested, it was still quite possible that Bush would have emerged the victor. Only if there were hand recounts in all the counties would a Gore win have been almost certain. And that did not happen.

But it almost did. Despite Gore's limited recount request, District Court Judge Terry Lewis was apparently set to order a full hand recount across the state of both the undervotes and overvotes when the Supreme Court ordered all counties in Florida to stop whatever recount efforts were under way.[19] As Florida Representative Peter Deustch said at the congressional hearing, "the Supreme Court's political decision of stopping the counting of the votes was in fact influenced by the missed [network] calls of calling Bush the President. If there was no winner after November 7, I think the political decision very well might have been different."[20]

The logic behind such an assertion comes from the justification for the recount halt, authored by Justice Antonin Scalia, which essentially assumed that Bush was the real winner in Florida. Scalia wrote that to continue the counting would "threaten irreparable harm to the petitioner [Bush] and to the country, by casting a cloud upon what he claims to be the legality of his election."[21] That is an amazing assertion, for it clearly assumes what the vote count had not definitively demonstrated—that Bush had won more votes in Florida than Gore. Not to allow the recount would have been of "irreparable harm" to Gore, and also to the country, if one assumes that Gore might have emerged the winner. Only if one assumes that Bush was the real winner would Scalia's justification be defensible. But on what grounds could Scalia and the other four justices assume that Bush was the real winner? It would appear that the networks' miscall, and the resulting political environment in Florida and Washington, D.C., which treated Gore's fight for a vote recount as doomed and destructive, helped shape, if not determine, the Supreme Court's decision.

The argument against this theory is that the five justices who voted to give Bush the election would have done so regardless of what the networks did or the what the political environment happened to be. But Justice David Souter believed that he was very close to persuading Justice Anthony Kennedy to send the case back to the Florida justices to fix whatever was necessary to have a fair count. Kennedy had initially joined with Justices William Rehnquist, Clarence Thomas, Antonin Scalia, and Sandra Day O'Connor to temporarily halt the recount, but in the final decision he seemed to be wavering. Souter told a group of prep-school students a month after the Supreme Court decision that if he'd had "one more day—just one more day," he might have prevailed. But Kennedy thought that the prospect of more political fighting was too much for the country to endure.[22] It's also true that had the political environment been different, and had the presidential contest been seen as the tie it was rather than as a fight by a sore loser who had conceded, and then un-conceded, and was now trying to hang onto power, Kennedy's objection to the continued political fighting would have been moot. With no presumed winner, the only fair way to determine who won would be to let the votes decide. Only if Kennedy assumed that the winner had already been identified could he justify his argument against continuing the recount.

Many commentators expressed astonishment that FOX would hire a person so closely related to one of the two principal candidates to head its decision desk. This was an obvious conflict of interest, which FOX never acknowledged, but instead defended as non-discrimination against relatives of politicians. The person who invented exit polls in the 1960s and developed the projection system the networks were using that night was Warren Mitofsky, who characterized Ellis' actions—conferring with his cousins while heading the FOX decision desk—as "the most unprofessional election night work I could ever imagine. He had no business talking to the Bush brothers or to any other politician about what he was doing."[23]

One might have expected FOX and Ellis to take a serious hit in the journalistic and polling community because of Ellis' behavior that evening, but that didn't happen. They were let off the hook, ironically, by Mitofsky himself, who on Election Night 2000 was the co-director of the joint CBS/CNN decision desk. He told Seth Mnookin of *Brill's Content* that, "this business about FOX pressuring other people to call, I never made a projection in my life because of some other network. When I heard.they put it [the projection for Bush] out there, I was disappointed, because I wanted to do it . . . we were about to make the projection."[24]

From that comment and other reviews of the data provided by VNS (Voter News Services) on election night, it soon became the accepted wisdom that if FOX had not made the call at the time it did, the other networks would have done so not much later. *Slate's* Jack Shafer wrote a week after the election: "It's somewhat hilarious that the press ethicists are calling for the head of John Ellis, the FOX News prognosticator and Bush cousin who gave Florida to Bush contemporaneously with the networks. Although Ellis has been fairly upfront about rooting for his cousin, we need to remember that he was looking at the same data as Mitofsky and the other network seers who made the same call."[25]

But a closer investigation into how the networks made the calls suggests that, contrary to conventional wisdom, had FOX not made the call, the other networks would have also refrained. NBC was the second network to make the call, but at the time of FOX's announcement, the NBC decision team leader, Sheldon Gawiser, was on the phone with Murray Edelman, the editorial director of VNS. Edelman was explaining why it would not be a good idea to call Bush the winner, but when FOX's announcement hit the air, Gawiser cut the connection to call the election for Bush. At that moment, I was sitting next to Mitofsky and Lenski, who were reviewing the computer screens, to see whether they wanted to follow FOX. When NBC made its call, Mitofsky immediately announced that CNN and CBS would do so as well. Despite the other networks' projections, the ABC decision desk was against making a projection, but an ABC executive over-rode that decision and called Bush the winner in Florida, just four minutes after FOX. The Associated Press and VNS refrained from hopping on the FOX bandwagon. Two hours later, they were vindicated when all the networks rescinded their projections.

Although the networks all agreed that their actions on Election Night 2000 harmed the electoral process, they have done little to prevent similar blunders in the future. They blamed VNS for the problems, essentially excusing their decision teams for making hasty decisions and avoiding the real issue of network competition. Yet, it was competition more than any other factor that gave rise to the most serious blunder—the projection of Bush as the winner in Florida, which created havoc in the post-election fight for the presidency. By 2004, the networks had disbanded VNS and signed on with a new election night projection system, headed by Mitofsky and Lenski.[26] But the networks refused to close down their individual decision teams. They continue to compete with each other and risk making miscalls in the process. As Murray Edelman said of the decision teams, "They were careful in 2004. The 2000 election was still fresh. But they will start edging back . . . they have a culture of competition. How long before they call another race incorrectly? It's just a matter of time."[27]

NOTES

1. See Mark Crispin Miller, *Fooled Again: The Real Case for Electoral Reform* (New York: Basic Books, 2007) for a look at current problems with stealing elections, and Andrew Gumbel, *Steal This Vote: Dirty Elections and the Rotten History of Democracy in America* (New York: Nation Books, 2005) for an account of how votes and elections have been stolen throughout American history.

2. Gregg Palast, *The Best Democracy Money Can Buy: An Investigative Reporter Exposes the Truth About Globalization, Corporate Cons, and High-Finance Fraudsters* (New York: Plume, Expanded Election Edition, May 2004).

3. Lance deHaven-Smith, *The Battle for Florida* (Gainesville, FL: University Press of Florida, 2005).

4. See Alan M. Dershowitz, *Supreme Injustice: How the High Court Hijacked Election 2000* (New York: Oxford University Press, 2001), Bruce Ackermann, *Bush v. Gore: The Question of Legitimacy* (New Haven: Yale University Press, 2002), and Vincent Bugliosi, *The Betrayal of America: How the Supreme Court Undermined the Constitution and Chose the Next President* (New York: Thunder Mouth's Press/Nation Books, 2001).

5. Jane Mayer, "Dept. of Close Calls," *The New Yorker*, Nov. 20, 2000, p. 38.

6. John Ellis, "A Hard Day's Night: John Ellis' Firsthand Account of Election Night," *Inside* magazine, Monday Dec. 11, 2000 10:52 AM The article appeared in the Dec. 26 issue of *Inside* magazine.

7. All references to Cynthia Talkov's views are based on personal interviews with her, April 15 and April 28, 2005.

8. Jeffrey Toobin, *Too Close to Call: The Thirty-Six Day Battle to Decide the 2000 Election* (New York: Random House, 2001), p. 20.

9. The study was sponsored by *The Washington Post, The Chicago Tribune, The New York Times, The Wall Street Journal, The Palm Beach Post, The St. Petersburg Times* and *The Associated Press*.

10. "Chads, Scanners, and Votes," CBS News Web site, Nov. 12, 2001; http://www.cbsnews.com/stories/2001/11/12/politics/main317662.shtml. See also Robert Tanner and Sharon L. Crenson, "Florida Review Shows Narrowest Margin," *Associated Press* news release, in *Portsmouth Herald*, November 12, 2001; http://www.seacoastonline.com/2001news/11_12_w2.htm.

11. John F. Harris, "A Symbolic but Muddled Victory," *The Washington Post*, November 12, 2001, p. A11; http://www.washingtonpost.com/ac2/wp-dyn/

A12604-2001Nov11?language=printer.

12. Toobin, *op.cit.*, p. 25.

13. Reed Irvine and Cliff Kincaid, "Lasting Damage From Election Night Numbers," Media Monitor on www.aim.org, Nov. 24, 2000.

14. Cited in Daphne Eviatar, "Murdoch's FOX News," *The Nation*, March 12, 2001, posted on www.thenation.com.

15. Irvine and Kincaid, op. cit.

16. David A. Kaplan, *The Accidental President* (New York: William Morrow, 2001), p. 28.

17. Toobin, op. cit., pp. 35, 56–57.

18. Todd Gitlin, "How TV Killed Democracy on Nov. 7," *Los Angeles Times*, Feb. 14, 2001.

19. Mickey Kaus, "Everything the *New York Times* Thinks About the Florida Recount Is Wrong! It turns out the U.S. Supreme Court really did cast the deciding vote...," *Slate* posted Tuesday, Nov. 13, 2001.

20. Representative Peter Deutsch, in remarks at the hearing before the House Committee on Energy and Commerce, Feb. 14, 2001.

21. Cited in Vincent Bugliosi, *The Betrayal of America: How the Supreme Court Undermined the Constitution and Chose Our President* (New York: Thundermouth's Press/Nation Books, 2001), p. 51.

22. Kaplan, op. cit., pp. 284–285.

23. Warren Mitofsky, written comments to a colleague, shortly after the November 2000 election.

24. Seth Mnookin, "It Happened One Night," *Brill's Content*, February 4, 2001.

25. Jack Shafer, "Defending the Projectionists," *Slate*, posted Nov. 15, 2000, at 2:24 P.M. PT.

26. Warren Mitofsky died in 2006, before the mid-term elections, but the National Election Pool (NEP) continues with the same election night operation, still under the name of Edison/Mitofsky.

27. Personal interview with Murray Edelman, Mar. 14, 2006.

FLORIDA 2000: BEGINNINGS OF A LAWLESS PRESIDENCY

★

LANCE DEHAVEN-SMITH

The moral significance of the disputed 2000 presidential election did become fully evident until midway through the second term of the Bush Administration, when the Administration's breathtaking criminality was finally exposed in a series of scandals. Back in 2000, many Americans realized that the presidential election had somehow been sidetracked, and that top officials in Florida, while claiming to be following the law, had slanted their decisions to favor Bush. But in the aftermath of the election, few people were willing to believe that Bush's supporters in Florida had actually set in motion the events that had culminated in the election breakdown. Instead, the general consensus was that Bush had ended up president by a fluke.

Now, however, much more is known not only about the 2000 election, but also about George W. Bush and his closest associates. The Bush Administration has been revealed to be one of the most criminally lawless regimes in American history. If the 2000 presidential election had been investigated thoroughly in 2001, some of these abuses of power might have been prevented. Certainly, other political elites and the public would have been wary of the new president and his team, for they would have learned that Bush had been carried to the presidency by a criminal conspiracy.

The conspiracy began with high-ranking elected officials in Florida who were probably guided by strategists for the campaign of George W. Bush. This group implemented a felon disenfranchisement program that was intentionally flawed so as to target Democrats and also cause havoc on Election Day in urban areas where Democrats were concentrated.<1> Later, during the post-election dispute, the core conspirators were joined by members of Congress, overseas military personnel, and the Speaker of the Florida House to stymie the recount, deliver overseas military ballots to Florida that had been cast illegally, slant the counting of overseas military ballots at the county level to favor Bush, and create the appearance of a constitutional crisis to draw in the U.S. Supreme Court when the recount could not be blocked by other means.[2]

CHANGING DEMOGRAPHICS

The Republican criminality in Florida's disputed 2000 presidential election grew in part from bitter partisan struggles of the previous two decades. Like the rest of the old confederacy, Florida had been staunchly Democratic until the 1960s, when the state began to move gradually toward the Republican column after passage of the 1964 Civil Rights Act. George W. Bush's brother, Jeb, lost his first race for governor when he was defeated in 1994 by incumbent Lawton Chiles, who won by less then 64,000 votes out of more than 5 million votes cast. At the time, this was the second closest election in modern Florida history, and Chiles had resorted to dirty tactics to eek out his narrow, and tainted, victory. Early in the campaign, he had made unsubstantiated accusations about Jeb's business dealings, and the week before Election Day he had resorted to push polls. Jeb ran again in 1998 and won easily against Buddy MacKay, Chile's Lieutenant Governor. Jeb's victory meant that, for the first time since Reconstruction, Republicans had control of Florida's top executive office and both houses of the legislature.

Still, even in their hour of victory, Jeb and other top Republicans could see that population trends were running against them. Since the 1950s, Florida has been experiencing rapid population growth, and in the decades preceding the 2000 election, the state had become steadily older and more diverse racially and ethnically.[3] Although Republicans had been successful in attracting support from native white Floridians, in-migrating Midwesterners and Cuban Americans, the GOP had not done well with non-Cuban Hispanics, Caribbean blacks, African Americans, or senior citizens from the Northeast. Yet, growth among all of these Democratic constituencies, especially the minorities, was outpacing the much slower growth of the Republican base. By 2025, minorities are expected to make up 40% of state residents, up from 32% in 2000.[4]

In the face of rapid population growth among Democratic constituencies, Republicans became intent on solidifying their hold on the state's political institutions. They sought to centralize power in the governor's office, change election laws to weaken Democratic voting power, facilitate absentee voting, stifle criticism from government analysts, and use privatization to replace Democratically-inclined state workers with private service providers whose dependence on government contracts would keep them loyal to the Republican power structure.

These and other tactics culminated in the 2000 election fiasco. The election, however, was not the Republicans' exclusive, or even their primary target. The actions they took that undermined the integrity of the 2000 election were part of a much larger assault on Florida's political institutions and civic culture. In this respect, Florida's experience under Jeb Bush presaged the nation's experience under Bush-Cheney. Jeb and other Republican leaders in the state initiated a long-term, multi-pronged effort to insert partisan Republican interests and people at key points throughout the state government, so they could use government resources and power to enforce party discipline, control public discourse, restrict access to information, and build support among doctors, state troopers, firefighters, and other groups amenable to Republican policies and seeking Republican favors.

FELON DISENFRANCHISEMENT

The only government agency to investigate Florida's administration of the disputed 2000 presidential election was the United States Civil Rights Commission. It was also the only agency to use subpoena powers and require sworn testimony. The Commission conducted hearings in January and February 2001, which turned up evidence of a possible conspiracy by Secretary of State Katherine Harris and other high-ranking Republican officials, perhaps including Jeb Bush, to illegally remove predominantly Democratic voters from the registration rolls under the guise of removing felons, who by Florida law are ineligible to vote unless they have their civil rights restored by the Governor and Cabinet.[5]

In 1998, Florida's Republican-controlled legislature enacted legislation requiring the registered-voter list to be purged by a private company rather than by professionals in the Division of Elections. At no previous time in Florida history had the determination of voter eligibility been placed in private hands. The company that received the contract to work with the Florida Secretary of State and the Director of the Division of Elections to identify ex-felons on registered-voter rolls was Database Technologies (DBT). The Civil Rights Commission subpoenaed the company's vice president, George Bruder, and required him to testify under oath.[6]

In recounting his experiences with the project, Bruder explained that, as DBT began to match names and other information on lists of convicted felons with those on Florida's list of registered voters, he became concerned that the match criteria DBT had been instructed to use were too loose and resulted in "false positives." However, the Division of Elections insisted that DBT use the loosest criteria permissible within the scope of its contract, which called only for the use of first names, last names, and birthdates. The Division instructed DBT not to require that first and middle names be in any particular order to match. In other words, John Andrew Smith would be considered to match Andrew John Smith. The Elections Division also insisted that matches be allowed even when the last names of individuals on the list of ex-felons only approximated the last names of registered voters. The spelling needed to be just "90 percent" the same. This meant that John Andrew Smith would be counted as a match with John Andrew Smythe, Andrew John Smythe, John Andrew Smitt, Andrew John Smitt, and so on. Bruder summed up this part of his testimony by saying that "the State dictated to us that they wanted to go broader and we did it in the fashion that they requested."

The loose match criteria used by DBT under the direction of the Division of Elections resulted in a highly erroneous list of registered voters who were thought to be ex-felons. County elections supervisors were sent the names of the purported felons who were registered to vote in their particular county. The supervisors were instructed to verify the information and remove voters from the rolls accordingly. How much care was taken by the supervisors is not known, but the investigation by the Civil Rights Commission found that procedures varied widely across the counties.

By June of 2000, it had become obvious to a number of the local supervisors of elections that tjhe lists they had been given were full of errors. Numerous examples of problems are chronicled in the Civil Rights Commission's report. In addition to the loose match criteria, one source of many errors was the mistaken inclusion of misdemeanants on the list of felons from, of all states, Texas. This error alone caused more than 8,000 Florida voters to be improperly identified for removal from the registered voter rolls.

These and other problems were brought to the attention of the Division of Elections, which sent letters to all supervisors advising them of the mistakes. But many of the problems were never corrected at the county level, and thousands of voters were removed from the rolls improperly. Often, the first time voters learned that their voter registration had been revoked was when they arrived at the polls to cast their ballots in the 2000 presidential election. This accounts for much of the chaos that day.

The findings of the Civil Rights Commission were certainly sufficient to warrant a full investigation of the actions of Florida Secretary of State Katherine Harris, Florida Governor Jeb Bush, and Elections Division Director Clay Roberts. Either singly or in combination, all three may have used their offices to improperly influence the outcome of the 2000 election—a felony under the state's election laws. At the very least, one or more of them appear to have been guilty of either misfeasance or nonfeasance in issuing a contract that did not contain performance criteria regarding the accuracy of DBT's work, in failing to correct the problems with the felon disenfranchisement initiative once they became visible, and in not assuring that polling places were adequately staffed on election day in 2000 to handle the resulting confusion. If Harris or others took these steps with the intention of weakening the voting power of African Americans—and this certainly appears to be the case—they violated federal voting rights laws.

However, no follow-up investigation was ever conducted. Incredibly, the hearings of the U.S. Civil Rights Commission received no live television coverage, and media stories about them always included Republican accusations that the Commission was biased because a majority of its members were Democrats or Democratic appointees.

DESPITE THE OBSTACLES, GORE WON

Florida election officials ultimately declared George W. Bush the winner in 2000 by a margin of 537 votes, but during and after the election dispute, questions remained about the uncounted ballots of 175,010 voters, ballots that had been rejected by error-prone tabulating machines employed in many Florida counties. Confusion and conflict, much of it generated by Republican intrigue, prevented these ballots from being counted during the election controversy. However, in 2001, every uncounted ballot was carefully examined in a scientific study by the University of Chicago, which found that when all the votes were counted, more votes had been cast for Gore than for Bush.[7]

The source of Gore's winning margin resided in an unexpected place. During the election dispute, when ballots were being recounted by hand, the focus had been on "undervotes" among punch card ballots. Undervotes are ballots rejected by machine tabulators because they appear to include no vote for one of the presidential tickets. Vote-tabulation machines read punch cards by shining a light on the cards as they are fed through the machine. Votes are registered by the tabulators when the light shines through holes that are made in the cards when voters punch out the "chad" next to the candidates of their choice. If chads are only partially broken free, they can become like swinging doors that may open or close when they are run through the counter. Often, a valid vote can be missed by a tabulating machine if the chad is left hanging, because a door-like, swinging chad can be folded closed as the ballot goes through the machine. This phenomenon is well known to election officials and is why many states, including Florida, have procedures for ballots to be recounted by hand when elections are very close.

Manual recounts of punch card ballots were controversial in the 2000 election dispute because Florida had no statewide standards for handling ballots with partially punched chads. State law called for county-level election boards to handle recounts by examining ballots visually and, where possible, determining the intention of the voter. During the recount, Palm Beach County treated hanging chads more restrictively than Broward County, which liberalized its criteria partway through the process. These differing and changing standards made the recounts appear arbitrary and vulnerable to manipulation. This was the reason given by the U.S. Supreme Court when it intervened to end the statewide recount that had been ordered by the Supreme Court of Florida in early December. When it issued its final decision on December 12, the U.S. Supreme Court endorsed manual recounts, but it said that Florida needed statewide standards. It also ruled that the statewide recount ordered by the Florida Supreme Court could not continue to completion because time had run out for submitting new results to Congress.

Ironically, we now know that the outcome of the 2000 presidential election did not hinge on hanging chads. About one-third of the machine-rejected ballots were undervotes. The University of Chicago found that ballots with partially punched chads split more or less evenly between Gore and Bush regardless of the standards used to judge hanging chads. Gore's winning margin was in an entirely different set of machine-rejected ballots—in what are now called "write-in overvotes." These were ballots on which a selection had been made from the list of candidates and then a name had also been printed in the space for write-ins. Although write-in overvotes were automatically excluded by tabulating machines, they contained unambiguous and legally valid votes whenever the write-in candidate matched the candidate chosen from the list preceding it. In its comprehensive study of all the uncounted ballots, the University of Chicago found that write-in overvotes heavily favored Gore. Thus, a full recount would have determined unambiguously that Gore had won.[8]

BIAS DURING THE CONTEST

When Election Day ended with no clear winner, Republican officials in Florida continued to behave just as they had before the election, which is to say, criminally. The very people who were supposed to be administering the election process to assure fairness, and who had sworn an oath to uphold the Constitution, entered into a conspiracy to secure the election for George W. Bush. A series of articles published in the *Washington Post* a few weeks after the election controversy had been decided revealed that at least some of the actions and decisions of Jeb Bush and Katherine Harris were coordinated directly or indirectly with the strategies of George W.'s legal team.[9] Jeb Bush and Harris became part of a conspiracy to prevent the votes cast on Election Day from being fully and fairly counted even though, or precisely because, they realized that a careful review might show that Gore had won.

The *Post* series was followed in the summer of 2001 by a series in the *New York Times* suggesting the possibility of a conspiracy between Republican officials in Tallahassee, Republican members of Congress, and military personnel at home and abroad.[10] The *Times* revealed that military personnel had been encouraged to vote after election day; that the delivery of overseas military ballots, at least some known to contain votes cast illegally, had been expedited in order to get to Florida in time to be counted; and that Republican operatives sent into Florida by the Bush campaign to pressure county canvassing boards had successfully pushed for improperly completed oversees ballots to be counted in Republican counties and rejected in Democratic counties.

At the center of these apparent conspiracies was Katherine Harris. As Secretary of State, she was probably most to blame for the election and post-election disorder—even if she had not been party to criminal conspiracies—because she had had overall responsibility for administering Florida's election process. To give her advice as the election dispute unfolded, Harris brought into her inner circle one of the state's best-known Republican strategists, Mac Stipanovich, who has not denied being in regular contact with George W. Bush's legal team during the controversy. To be sure, during the dispute, accusations were hurled at Harris publicly—for example, that she was helping George W. in return for a promised ambassadorship. Rumors also circulated in Tallahassee that she and Jeb Bush had had an affair on one of their joint trips out of state during the primaries.[11] At the time, however, these accusations all seemed to have been contrived by her political enemies. However, once Stapanovic's role behind the scenes had come to light, Harris' repeated rulings that benefited Bush could no longer be easily dismissed as innocent expressions of her best judgment unfairly depicted as partisan sabotage.

For his part, Jeb Bush recused himself from the Election Commission, but nevertheless played a very active role helping his brother behind the scenes. If his aid to George W. had been limited to offering advice and emotional support, Jeb's behavior would have been beyond public reproach. But, in fact, some of his actions appear to have been violations of Florida law. While employed by the state, he personally attended meetings with his brother's lawyers. Worse, he instructed or, at the very least, allowed his legal staff, while they too were working on state time, to contact the state's biggest law firms and discourage them from working for Gore.[12] These calls involved more than a misappropriation of state resources for partisan political activities. Given that the law firms in question drew considerable income from state contracts and lobbying contracts requiring access to the governor, the firms would have perceived these calls as veiled threats. Using public office for coercion is a felony.

Although less extensive and more attenuated, partisanship was also evident among the Democrats. Attorney General Bob Butterworth, a Democrat, had regular contact with the Gore team, went on television to defend the recounts, and had his staff suggest to the Palm Beach County canvassing board that it request an opinion from him about the recount deadline imposed by the

Secretary of State. On the other hand, Butterworth also took actions that worked against Gore. In particular, he stated in writing and on television that requirements in Florida election requiring absentee ballots to have postmarks should be waived, because the mail of some members of the military stationed overseas and on ships would not have been stamped. Butterworth also demonstrated insight by arguing that equal treatment requirements in the U.S. Constitution needed to be addressed by conducting manual recounts statewide. Still, Butterworth's frequent contacts with the Gore legal and political team were inconsistent with the independence expected of his office.

In short, the officials who were supposed to keep Florida's election process fair and open did not appear neutral, and they were not neutral in fact. *The Washington Post* summed up the role of partisanship as follows:

> What is clear is that Bush enjoyed an enormous advantage because of the presence of his brother in the governor's office and Katherine Harris as secretary of state. The role Jeb Bush and his team played in rounding up legal talent, providing political analysis and offering strategic advice is all the more clear from post-election interviews. With Jeb Bush as governor, the Republicans controlled the machinery of state government and with it the power to set deadlines, enforce election laws in ways that were beneficial to the then-Texas governor and put obstacles in Gore's path. Secretary of State Harris also relied on advice from one of the leading Republican strategists in the state—J.M. "Mac" Stipanovich, a well-connected Republican lobbyist who was an ally of Jeb Bush.[13]

The evidence is clear that the 2000 presidential election was stolen. It was stolen mainly by sabotage, but also by plain old-fashioned vote fraud. Moreover, the evidence implicates men and women who held high public offices before and during the election dispute. Under the statute of limitations, these people may no longer be punishable for their crimes, but for the nation's sake, these crimes still need to be investigated so that the truth will be known and reforms can be devised to prevent similar criminality in the future.

Equally important is for Americans to learn from this experience. When a candidate and his or her supporters appear willing to break laws, ignore the Constitution, disenfranchise qualified voters, and in other ways degrade the political process to gain power, the appropriate response is not to "move on," but to investigate, for people who are willing to cheat and lie to win an election will certainly be willing to do the same or worse once they are in office. This is the lesson from the 2000 presidential election and the shameful administration of George W. Bush.

NOTES

1. U.S. Civil Rights Commission, *Voting Irregularities in Florida During the 2000 Presidential Election*, June 2001.

2. David Barstow and Don Von Natta, Jr., "How Bush Took Florida: Mining the Overseas Absentee Vote," *New York Times*, July 15, 2001.

3. David Colburn and Lance deHaven-Smith, *Florida's Megatrends* (Gainesville: The University Press of Florida, 2002).

4. Detailed Bulletin 145, *Florida Population Studies 2006* (Gainesville: Bureau of Economic and Business Research, 2006).

5. U.S. Civil Rights Commission, *Voting Irregularities in Florida During the 2000 Presidential Election*, June 2001. See also, S.V. Date, *Jeb: America's Next Bush* (New York: Penguin, 2007), pp. 120-124.

6. Transcript, U.S. Commission on Civil Rights, *Hearing on Allegations of Election Day Irregularities in Florida*, Tallahassee, Florida, January 11, 2001.

7. For a detailed review and analysis of the study's data see Lance deHaven-Smith, *The Battle for Florida: An Annotated Compendium of Materials from the 2000 Presidential Election* (Gainesville: The University Press of Florida, 2005).

8. deHaven-Smith, pp. 38-42. See also, Steven F. Freeman and Joel Bleifuss, *Was the 2004 Presidential Election Stolen? Exit Polls, Election Fraud, and the Official Count*, pp. 33-54.

9. David Von Drehle, Dan Balz, Ellen Nakashima and Jo Becker, "A Wild Ride Into Uncharted Territory," *Washington Post,* January 28, 2001. Dan Balz, David Von Drehle, Susan Schmidt and Roberto Suro, "The Inside Story of America's Closest Election," *Washington Post,* February 4, 2001. David Barstow and Somini Sengupta, "The Florida Governor: With Tallahassee All Astir, Jeb Bush Keeps Distance," *New York Times,* November 17, 2001.

10. David Barstow and Don Von Natta, Jr. "How Bush Took Florida: Mining the Overseas Absentee Vote." *New York Times,* July 15, 2001.

11. Jake Tapper, *Down and Dirty: The Plot to Steal the Presidency* (New York: Little, Brown and Company, 2001). Douglas Kellner, *Grand Theft 2000: Media Spectacle and a Stolen Election* (New York: Rowman & Littlefield, 2001).

12. David Von Drehle, Dan Balz, Ellen Nakashima and Jo Becker, "A Wild Ride Into Uncharted Territory," *Washington Post,* January 28, 2001.

13. Dan Balz, David Von Drehle, Susan Schmidt and Roberto Suro, "Epilogue: Last in a Series on the 2000 Election," *Washington Post,* February 4, 2001.

2002

★

Having lost control of the Senate when Jim Jeffords left the GOP on May 24, 2001, the Republican Party went all-out to get it back, and then some, in the off-year elections. Thus there were big surprises, major mysteries and whopping improprieties in several states—including New Hampshire, where party operatives would later be convicted for a phone-jamming scheme that helped to slash the Democratic turnout early on the morning of Election Day. The strangest race of all, however, was in Georgia, where the well-liked Democratic Senator Max Cleland, a decorated veteran, was unexpectedly "defeated" by chicken hawk Saxby Chambliss.

In 2003, a computer engineer named Rob Behler, who had worked the previous summer as Diebold's deployment manager in Georgia, came out with a startling claim: that, just a few weeks prior to the election, Bob Urosevich, president of Diebold's e-voting division, had flown in from Texas to direct the surreptitious placement of a software patch on several thousand of the company's machines. Behler told his story on ABC's *Nightline*, and in an article by Ronnie Dugger in *The Nation*—and then both he and his account slipped down the memory hole.

In this section, Robert F. Kennedy, Jr. revisits the Georgia story, reconfirming and expanding Behler's story with the testimony of Chris Hood, another former Diebold manager. Kennedy uses Hood's account to demonstrate the lack of security of DRE machines, which were shortly to be used throughout the nation on Election Day, 2002. Notwithstanding the extreme importance of that issue, Kennedy's exposé made little news; Chris Matthews yelled at him on *Hardball*, and that was it.

That year, the Republican Party also fixed the vote in certain state elections: most vengefully, it seems, in Alabama, where Governor Don Siegelman, a popular reformist Democrat, was cheated of his re-election—and later prosecuted on imaginary charges, and then hustled off to federal prison, where he sits today, held incommunicado and with no right of appeal. Dubbed "the Man in the Iron Mask" by Scott Horton of *Harper's*, Siegelman is a political prisoner, and yet his plight has been ignored almost completely by the press. In a pair of interconnected essays, Larisa Alexandrovna sheds a bright light on the Republican cabal that runs the Yellowhammer State, with guidance from the Bush machine in Washington, while James Gundlach tells us how the Alabama vote was evidently fixed in 2002.

DIEBOLD AND MAX CLELAND'S "LOSS" IN GEORGIA

★

ROBERT F. KENNEDY JR.

The debacle of the 2000 presidential election made it all too apparent to most Americans that our electoral system was broken. And private-sector entrepreneurs were quick to offer a fix: Touch-screen voting machines, promised the industry and its lobbyists, would make voting as easy and reliable as withdrawing cash from an ATM. Congress, always ready with funds for needy industries, swiftly authorized $3.9 billion to upgrade the nation's election systems—with much of the money devoted to installing electronic voting machines in each of America's 180,000 precincts. But as the 2008 election approaches, electronic voting machines have made things worse instead of better, as studies have demonstrated that hackers can easily rig the technology to fix an election.

Even worse, many electronic machines don't produce a paper record that can be recounted when equipment malfunctions—an omission that practically invites malicious tampering. "Every board of election has staff members with the technological ability to fix an election," Ion Sancho, an election supervisor in Leon County, Florida, told me. "Even one corrupt staffer can throw an election. Without paper records, it could happen under my nose and there is no way I'd ever find out about it. With a few key people in the right places, it would be possible to throw a presidential election."

Chris Hood remembers the day in July 2002 that he began to question what was really going on in Georgia. An African-American whose parents fought for voting rights in the South during the 1960s, Hood was proud to be working as a consultant for Diebold Election Systems, helping the company promote its new electronic voting machines. During the presidential election two years earlier, more than 94,000 paper ballots had gone uncounted in Georgia—almost double the national average—and Secretary of State Cathy Cox was under pressure to make sure that every vote was recorded properly.

Hood had been present in May 2002 when officials with Cox's office signed a contract with Diebold, paying the company a record $54 million to install 19,000 electronic voting machines across the state. At a restaurant inside Atlanta's Marriott Hotel, he noticed the firm's CEO, Walden O'Dell, checking Diebold's stock price on a laptop computer every five minutes, waiting for a bounce from the announcement.

Hood wondered why Diebold, the world's third-largest seller of ATMs, had been awarded the contract. The company had barely completed its acquisition of Global Election Systems, a voting-machine firm that owned the technology Diebold was promising to sell Georgia. And its bid was the highest among nine competing vendors. Whispers within the company hinted that a fix was in.

"The Diebold executives had a news conference planned on the day of the award," Hood recalls, "and we were instructed to stay in our hotel rooms until just hours before the announcement. They didn't want the competitors to know and possibly file a protest" about the lack of a fair bidding process. It certainly didn't hurt that Diebold had political clout: Cox's predecessor as secretary of state, Lewis Massey, was now a lobbyist for the company.

The problem was, Diebold had only five months to install the new machines—a "very narrow window of time to do such a big deployment," Hood notes. The old systems stored in warehouses had to be replaced with new equipment, and dozens of state officials and poll workers had to be trained in how to use the touch-screen machines. "It was pretty much an impossible task," Hood recalls. There was only one way, he adds, that the job could be done in time—if "the vendor had control over the entire environment." That is precisely what happened. In late July, to speed deployment of the new machines, Cox quietly signed an agreement with Diebold that effectively privatized Georgia's entire electoral system. The company was authorized to put together ballots, program machines and train poll workers across the state—all without any official supervision. "We ran the election," says Hood. "We had 356 people that Diebold brought into the state. Diebold opened and closed the polls and tabulated the votes. Diebold convinced Cox that it would be best if the company ran everything due to the time constraints, and in the interest of a trouble-free election, she let us do it."

Then, one day in July, Hood was surprised to see the president of Diebold's election unit, Bob Urosevich, arrive in Georgia from his headquarters in Texas. With the primaries looming, Urosevich was personally distributing a "patch," a little piece of software designed to correct glitches in the computer program. "We were told that it was intended to fix the clock in the system, which it didn't do," Hood says. "The curious thing is the very swift, covert way this was done."

Georgia law mandates that any change made in voting machines be certified by the state. But thanks to Cox's agreement with Diebold, the company was essentially allowed to certify itself. "It was an unauthorized patch, and they were trying to keep it secret from the state," Hood told me. "We were told not to talk to county personnel about it. I received instructions directly from Urosevich. It was very unusual that a president of the company would give an order like that and be involved at that level."

According to Hood, Diebold employees altered software in some 5,000 machines in DeKalb and Fulton counties—the state's largest Democratic strongholds. To avoid detection, Hood and others on his team entered warehouses early in the morning. "We went in at 7:30 a.m. and were out by 11," Hood says. "There was a universal key to unlock the machines, and it's easy to get access. The machines in the warehouses were unlocked. We had control of everything. The state gave us the keys to the castle, so to speak, and they stayed out of our way." Hood personally patched fifty-six machines and witnessed the patch being applied to more than 1,200 others.

The patch comes on a memory card that is inserted into a machine. Eventually, all the memory cards end up on a server that tabulates the votes—where the patch can be programmed to alter the outcome of an election. "There could be a hidden program on a memory card that adjusts everything to the pre-ferred election results," Hood says. "Your program says, 'I want my candidate to stay ahead by three or four percent or whatever.' Those programs can include a built-in delete that erases itself after it's done."

It is impossible to know whether the machines were rigged to alter the election in Georgia, as Diebold's machines provided no paper trail, making a recount impossible. But the tally in Georgia that November surprised even the most seasoned political observers. Six days before the vote, polls showed Senator Max Cleland, a decorated war veteran and Democratic incumbent, leading his Republican opponent Saxby Chambliss—darling of the Christian Coalition—by five percentage points. In the governor's race, Democrat Roy Barnes was running a decisive eleven points ahead of Republican Sonny Perdue. But on Election Day, Chambliss won with 53 percent of the vote, and Perdue won with 51 percent.

Diebold insists that the patch was installed "with the approval and oversight of the state." But after the election, the Georgia Secretary of State's office submitted a "punch list" to Bob Urosevich of "issues and concerns related to the statewide voting system that we would like Diebold to address." One of the items referenced was "Application/Implication of '0808' Patch." The state was seeking confirmation that the patch did not require that the system "be recertified at national and state level" as well as "verifiable analysis of overall impact of patch to the voting system." In a separate letter, Secretary Cox asked Urosevich about Diebold's use of substitute memory cards and defective equipment, as well as widespread problems that caused machines to freeze up and improperly record votes. The state threatened to delay further payments to Diebold until "these punch list items will be corrected and completed."

Diebold's response was not made public, but its machines remained in place for Georgia's election in the fall of 2006. Hood says it was "common knowledge" within the company that Diebold also illegally installed uncertified software in machines used in the 2004 presidential primaries—a charge the company denied. Disturbed to see the promise of electronic machines subverted by private companies, Hood left the election consulting business and become a whistle-blower. "What I saw," he says, "was basically a corporate takeover of our voting system."

The United States is one of only a handful of major democracies that allow private, partisan companies to secretly count and tabulate votes using their own proprietary software. Today, 80 percent of all the ballots in America are tallied by four companies—Diebold, Election Systems & Software (ES&S), Sequoia Voting Systems and Hart InterCivic. In 2004, 36 million votes were cast on their touch-screen systems, and millions more were recorded by optical-scan machines owned by the same companies that use electronic technology to tabulate paper ballots. The simple fact is, these machines not only break down with regular-ity, they are easily compromised—by people inside, and outside, the companies.

Three of the four companies have close ties to the Republican Party. ES&S, in an earlier corporate incarnation, was chaired by Chuck Hagel, who in 1996 became the first Republican elected to the U.S. Senate from Nebraska in twenty-four years—winning a close race in which 85 percent of the votes were tallied by his former company. Hart InterCivic ranks among its investors GOP loyalist Tom Hicks, who bought the Texas Rangers from George W. Bush in 1998, making Bush a millionaire fifteen times over. And according to campaign-finance records, Diebold, along with its employees and their families, has contributed at least $300,000 to GOP candidates and party funds since 1998—including more than $200,000 to the Republican National Committee. In a 2003 fund-raising e-mail, the company's then-CEO Walden O'Dell promised to deliver Ohio's electoral votes to Bush in 2004.

The voting-machine companies bear heavy blame for the 2000 presidential-election disaster. Fox News' fateful decision to call Florida for Bush—followed minutes later by CBS and NBC—came after electronic machines in Volusia County erroneously subtracted more than 16,000 votes from Al Gore's total. Later, after an internal investigation, CBS described the mistake as "critical" in the network's decision. Seeing what was an apparent spike for Bush, Gore conceded the election—then reversed his decision after a campaign staffer investigated and discovered that Gore was actually ahead in Volusia by 13,000 votes.

Investigators traced the mistake to Global Election Systems, the firm later acquired by Diebold. Two months after the election, an internal memo from Talbot Iredale, the company's master programmer, blamed the problem on a memory card that had been improperly—and unnecessarily—uploaded. "There is always the possibility," Iredale conceded, "that the 'second memory card' or 'second upload' came from an unauthorized source."

Amid the furor over hanging chads and butterfly ballots in

Florida, however, the "faulty memory card" was all but forgotten. Instead of sharing culpability for the Florida catastrophe, voting-machine companies used their political clout to present their product as the solution. In October 2002, President Bush signed the Help America Vote Act (HAVA), requiring states and counties to upgrade their voting systems with electronic machines and giving vast sums of money to state officials to distribute to the tight-knit cabal of largely Republican vendors.

The primary author and steward of HAVA was Representative Bob Ney, then the GOP chairman of the powerful U.S. House Administration Committee. Ney resigned in November 2006 after a guilty plea to charges of conspiracy and making false statements in relation to the scandal surrounding disgraced lobbyist Jack Abramoff, whose firm received at least $275,000 from Diebold to lobby for its touch-screen machines. Ney's chief of staff, David DiStefano, also worked as a registered lobbyist for Diebold, receiving at least $180,000 from the firm to lobby for HAVA and "other election reform issues." Ney—who accepted campaign contributions from DiStefano and counted Diebold's then-CEO O'Dell among his constituents—made sure that HAVA strongly favored the use of the company's machines.

Ney also made sure that Diebold and other companies would not be required to equip their machines with printers to provide paper records that could be verified by voters. In a clever twist, HAVA effectively pressured every precinct to provide at least one voting device that had no paper trail—supposedly so that vision-impaired citizens could vote in secrecy. The provision was backed by two little-known advocacy groups: the National Federation of the Blind, which accepted $1 million from Diebold to build a new research institute, and the American Association of People with Disabilities, which pocketed at least $26,000 from voting-machine companies. The NFB maintained that a paper voting receipt would jeopardize its members' civil rights—a position not shared by other groups that advocate for the blind.

Before sinking in the sewage of the Abramoff scandal, Ney did one last favor for his friends at Diebold. When 212 members of Congress from both parties sponsored a bill to mandate a paper trail for all votes, Ney used his position as chairman to prevent the measure from even getting a hearing before his committee. The result was that HAVA—the chief reform effort after the 2000 disaster—placed much of the nation;s electoral system in the hands of for-profit companies. "This whole undertaking was never about voters," says Hood, who saw firsthand how the measure benefited Diebold's bottom line. "It was about privatizing elections. HAVA has been turned into a corporate-revenue enhancement scheme."

No case better demonstrates the dangers posed by electronic voting machines than the experience of Maryland. As in Georgia, officials there granted Diebold control over much of the state's election systems during the 2002 midterm elections. (In the interests of disclosure, my sister was a candidate for governor that year and lost by a margin consistent with pre-election polls.) On Election Night, when Chris Hood accompanied Diebold president Bob Urosevich and marketing director Mark Radke to the tabulation center in Montgomery County where the votes would be added up, he was stunned to find the room empty. "Not a single Maryland election official was there to retrieve the memory cards," he recalls. As cards containing every vote in the county began arriving in canvas bags, the Diebold executives plugged them into a group of touch-screen tabulators linked into a central server, which was also controlled by a Diebold employee.

"It would have been very easy for any one of us to take a contaminated card out of our pocket, put it into the system, and download some malicious code that would then end up in the server, impacting every other vote that went in, before and after," says Hood. "We had absolute control of the tabulations. We could have fixed the election if we wanted. We had access, and that's all you need. I can honestly say that every election I saw with Diebold in charge was compromised—if not in the count, at least in the security."

After the election, Maryland planned to install Diebold's AccuVote-TS electronic machines across the entire state—until four computer scientists at Johns Hopkins and Rice universities released an analysis of the company's software source code in July 2003. "This voting system is far below even the most minimal security standards applicable in other contexts," the scientists concluded. It was, in fact, "unsuitable for use in a general election."

"With electronic machines, you can commit wholesale fraud with a single alteration of software," says Avi Rubin, a computer-science professor at Johns Hopkins who has received $7.5 million from the National Science Foundation to study electronic voting. "There are a million little tricks when you build software that allows you to do whatever you want. If you know the precinct demographics, the machine can be programmed to recognize its precinct and strategically flip votes in elections that are several years in the future. No one will ever know it happened."

In response to the study, Maryland commissioned two additional reports on Diebold's equipment. The first was conducted by Science Applications International Corporation, a company that, along with Diebold, was part of an industry group that promoted electronic voting machines. SAIC conceded that Diebold's machines were "at high risk of compromise," but concluded that the state's "procedural controls and general voting environment reduce or eliminate many of the vulnerabilities identified in the Rubin report." Despite the lack of any real "procedural controls" during the 2002 election, then Governor Robert Ehrlich gave the state election board the go-ahead to pay $55.6 million for Diebold's AccuVote-TS system.

The other analysis, commissioned by the Maryland legislature, was a practical test of the systems by RABA Technologies, a consulting firm experienced in both defense and intelligence work for the federal government. Computer scientists hired by RABA to hack into six of Diebold's machines discovered a major flaw: The company had built what are known as "back doors" into the software that could enable a hacker to hide an unauthorized and malicious code in the system. William Arbaugh, of the University of Maryland, gave the Diebold system an "F" with "the possibility of raising it to a 'C'" with extra credit—that is, if they follow the recommendations we gave them."

But according to e-mails obtained by *Rolling Stone* in 2006, Diebold not only failed to follow up on most of the recommendations, it worked to cover them up. Michael Wertheimer, who led the RABA study, now serves as an assistant deputy director in the Office of the Director of National Intelligence. "We made numerous recommendations that would have required Diebold to fix these issues," he wrote in one e-mail, "but were rebuffed by the argument that the machines were physically protected and could not be altered by someone outside the established chain of custody."

In another e-mail, Wertheimer said that Diebold and state officials worked to downplay his team's dim assessment. "We spent hours dealing with Diebold lobbyists and election officials who sought to minimize our impact," he recalled. "The results were risk-managed in favor of expediency and potential catastrophe."

During the 2004 presidential election, with Diebold machines in place across the state, things began to go wrong from the very start. A month before the vote, an abandoned Diebold machine was discovered in a bar in Baltimore. "What's really worrisome," says Hood, "is that someone could get hold of all the technology—for manipulation—if they knew the inner workings of just one machine."

Election Day was a complete disaster. "Countless numbers of machines were down because of what appeared to be flaws in Diebold's system," says Hood, who was part of a crew of roving technicians charged with making sure that the polls were up and running. "Memory cards overloading, machines freezing up, poll workers afraid to turn them on or off for fear of losing votes."

Then, after the polls closed, Diebold technicians who showed up to collect the memory cards containing the votes found that many were missing. "The machines are gone," one janitor told Hood—picked up, apparently, by the vendor who had delivered them in the first place. "There was major chaos because there were so many cards missing," Hood says.

Even before the 2004 election, experts warned that electronic voting machines would undermine the integrity of the vote. "The system we have for testing and certifying voting equipment in this country is not only broken but is virtually nonexistent," Michael Shamos, a distinguished professor of computer science at Carnegie Mellon University, testified before Congress that June. "It must be re-created from scratch."

Two months later, the U.S. Computer Emergency Readiness Team—a division of the Department of Homeland Security—issued a little-noticed "cyber-security bulletin." The alert dealt specifically with a database that Diebold used in tabulating votes. "A vulnerability exists due to an undocumented backdoor account," the alert warned, citing the same kind of weakness identified by the RABA scientists. The security flaw, it added, could allow "a malicious user [to] modify votes."

Such warnings, however, didn't stop states across the country from installing electronic voting machines for the 2004 election. In Ohio, jammed and inoperable machines were reported throughout Toledo. In heavily Democratic areas of Youngstown, nearly 100 voters pushed "Kerry" and watched "Bush" light up. At least twenty machines had to be recalibrated in the middle of the voting process for flipping Kerry votes to Bush. Similar "vote hopping" was reported by voters in other states.

The widespread glitches didn't deter Secretary of State J. Kenneth Blackwell—who also chaired Bush's re-election campaign in Ohio—from cutting a deal in 2005 that would have guaranteed Diebold a virtual monopoly on vote counting in the state. Local election officials alleged that the deal, which came only a few months after Blackwell bought nearly $10,000 in Diebold stock, was a violation of state rules requiring a fair and competitive bidding process. Facing a lawsuit, Blackwell agreed to allow other companies to provide machines as well.

Electronic voting machines also caused widespread problems in Florida, where Bush bested Kerry by 381,000 votes. When statistical experts from the University of California examined the state's official tally, they discovered a disturbing pattern: "The data show with 99.0 percent certainty that a county's use of electronic voting is associated with a disproportionate increase in votes for President Bush. Compared to counties with paper ballots, counties with electronic voting machines were significantly more likely to show increases in support for President Bush between 2000 and 2004." The three counties with the most discrepancies— Broward, Palm Beach and Miami-Dade—were also the most heavily Democratic. Electronic voting machines, the report concluded, may have improperly awarded as many as 260,000 votes to Bush. "No matter how many factors and variables we took into consideration, the significant correlation in the votes for President Bush and electronic voting cannot be explained," said Michael Hout, a member of the National Academy of Sciences.

Charles Stewart III, an MIT professor who specializes in voter behavior and methodology, was initially skeptical of the study—but was unable to find any flaw in the results. "You can't break it—I've tried," he told *The Washington Post*. "There's something funky in the results from the electronic-machine Democratic counties."

Questions also arose in Texas in 2004. William Singer, an election programmer in Tarrant County, wrote the secretary of state's office after the vote to report that ES&S pressured officials to install unapproved software during the presidential primaries. "What I was expected to do in order to 'pull off' an election," Singer wrote, "was far beyond the kind of practices that I believe should be standard and accepted in the election industry." The company denied the charge, but in a 2006 e-mail, Singer elaborated that ES&S employees had pushed local election officials to pressure the secretary of state to accept "a software change at such a last minute there would be no choice, and effectively avoid certification." Despite such reports, Texas continues to rely on ES&S.

In October 2005, the Government Accountability Office issued a damning report on electronic voting machines. Citing widespread irregularities and malfunctions, the government's top watchdog agency concluded that a host of weaknesses with touch-screen and optical-scan technology "could damage the integrity of ballots, votes and voting-system software by allowing unauthorized modifications." Some electronic systems used passwords that were "easily guessed" or employed identical passwords for numerous systems. Software could be handled and transported with no clear chain of custody, and locks protecting computer hardware were easy to pick. Unsecured memory cards could enable individuals to "vote multiple times, change vote totals and produce false election reports."

An even more comprehensive report released in June, 2006 by the Brennan Center for Justice, a nonpartisan think tank at the New York University School of Law, echoed the GAO's findings. The report—conducted by a task force of computer scientists and security experts from the government, universities and the private sector—was peer-reviewed by the National Institute of Standards and Technology. Electronic voting machines widely adopted since 2000, the report concluded, "pose a real danger to the integrity of national, state and local elections." While no instances of hacking have yet been documented, the report identified 120 security threats to three widely used machines—the easiest method of attack being to utilize corrupt software that shifts votes from one candidate to another.

Computer experts have demonstrated that a successful attack would be relatively simple. In a study released in September, 2006, computer scientists at Princeton University created vote-stealing software that could be injected into a Diebold machine in as little as a minute, obscuring all evidence of its presence. They also created a virus that could "infect" other units in a voting system, committing "widespread fraud" from a single machine. Within sixty seconds, a lone hacker could own an election.

In 2005, comedian Bill Maher stood in a Las Vegas casino and looked out over thousands of slot machines. "They never make a mistake," he remarked to me. "Can't we get a voting machine that can't be fixed?"

Indeed, there is a remarkably simple solution: equip every touch-screen machine to provide paper receipts that can be verified by voters and recounted in the event of malfunction or tampering. "The paper is the insurance against the cheating machine," says Rubin, the computer expert.

In Florida, an astonishing new law actually makes it illegal to count paper ballots by hand after they've already been tallied by machine. But twenty-seven states now require a paper trail, and others are considering similar requirements. In New Mexico, Governor Bill Richardson has instituted what many consider an even better solution: Voters use paper ballots, which are then scanned and counted electronically. "We became one of the laughingstock states in 2004 because the machines were defective, slow and unreliable," says Richardson. "I said to myself, 'I'm not going to go through this again.' The paper-ballot system, as untechnical as it seems, is the most verifiable way we can assure Americans that their vote is counting."

Paper ballots will not completely eliminate the threat of tampering, of course—after all, election fraud and miscounts have occurred throughout our history. As long as there has been a paper trail, however, our elections have been conducted with some measure of public scrutiny. But electronic voting machines are a hacker's dream. And today, for-profit companies are being given unprecedented and frightening power not only to provide these machines, but to store and count our votes in secret, without any real oversight.

You do not have to believe in conspiracy theories to fear for the integrity of our electoral system. The right to vote is simply too important—and too hard won—to be surrendered without a fight. It is time for Americans to reclaim our democracy from private interests.

THE ORDEAL OF
DON SIEGELMAN

★

LARISA ALEXANDROVNA

On Election Day 2002, the Alabama governorship seemed all but certain to be delivered to the Democratic incumbent, Don Siegelman. In a largely Republican state, the popular Siegelman had been the only person in Alabama history to hold all of the state's highest offices, having served as Attorney General, Secretary of State, Lieutenant Governor and finally, as Governor. When the polls closed on election night, and the votes were being counted, it seemed increasingly apparent that Governor Siegelman had been victorious in his re-election bid against the Republican challenger, Bob Riley. But, sometime in the middle of the night, a single county changed everything, and by the next morning, Alabamians awoke to find that Riley was their new governor.

According to CNN, the confusion over who the actual winner was stemmed from what appeared to be two different sets of numbers coming in from Baldwin County:

> "The confusion stems from two sets of numbers reported by one heavily Republican district," the network stated. "Figures originally reported by Baldwin County showed Siegelman got about 19,000 votes there, making him

the state's winner by about two-tenths of 1 percent," its reporter added. "But hours after polls closed, Baldwin County officials said the first number was wrong, and Siegelman had received just less than 13,000. Those figures would make Riley the statewide winner by about 3,000 votes."[1]

Riley's electoral victory had rested on a razor-thin margin of 3,120 votes. According to official reports, Baldwin County had conducted a recount sometime in the middle of the night, when the only county officers and election supervisors present were Republicans. While there were many electronic anomalies across the state, the Baldwin County recount had put Riley over the finish line.

State and county Democrats quickly requested another Baldwin County recount with Democratic observers present, as well as a statewide recount. But before the Baldwin County Democratic Party canvassing board could act, Alabama's Republican Attorney General William Pryor had the ballots sealed. Unless Siegelman filed an election contest in the courts, Pryor said, state county canvassing boards did not have the authority "to break the seals on ballots and machines under section 17-9-31" of the state constitution.[2]

FRAMING A POLITICAL OPPONENT

Pryor had won his reelection bid in 1998 to Alabama's top legal office with the help of two campaign managers, one of whom is remarkably well known because he would later go on to lead the George W. Bush victory in the 2000 election: Karl Rove. Pryor's other campaign manager was a longtime GOP operative by the name of Bill Canary. Canary would emerge as the campaign manager for Siegelman's opponent, Bob Riley, in the 2002 election.

After Pryor was re-elected in 1998, he almost immediately

began investigating Siegelman, who was then Lieutenant Governor. Siegelman appears to have made an enemy of Pryor as early as 1997, when he criticized the latter's close relationship with the tobacco industry. Pryor's history and relationship with Canary and Rove should have been reason enough for the Alabama Attorney General to recuse himself from the November 2002 election controversy. But Pryor refused.

A year earlier, in 2001, President Bush had appointed Leura Canary to serve as U.S. Attorney for the Middle District of Alabama. If that last name sounds familiar, it is because her husband is Bill Canary. Leura Canary had begun working on Siegelman's case almost as soon she took office, when she federalized Attorney General Pryor's ongoing state probe. After spending six months investigating Siegelman, Leura Canary was forced to formally recuse herself from the investigation because of her husband's connections to the Riley campaign. At least she gave the appearance of recusing herself; no evidence of this recusal has ever been found, and all requested documents from the Department of Justice are MIA. By all accounts, Leura Canary continued to conduct the investigation from behind the scenes.[3] This resulted in her delivering an indictment in 2004 of conspiracy and fraud in which Siegelman and two alleged co-conspirators were said to have rigged Medicaid contracts in 1999. However, only a few months after filing the indictment, the U.S. Attorney's prosecuting the case were held in contempt of court, and the case against Siegelman was dismissed.[4]

FINDING A MORE RECEPTIVE JUDGE

After Siegelman indicated his intention to seek reelection, Canary's original investigation resurfaced in 2005. (Canary had never stopped pushing the investigation along, even against the advice of her professional staff.) As a result, in October 2005, Don Siegelman was once again indicted by a federal grand jury, on 32 counts of bribery, conspiracy and mail fraud.

Siegelman was accused of accepting a $500,000 donation from HealthSouth founder Richard M. Scrushy in exchange for an appointment to the Alabama hospital regulatory board. That donation supposedly went to pay off a debt incurred by a non-profit foundation set up by Siegelman and others to promote an education lottery in a state referendum. However, Siegelman's attorney argued that Siegelman did not control the foundation by which the debt was incurred, nor did he take money from or profit from the foundation.

The case was assigned to Judge Mark Fuller, whom George W. Bush had nominated for a federal judgeship to the U.S. District Court for the Middle District of Alabama in 2002. Prior to his promotion to the federal bench, Fuller had served as District Attorney for Alabama's 12th Circuit. Fuller had been replaced as D.A. by Gary McAliley, who in investigating his predecessor's accounting practices, found that Fuller had been defrauding the Alabama retirement system by spiking salaries.[5]

There were many irregularities during the trial, including strong indications of jury tampering involving two jurors. Eventually, in June 2006, Siegelman was convicted of seven of the charges against him, after the jury had deadlocked twice and been sent back each time to deliberate by Judge Fuller. When it came time for sentencing, Fuller imposed a sentence of seven years and four months, and would not allow Siegelman to remain free while his case was under appeal. Within hours of his sentencing, Siegelman had been taken to a federal penitentiary in Atlanta.

A letter sent to then-U.S. Attorney General Alberto Gonzales by members of the U.S. House Judiciary Committee revealed numerous questions about the indictment and the trial:

> "There have been several reported irregularities in the case against Mr. Siegelman that raise questions about his prosecution. In 2004, charges against Mr. Siegelman were

dropped by the U.S. Attorney's Office in the Northern District of Alabama before the case went to trial, and the judge harshly rebuked prosecutors bringing that case. In the RICO case filed in the Middle District of Alabama in 2005, there have been allegations of jury tampering involving two of the jurors who convicted Mr. Siegelman. These and other irregularities prompted 44 former state attorneys general to sign a petition 'urging the United States Congress to investigate the circumstances surrounding the investigation, prosecution, sentencing and detention' of Mr. Siegelman."[6]

However, this story became even more twisted when a long time Alabama Republican attorney who had handled opposition research for Bob Riley's 2002 campaign against Siegelman came forward with some astonishing allegations.

Dana Jill Simpson had spent the 2002 election cycle digging into Don Siegelman's background. In 2007, Simpson filed an affidavit in which she alleged direct White House involvement in the 2002 Alabama election. According to Simpson's affidavit, Siegelman had conceded the election and did not push for a recount because Riley's team had threatened him with prosecution if he did not withdraw from the race. In addition, Simpson also revealed an alleged conference call that took place on November 17, 2002 between herself, Bill Canary, Rob Riley—Governor Bob Riley's son—and other members of the Riley campaign:

> "Rob Riley told her in early 2005 that his father and a Republican operative met with Rove months earlier to discuss Siegelman's prosecution. Simpson said Rob Riley told her Rove spoke to Bob Riley and William Canary. 'He proceeds to tell me that Bill Canary and Bob Riley had had a conversation with Karl Rove again, and that they had this time gone over and seen whoever was the

head of the department' at Justice overseeing the Siegelman prosecution, Simpson testified."[7]

Expanding on her original allegations, Simpson testified
on September 14, 2007 before lawyers for the House Judiciary
Committee and dropped a bombshell revelation. Describing a
conference call among Bill Canary, Rob Riley and other Riley
campaign aides, which she said took place on November 18,
2002—the same day Don Siegelman conceded the election—
Simpson alleged that Canary had said that "Rove had spoken
with the Department of Justice" about "pursuing" Siegelman and
had also advised Riley's staff "not to worry about Don Siegelman"
because "'his girls' would take care of" the governor.

The "girls" allegedly referenced by Bill Canary were his wife,
Leura, and Alice Martin, another 2001 Bush appointee as the
U.S. Attorney for the Northern District of Alabama. Simpson
added that she was told by Rob Riley that Judge Mark Fuller was
deliberately chosen when the Siegelman case was prosecuted in
2005, and that Fuller would "hang" Siegelman.[8]

Before Simpson testified before the House Judiciary Committee, her house was burned down and her car was run off the
road. Simpson was not the only one to have had experienced such
bizarre misfortune. Dana Siegelman, Don Siegelman's daughter,
said that her family's home was twice broken into during the trial
and that Siegelman's attorney had had his office broken into as
well.[9]

In the end, what then are we to make of the Alabama election of 2002 and its aftermath, during which not only did Don
Siegelman lose, but so did those of us who believe in the rule of
law, the Constitution, fair elections, and a Justice System above
politics? Is this the type of story you expect to read about in the
United States of America?

NOTES

1. CNN, "Two lay claim to Alabama governor's mansion," November 5, 2002, http://cnnstudentnews.cnn.com/2002/ALLPOLITICS/11/06/elec02. alabama.governors/

2. Steve McConnell, "The Changing of The Guards: Bay Minette, Election Night,"*Badwin County Now*, July 20, 2007, http://baldwincountynow.com/articles/2007/07/25/local_news/doc469fbb5bd2a7f444039407.txt

3. Scott Horton, "The Remarkable 'Recusal' of Leura Canary, *Harpers Magazine*, September 14, 2007, http://www.harpers.org/archive/2007/09/hbc-90001209

4. John Davis, "Siegelman On Trial Today," *Montgomery Advertiser*, October 4, 2004, http://www.montgomeryadvertiser.com/specialreports/siegelman/storyV5SIEGELMAN04W.htm

5. Alliance for Justice, "Statement on House Judiciary Subcommittees Joint Hearing on 'Allegations of Selective Prosecution," October, 22, 2002, http://www.afj.org/about-afj/press/10222007.html

6. House Judiciary Committee, "Judiciary Members Ask AG for Documents, Information on Alabama's Siegelman Case and Allegations of Other Selective Prosecutions," The Gavel: House Speaker Pelosi's Web Site, July 17, 2007, http://www.speaker.gov/blog/?p=595

7. Brett J. Blackledge, Mary Orndorff and Kim Chandler, "Lawyer adds to her affidavit on Siegelman," *The Birmingham News*, October 10, 2007, http://www.al.com/printer/printer.ssf?/base/news/1192005492139550.xml

8. Muriel Kane and Larisa Alexandrovna, "The Permanent Republican Majority Part One: How A Coterie Of Republican Heavyweights Sent A Governor To Jail," *The Raw Story*, November 26, 2007, http://rawstory.com/news/2007/timeline_don_siegelman_1126.htm

9. Larisa Alexandrovna, "The Permanent Republican Majority Part II: Daughter Of Jailed Governor Sees White House Hand In Her Father's Fall," *The Raw Story*, November 27, 2007, http://rawstory.com/news/2007/The_permanent_Republican_majority_Daughter_of_1127.html

A STATISTICL ANALYSIS OF THE GUBERNATORIAL VOTE IN BALDWIN COUNTY, ALABAMA IN 2002

★

JAMES H. GUNDLACH

The 2002 Governor's race in Alabama erupted into controversy when Baldwin County first reported results that suggested that the Democratic incumbent, Don Siegelman, had defeated the Republican challenger, Bob Riley, by a margin of 3,120 votes out of 1,364,602 cast and a few hours later reported results that reversed the outcome of the election. In this essay, I demonstrate how relatively simple statistical techniques can identify apparent systematic electronic manipulation of voting results. This essay consists of four parts. The first part is an overview of the election. The second part is an analysis of county level data that suggests that both sets of results from Baldwin County were anomalous. The third part is a set of analyses of results from voting districts that identify and describe some clear patterns in the anomalous Baldwin County final results. The final part of this essay discusses the possibilities of electronic vote manipulation and suggests mechanisms for preventing it in the future.

SOME ELECTION BACKGROUND

I first looked at the election results by dividing the state into two components: Baldwin County and the rest of the state. I then looked at the results of the 1998 and 2002 governor's races for these two components. In the 1998 election, Don Siegelman had received 742,766 votes in the rest of Alabama compared to 533,772 votes for the Republican, Fob James. In Baldwin County, which is where Fob James lived, Siegelman received 17,389 votes, compared to 21,004 votes for James. In 2002, Siegelman received 635,545 votes compared to 623,145 for Bob Riley in the rest of Alabama. In the first set of returns for Baldwin County, Siegelman received 19,070 votes to 31,052 for Riley. In the second set of returns, Siegelman was reported as receiving 12,736 votes while Riley's total did not change.

In addition to the issues reported in the press, this review suggests three points about Baldwin County's election results that should make one suspicious. One was the unusually large increase in votes for the Republican candidate from 1998 to 2002. While Riley ran better across the state than James did, the only other county that showed such a large increase was Riley's home, Clay County, which went from 2,122 to 3,176. The second factor that raises suspicions is the size of the decline in Siegelman's reported vote. The difference between the two reported votes was a decline of almost one-third of the total votes finally reported for Siegelman. A one-third reduction is rarely the result of random errors, but is commonly found in data that has been intentionally changed.

The final point that raises suspicion is that there should be no way to produce two different results with the computerized vote tabulation. That is, the system should not allow access to computer code or procedures that can produce different results. Computers do not accidentally produce different totals unless someone is controlling the computer in order to produce different results. Once the same computer produces different election results, the results should be considered too suspect to certify without an independently supervised recount.

A COUNTY LEVEL ANALYSIS: BALDWIN COUNTY AS AN OUTLIER

The primary method of analysis examines changes in the level of votes for the Democratic candidate between 1998 and 2002. The data were obtained from the elections page of the web site of the Secretary of State of Alabama.

The first set of analyses regresses the percent of the county vote for the Democratic candidate in 2002, using both sets of Baldwin County's returns, on the percent of the county vote for the same candidate for Governor in 1998. The results of these analyses are presented below:

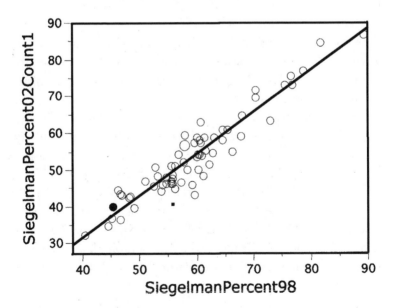

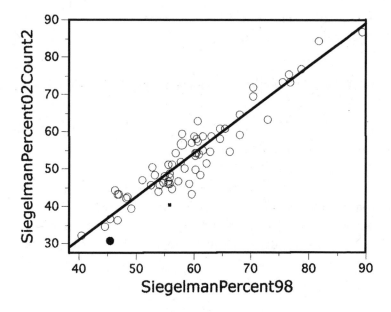

The first plot shows the relationship for the initial returns and the second shows the results for the second set of Baldwin County returns. The solid dot is Baldwin County. Note that in the initial returns, Baldwin County fits closer to the line than most of the other counties. But, in the second set of returns, Baldwin County is further from the line along the vertical dimension than any other county. These results suggest that the changes made between releasing the first and second set of results made Baldwin County an outlier. This is exactly the opposite of what you would expect if the changes corrected an error in the data. An error usually makes the data point deviate from expected patterns, and fixing the error typically moves the data point back into the pattern. This kind of statistical irregularity deepens suspicions about the final Baldwin County election results.

However, there could have been other factors operating on the Republican side that may account for this. Baldwin County voters, like most in Alabama, had voted with strong majorities for President Bush in 2000, and Bush campaigned for Riley in Alabama in 2002. It can be argued that this change in the vote simply reflects the effect of Bush on Baldwin County voters. Analyses using the percent of vote for Bush in 2000 to predict the percent of vote for Riley in 2002 are presented below. The first scatter plot shows the Baldwin County percentage based on the first reported results. Again the first results—those giving the election to Don Siegelman—fit the pattern shown by the other counties. The second set of results has Baldwin County as an extreme outlier, showing that Riley is receiving about 15 percent more of the vote than predicted by the vote for Bush in 2000. The small square dot is Clay County, Riley's home. It is worth noting that the home county advantage is only about half as large as the second count given to Riley in Baldwin County. Thus, the analysis of the Republican side of the election also increases the suspicion that the Baldwin County results were manipulated.

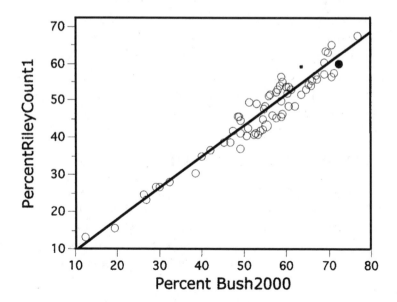

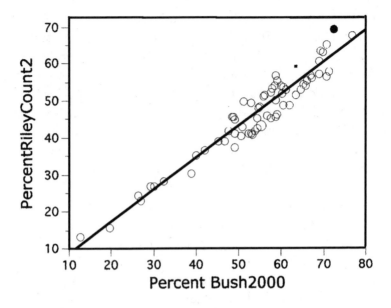

A third county, indicated by the circle just to the left of the Clay County mark, is Lee County, home to Auburn University. Siegelman lost substantial support in Lee County because of the controversial behavior of a university board member he had appointed. The details of how this cost Siegelman about as many votes that appear to be missing from Baldwin County are beyond the scope of this essay.

AN ANALYSIS OF VOTING DISTRICT DATA

Given that the county level analysis deepened suspicions that the Baldwin County results were manipulated to make Riley the winner, I extended the analysis to a set of voting districts to see if the suspicious pattern was a significant deviation from the expected results. For this analysis I produced a data set for comparable voting districts in Baldwin, Montgomery, and Shelby Counties for the governor's races in 1998 and 2002. It should be noted that determining which voting districts were comparable over two elections four years apart was difficult because several voting districts were changed either in name or boundaries—or both—between the two elections. Out of Montgomery and Shelby Counties'122 voting districts, I was able to verify sufficient consistency in names and boundaries in seventy. Of Baldwin County's sixty-five voting districts, I was able to produce thirty-nine that were comparable for both 1998 and 2002. Most of this reduction in numbers was due to aggregating boxes or beats to insure comparability. For example, Fairhope Civic Center had boxes for four voting districts that had shifted their boundaries from 1998 to 2002. By aggregating the four boxes into one geographic unit for both 1998 and 2002, I was able to create one comparable voting district for both years. I conducted regression analyses similar to the county level analyses above for two sets of voting districts, those outside of Baldwin County and those in Baldwin County. If the first reported results were accurate for Siegelman but inflated for Riley, you would expect the slope for Baldwin County to be about a third lower than the slope for the other voting districts. The results are shown below:

Regression of Percent Siegelman 2002 on Percent Siegelman 1998
Montgomery and Shelby County Voting District Results

Term	Estimate	Std Error	t Ratio	Prob>ltl	r
Intercept	7.8636457	23.97778	0.33	0.7440	0
Siegelman98	0.853541	0.029685	28.75	<.0001	0.961

Regression of Percent Siegelman 2002 on Percent Siegelman 1998
Baldwin County Voting District Results

Term	Estimate	Std Error	t Ratio	Prob>ltl	r
Intercept	-9.771301	11.75185	-0.83	0.4110	0
Siegelman98	0.697915	0.021321	32.73	<.0001	0.983

MONTGOMERY AND SHELBY COUNTY RESULTS

There are two important points to note in comparing these results. First, the correlations, r=. 96 and .98 are quite strong. That means that the 1998 Siegelman vote was an adequate predictor of his 2002 vote. Second is the difference in the estimates. The estimate, or slope, for the voting districts outside of Baldwin County is .85. This means that for each vote that Siegelman got in 1998, he got .85 votes in 2002. The fact that this matches the pattern in the state outside Baldwin County suggests that the selected voting districts adequately represent the rest of the state.

Remember that in the first part of the essay, I showed that Siegelman got 85 percent of the vote in 2002 that he got in 1998. The regression for the Baldwin County voting districts shows a slope of .697. This means that results for Baldwin County are substantially different from the voting districts outside of Baldwin County. A significance test for the difference between the slopes shows that the two slopes are significantly different from each other, $t=6.19$, $p<.0001$. The combined findings of a strong relationship between the 1998 and 2002 votes in Baldwin County as well as outside, and the different slope, strongly suggests a systematic manipulation of the voting results. In addition, a comparison of the slopes provides a way to estimate the apparent nature of the manipulation. By dividing the Baldwin County slope, .697, by the slope for the other voting districts, .854, and subtracting the results from 1.00, you get an estimate of the proportion of the Siegelman vote in each voting district that apparently disappeared from the official Baldwin County results. This yields a result of .18, which is about half as much as predicted from the hypothesis based on the first reported results. This raised the question of how could a process of moving X number of votes from one candidate to the other result in the mysterious production of erroneous results that were 2X above the final reported results?

My hypothesis is that someone was moving a little more than

3,000 Baldwin County votes from Siegelman to Riley by calculating a fifth of Siegelman's votes in each voting district, rounding it to a whole number, adding the resulting value to Riley's votes in that district, and then subtracting that number from Siegelman's vote. However, instead of subtracting the calculated number, they added it to the vote for Siegelman. This is a common error created by using copy and paste to produce the invisible formulas for spreadsheet cells. The result was a first report of county vote totals that had percentage distributions close to what was expected, but a total vote that much higher than expected. Once they went back and fixed the procedure so that it performed as they desired—a reasonable total vote and Riley winning the election—the difference between the first and second reporting of Siegelman's vote was twice the number of electronically shifted votes. If what I hypothesized happened, then the total votes for Baldwin County were 27,866 for Riley and 15,283 for Siegelman. This would have produced state totals of 669,039 votes for Riley and 671,652 votes for Siegelman. The only way we will know for sure if this result is accurate is if the paper ballots for Baldwin County are recounted.

HOW BALDWIN COUNTY RESULTS COULD HAVE BEEN MANIPULATED

When Baldwin County reported two sets of results, it was clear to me that someone had manipulated the vote. There is simply no way that electronic vote counting can produce two sets of results without someone using computer programs in ways that they were not intended. In other words, the fact that two sets of results were reported is sufficient evidence in and of itself that the vote tabulation process was compromised.

The system employed in Baldwin County works much like a digital camera that stores pictures on a computer chip that is then physically removed from the camera and inserted into a reader that is attached to a personal computer that then transfers the images to the hard drive of the personal computer to be edited and used. The voting machine reads a paper ballot and writes the information on a cartridge that saves the results of all the ballots cast on that machine. After the polls close, the cartridge is transported to the county courthouse where it and all the other cartridges from all the county voting machines are inserted into a reader attached to the tabulating computer and the files are transferred from the cartridge to the hard drive of the tabulating computer. Once all the files have been transferred to the hard drive of the tabulating computer, a program reads the files from the individual voting machines and produces summary tabulations.

This system provides several points at which the data can be tampered with. First, and perhaps the least likely, is altering the recorded information on the cartridges between the polling place and the county courthouse. This is especially difficult to do if the results of all the voting boxes are to be changed. And, it would require using a computer that could emulate the output from the voting machine.

A second way would be to install something like a computer worm or virus on the tabulating computer that would intercept the data stream when the cartridges were being read, modify the data in a desired way, and send the modified data to the hard drive. This would require someone with a high level of computer programming skills, and would be fairly labor intensive. It would also be difficult to specify the amount that the results should be fudged. But it would be a modification that once created and put in place could well alter the results in every county that uses this system.

The third approach would simply require access to a program to edit the data files once they are stored on the computer hard drive, using the keyboard and monitor attached to the tabulating computer. This would require a relatively long period of unobserved access to the tabulating computer between reading the cartridges and tabulating the final results. News reports suggest the opportunity for this kind of manipulation was available.

The fourth approach, and the one I would take if I were to do it, would be to install a wi-fi card on the tabulating computer, along with enabling software, and use a similarly equipped laptop in a nearby room to modify the data files immediately after they were read from the cartridges. This would simply require access to the tabulating computer at some time before the election to install the card, and after the election to remove the card.

CONCLUSION

In this essay, I have shown how some relatively simple statistical analysis techniques can be used to identify probable electronic manipulation of voting results. The Baldwin County results attracted attention because two results were reported. This was probably due to mistakes made in the data manipulation procedures. If this kind of electronic ballot stuffing is done in the future, voters and candidates cannot count on similar errors to serve as flags to bring the process under review. With a little work before an election building necessary data sets and some more work entering returns on election night and over the following few days, statistical analysis can point to probable ballot stuffing, electronic or otherwise. This could lead to more honest vote counting, as well as greater trust in the electoral process, and government in general.

2004

★

Despite the myth that Bush won Florida in 2000, the recognition that he stole it still gnaws at many Democrats (or those who aren't still sticking pins in their Ralph Nader dolls). Loath to face the true extent of the Republican assault on voting rights, such Democrats have largely blamed the Supreme Court alone for Bush's "victory"; and they have done so very quietly, lest they be called "sore losers."

By and large, such Democrats have also winked at Bush's "re-election," preferring masochistically to blame themselves, and/or the people, for that inexplicable surprise—even though the second race was far more broadly and explicitly subverted than the first, the Republican Party using every kind of fraud tactic to suppress the Kerry vote and pad the Bush vote nationwide. As Michael Collins demonstrates meticulously in "The Urban Legend," Bush's "win" was based on the concoction of at least 4 million phantom votes—a feat of national disenfranchisement unprecedented in the history of U.S. elections. Based on an article first posted on the Website scoop.co.nz in June of 2007 (and researched with the help of Alastair Thompson, Scoop's editor), Collins's essay helps us grasp the mammoth scale of Bush's second coup, which certainly took place not only in Ohio.

Those reluctant to believe that this could happen here have often argued that so huge a rip-off would require a national army of devoted henchmen, some of whom would surely have been caught. For one thing, some election fraudsters have been caught (as in New Hampshire in 2002, and Ohio's Cuyahoga County, where two election clerks were sent to prison for obstructing the court-ordered recount in 2005). With e-voting machines, moreover, just one person can annul the votes of millions. More generally, the upset in 2004 depended largely on the silent partnership of just a few committed partisans, as Dave Griscom argues in his keen analysis of the subverted vote in Arizona. In his essay, Griscom shows that the machines were likely "hacked and stacked" through the collaboration of the Republican Party leadership (Secretary of State Jan Brewer also served as co-chair of the Bush campaign in Arizona) with Christianist poll workers eager to protect their sites from any prying eyes.

The Republican Party's eagerness to steal the vote in 2004 was particularly clear in Nevada, where high-placed partisans worked hard throughout the months before Election Day to get Nevada to adopt the Sequoia electronic voting system: one so insecure, despite its innovative "paper trail," that it repeatedly failed laboratory tests. That dismal record was deliberately kept secret from the press and the people of Nevada, a cover-up that extended all the way up to the Election Assistance Commission, as Brad Friedman and Michael Richardson, with research assistance from John Gideon, demonstrate in their essay, "The Selling of the Touch-Screen 'Paper Trail': From Nevada to the EAC."

ELECTION 2004:
THE URBAN LEGEND

★

MICHAEL COLLINS

(Based on original unpublished research by Internet poster anax-archos, to whom I owe a debt of gratitude.)

On Election Night 2004, few in the country had the vantage point of network news commentators. Throughout the day, these experts received a stream of information from the exit polls of the National Election Pool (NEP). Sponsored by a media consortium consisting of the four major television networks plus CNN and the Associated Press, the NEP provided the most sophisticated polling data ever recorded, and was the only source on *"who* voted for each candidate; *why* the voters in each area made critical choices; and *where* geographical differences on candidates and issues were a factor."[1]

Right after the election, analyst Charles Cook practically gushed after he studied the exit polls, saying the Bush effort was "...unquestionably...the best planned, best executed presidential campaign ever."[2] He reflected that, "Perhaps the most interesting, and maybe puzzling, exit poll finding is that (compared to 2000) Kerry lost 11 points among the 13 percent of Americans who live in cities with populations over 500,000, while President Bush jumped up 13 points (since 2000)." Cook's analysis pinpointed the actual reason for the Bush victory: urban voters.

On election eve, however, a different story prevailed. While they had access to the same exit polls that Cook had, the news people did not notice the same trends and numbers. Instead, it was all about country versus city, red versus blue and white versus non white. While the media was right about an election, the election they were right about had taken place four years earlier, as the public received a regurgitation of election 2000 analysis for 2004. The follow up consensus was formed from this inaccurate analysis: The remarkable Rove had done it again with those energized evangelicals, in the process grabbing enough van driving suburban moms to make the difference.

USA Today[3] echoed much of this analysis when they concluded their election wrap up with this insight:

> In the end, the states broke for Bush much as they did in 2000. Bush lost one state that he won in 2000: New Hampshire. Late Wednesday, the Associated Press reported New Mexico went to Bush. Iowa was still undecided. Both states backed Gore in 2000.[4]

During the week following Election Day, there were additional flourishes added to the portrait of Bush's remarkable victory. He had captured the *values voters*, a new demographic. These voters had cast aside their normal allegiances and turned red in a full embrace of the values of the Bush administration. According to the National Exit Poll, Bush supposedly achieved another remarkable feat: He had moved the Latino vote from a Democratic mainstay to a competitive demographic. Unlike the typical 60-40 margins Democrats counted on, in 2004 Latino votes were divided 54-46 in favor of the Democrats, a twelve point swing. These two additional "findings" hinted at but did not address directly the Bush urban wave that Cook had noticed.

While there was no broad public debate on the legitimacy of the outcome, intensive debate on the Internet was stimulated by the accidental release of preliminary exit poll data throughout Election Day which showed Kerry winning 51%-48%. Totaling over 11,000 respondents, these polls were marked "Not for on air use." This fueled charges of election fraud. In addition, the debate also focused on what was called the *red shift*, Bush's victories in a number of key states, all of which were said to be outside the margin of error for the poll. However, aside from these interesting, but largely ignored exchanges, Americans settled in for four more years of George Bush.

IS THIS WHAT ACTUALLY HAPPENED?

According to the final National Exit Poll, there was a lot more to the 2004 election than red versus blue:

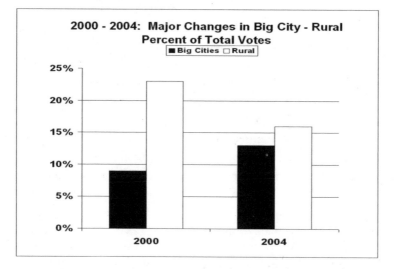

Figure 1. The 2004 rural vote must have alarmed the Bush camp. It was less as a percentage of the overall vote, dropping from 23%-16%. Bush's total rural vote went from 14 million in 2000 to just short of 12 million in 2004. These totals added up to a devastating loss of 2 plus million votes from his base instead of an increase of 3 to 4 million that the campaign needed. This was very bad news for the White House. (All of the charts and figures presented come from the final 2000 and 2004 National Exit Polls.)

In 2000, Bush had a large margin of victory in rural America. This "red versus blue" narrative was also postulated as the basis for the 2004 victory. However, in reality, rural America provided both fewer voters and fewer votes for Bush in 2004. While he still won the rural segment of the population, it was hardly the overwhelming victory it had been in 2000. What had happened to the waves of born again Christians supposedly loyal to Bush? Did they stay home? Did they vote by not voting, a time honored American practice? Did they sit out this most critical of elections despite their spirited performance in 2000, and the exhortations from pulpits and the Republican Party?

In high turnout elections, the candidate who loses a big chunk of his base constituency loses the election. There have been no exceptions to this in modern election history. While the drop in his core constituency from 23%-16% was bad enough for Bush, according to the NEP, Bush also lost expected votes. With 23 percent of the vote in 2000, Bush had garnered 14.1 million rural votes. At 16 percent of the vote in 2004, the rural segment provided only 11.6 million votes. This was an absolute loss of 2.5 million votes in an election that had a 16 percent increase in turnout compared to 2000.

According to the declared vote count, Bush won the election. Yet he did so with fewer votes from his core constituency in actual terms, and fewer votes as a percentage of total votes. It is important to keep this in mind as we move forward because these novelties compound one upon another to present an outcome that is simply not believable.

Bush also lost significant ground in "small towns," the other element of his "values" coalition. Small towns are defined as towns of between 10,000 and 50,000 residents.

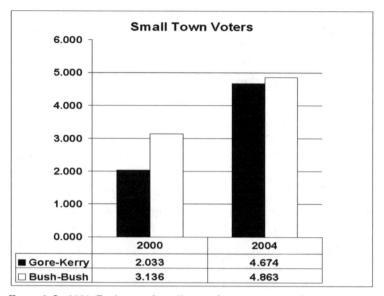

Figure 2. In 2000, Bush owned small town America, beating Gore 60%-40% and walking away with a 1.0 million vote margin. In 2004, turnout increased dramatically, but the race evened with the Bush margin at just below 200,000 votes.

Small towns were another significant part of the Bush "base." While many rural voters expressed their disenchantment, according to the exit polls, by staying home, the citizens of small towns increased their turnout by 88 percent in 2004, and evened the playing field by voting in near equal numbers for John Kerry. Bush had 4.9 million small town votes to Kerry's 4.7 million, for a total of 9.5 million. By comparison, in 2000, Bush had received 1.1 million more small town votes than Gore (3.1 million to 2.0 million).

The suburbs were only somewhat better for Bush in 2004 than in 2000. His victory margin there was 5 percent over Kerry, where it had been just 2 percent over Gore in 2000. The suburbs comprised nearly half of the total votes. Given the decay in the rural and small town margins and the historical Democratic majority in the cities, the 2004 presidential contest was as good as lost for Bush.

Here, however, the exit poll narrative changes. According to the polls, Bush made very surprising gains in cities with a population of between 50,000 and 500,000. In 2000, Bush had trailed Gore by seventeen points in the smaller cities, 12.0 million votes to 8.4 million votes. In 2004 however, the smaller cities were almost even, with Kerry at 11.36 million and Bush at 11.39 million. (Turnout was up just 9 percent.) It is very difficult to explain such a trend. Nevertheless, taking the rural voters, the suburbs, and the break even smaller cities as a group, Bush was still in real trouble heading into the larger cities. Had Kerry just held Bush close to the Gore margins for 2000 in those Democratic friendly venues, he would have won the election.

And why not expect a strong Kerry showing? Bush had not been a city-friendly president, and had not gone out of his way to help large cities with any initiatives of note. In New York, for example, things looked particularly bad, as a 2003 poll showed that over 50 percent of the city's residents thought that the administration had had foreknowledge of the 9/11 attacks and had done nothing to prevent them. This was hardly a predictor of great success for Bush in the largest of large cities.

But then something very unusual happened, as Charles Cook pointed out. According to the NEP, Bush made incredible gains in the large cities over his 2000 vote share. These gains were large enough to offset his drop in core support in rural areas and give him a 3 percent victory. In addition, big city voters must have been "motivated" by something, as turnout in cities with over 500,000 in population increased by 66 percent. What was this all about? The answer to that question and the plausibility of the answer to that question are vital in understanding the story we were told of the 2004 election results.

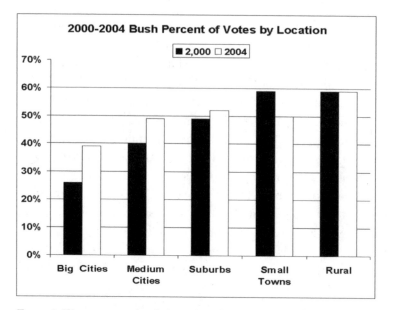

Figure 3. We are expected to believe that after doing poorly in the rural areas and small towns, that Bush attracted several million new big city voters and pulled off a last minute victory. In the small towns he was well below his 2000 performance for total votes. In the "red" zone, rural America, he got fewer votes in 2004 than he did in 2000 while turnout was up across the nation.

According to the exit poll, the real kill shot for the Bush victory came from large urban areas, "big cities," defined as those with a population of half a million or more, e.g., New York, Chicago, Detroit, etc. These cities had been the strongest base for Democrats since the Great Depression. While there had been variations in turnout from presidential election to election, the Democratic margins in the large cities had always remained strong.

THE BUSH URBAN WAVE OF 2004 BY THE NUMBERS

The most instructive way to look at the remarkable and certainly unpredictable Bush urban wave is to take his cumulative margin starting with the rural areas and move to progressively more dense population areas, ending up with the big cities.

In 2000, with 105 million overall votes cast, Bush had a 5 million vote advantage in rural America. In 2004, however, with 122 million votes cast, this same constituency gave him only a 3.9 million margin. There had been 23.8 million votes cast in the rural segment in 2000, and just under 20 million in 2004. Given the very high rural turnout rates from 2000 and the nationwide turnout increase in 2004, who would have expected the rural votes and share to decline in 2004? Yet it did. Towns with a population of between 10,000 and 50,000 accounted for 5 million votes in 2000, with Bush taking this group 60%-40% over Gore. In 2004, vote totals in this segment reached nearly 10 million, with 50 percent voting for Bush and 48 percent voting for Kerry. However, this added just 175,000 votes to the *accumulated* margin for Bush in 2004. In 2000, by comparison, he added 1.1 million votes to his margin from this segment.

According to this electoral math, things were looking grim for George W. Bush. His rural base had stayed home and small town voters, while nearly doubling their 2000 vote totals, had voted in almost equal numbers for Kerry. After those Republican core area totals, Bush was up by 4 million votes; at the same juncture in 2000, he had been up 6.3 million votes, with a smaller electorate.

The suburbs, the largest voting block, showed slight improvement for Bush in 2004. He increased his 2000 victory margin there from 2%-5%, and the suburban share went from 43%-45%. Yet his cumulative margin at this juncture was 6.8 million, compared to 7.3 million in 2000.

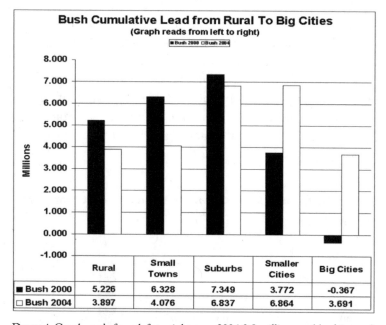

Bush Cumulative Lead from Rural To Big Cities
(Graph reads from left to right)

■ Bush 2000 □ Bush 2004

	Rural	Small Towns	Suburbs	Smaller Cities	Big Cities
■ Bush 2000	5.226	6.328	7.349	3.772	-0.367
□ Bush 2004	3.897	4.076	6.837	6.864	3.691

Figure 4. Graph reads from left to right, e.g., 2004 3.8 million rural lead in rural areas; adding the small town margin, Bush has only a 4.0 million cumulative-net lead when the 2004 small town votes are factored in. This shows that Bush "won" not by building up a huge lead that was eroded in urban areas, but by building up a much smaller lead that was not nearly as dramatically "eroded" in the cities.

Gore had fared worse than Kerry in rural and small town America, but had broken even in the suburbs. Once he hit the smaller and larger cities, Gore was on a roll and pulled out his half million popular vote victory. In 2004, Bush struggled in the rural and small town segments, and gained a modest advantage in the suburbs. Overall, things weren't looking good compared to his 2000 performance.

Then the urban wave began to form. According to the final exit poll, despite being abandoned by his 2000 base, which had been specifically targeted in 2004, Bush rallied in the smaller cities. He went from a loss of 60%-40% in 2000 to a dubious break even in 2004. Instead of an inadequate 3.8 million advantage in 2000, Bush went downtown, so to speak, with a seemingly staggering 6.8 million vote advantage over Kerry.

Remarkably, this was still not going to be enough for a Bush win. Had Kerry maintained the Gore big city margin of 2000—coupled with the 60 percent increase in turnout—he would have won the election easily, both numerically and in terms of electoral votes.

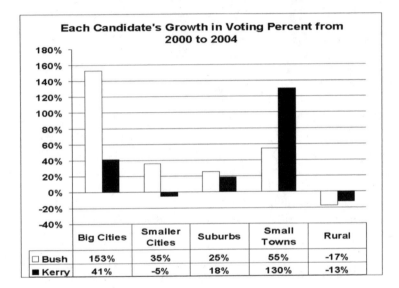

	Big Cities	Smaller Cities	Suburbs	Small Towns	Rural
☐ Bush	153%	35%	25%	55%	-17%
■ Kerry	41%	-5%	18%	130%	-13%

Figure 5. Unprecedented! That's the only word necessary to show the dichotomy of 2004—Bush losing actual votes in his base, rural America, while gaining an exponential increase in big cities.

But then something happened. While Bush's rural, conservative, white, Christian voters were staying home or changing candidates, his appeal to urban voters apparently went off the charts. He increased his big city vote total from 26%-39%, from 2.7 million total votes in 2000 to 5.9 million in 2004.

Running behind his 2000 totals among his base, Bush had little hope of victory until the returns from the cities came in. The large cities were filled with voters who were typically part of the core Democratic constituency. Despite this historical pattern, inner city Americans came to the polls in record numbers, then supposedly voted more Republican than before or since, giving George Bush the necessary votes for his victory in 2004.

Accepting this strange sequence of events requires believing that a precedent setting election occurred in 2004. While the Democrats have in the past seen retreats in urban turnout and vote share, these retreats have *never* been accompanied by retreats in the Republican base. The two phenomena just don't happen in the same election. In 2004, Democrats increased their votes in the diminished rural voting block, significantly improved their performance in the small towns, and held close in the suburbs. They were taking three out of every five new voters around the country—but then we are expected to believe that they lost the election in the big cities after taking a similar beating in the smaller cities. This combination of events has never happened before in American history. It is unprecedented . . . and unbelievable.

AN URBAN LEGEND OR A POTEMKIN VILLAGE?

If this Bush urban wave actually materialized, you would have expected to see both a general and a proximate cause. The general cause would have come in the form of an issue or issues that moved voters to such a degree that they abandoned decades of party loyalty, or that candidate preference held sway over party loyalty. The proximate cause would have shown up as big city activity focused on get out the vote efforts combined with advertising and major campaign events. You would have seen Bush in the cities, laying on the charm, so to speak, and announcing a few high profile federal projects. How could Bush make huge gains in admittedly hostile territory without these efforts?

However, there was no apparent general cause for a shift in voting loyalties in big cities. Unlike Ronald Reagan, who emphasized big city enterprise zones, Bush seemed indifferent to the needs of urban dwellers. He was not a city type of guy, and rarely went to New York, Chicago, or Los Angeles for anything other than high level events. Not big on mixing with the masses, he demonstrated a clear preference for the solitary activity of clearing trees and brush from the Texas ranch he had acquired just before the 2000 primaries. To the extent that 9/11 sensibilities may be considered an issue in the cities, they seem to have been a far larger factor in the suburban vote, at least as far as the exit polls indicated.

As for the proximate causes needed to turn opinion and attitude into an actual voting experience for the converted, they were also not evident. The Republican focus was always on ramping up the rural base and increasing the suburban vote. Thus, there was little if any comment in the Republican media machine about push polls, or new programs for or special events in big cities to drive the vote. In short, the big city strategy was not a featured item in the 2004 Republican playbook.

Finally, the black, Latino, and Jewish voting blocks in the large cities remained essentially unchanged from 2000, voting overwhelmingly Democratic.

So the question remains: how do we account for the election-winning increases for Bush in the big city vote share? If black, Latino, and Jewish voters in the big cities were strongly in favor of Kerry, there was only one remaining big city voting block left who could have pushed Bush over the top: There had to have been an unprecedented outpouring of white voters in large urban areas.

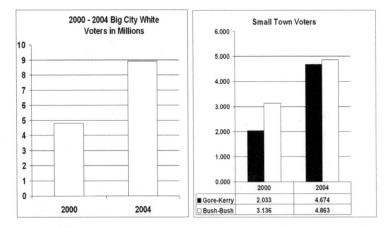

Figures 6 and 7. According to the NEP, white voters contributed less than 5 million votes to the big city segment in 2000, but almost 9 million in 2004, accounting almost exclusively for the increase from 2.3 million to 5.9 million big city votes for Bush from 2000 to 2004.

THE NATURE OF THE BUSH WHITE URBAN WAVE

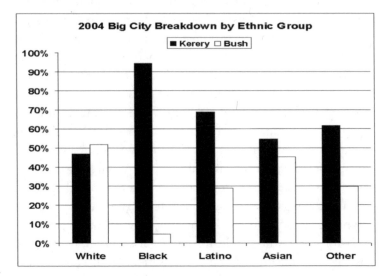

Figure 8. The Black and Latino vote in big cities didn't shift much from 2004. Bush lost big again. But he did much better among big city whites than in 2000.

Where then did the Bush urban wave come from? The simple answer is that it was *weighted* into existence. The act of reconciling the exit polls to the official vote count *created* it. The Bush urban voters came into existence because they had to . . . otherwise the official vote count would be wrong.

Weighting is a practice used by the U.S. Census, political consultants, public health officials and others who conduct large scale survey research. If you collect data on a population, and your data is unrepresentative of a subset of that population, you can "weight" certain responses by a multiplier greater or less than one to make your poll consistent with the population measured. The problem is when weighting is used to reconcile polling data with a "known fact" that may not be known at all, which in this case was that the NEP assumed that the official vote count was correct.

During the 2004 election, the weighting process was conducted after the national exit polls were found to be inconsistent with the announced vote tallies. After all, how could the unintentionally released Election Day NEP be right in showing a 3 percent Kerry overall victory margin when the vote tabulators showed a 3 percent Bush win? Rural America didn't produce that margin. Neither did the small towns or the suburbs. Even the improvement in the smaller cities wasn't enough. The big cities, according to the announced totals, delivered the vote for Bush.

The Bush campaign had focused its efforts almost exclusively on rural areas and suburbs in order to counter the anticipated big city Democratic margins. But then, just when it was needed, white ghosts emerged from parking lots, alleys and perhaps even graveyards in big cities across the country to give George W. Bush a stunning victory. It had to be this way, otherwise the vote count was wrong and who would tolerate such a notion, despite the clear signs on the ground and in the National Exit Poll? But the convenient and wide-spread red versus blue story of election eve was maintained through inertia. For those with nagging questions, that story was replaced by the Urban Legend of 2004: Bush won the 2004 presidential election in big cities.

Yet, it borders on the absurd to believe that Bush won reelection on the basis of this huge increase in big city votes and vote share. We're supposed to believe that he went from 2.3 million big city votes in 2000 to 5.4 million in 2004, a 153 percent increase. This artifact of the NEP's weighting process strains the limits of credulity. However, while there was something very wrong with the NEP weighting process, specifically in the big city results, there was something much more troubling about the vote total.

AND THIS IS THE PROBLEM

There have been heated debates on the Internet regarding the outcome of the 2004 election. Much of the analysis focuses on the disparity between released and unreleased national exit polls. The mainstream media did not and has not covered this controversy. Yet by August 2006, more than half of Americans expressed doubts that the 2004 results were fair, according to a Zogby Poll of 1018 registered voters nationwide.[5]

For this essay, I chose the less controversial approach of using the final, revised exit poll data with a focus on two of the stated purposes of the exit poll, i.e. *who* were the voters and *where* did they cast their ballots. Yet after careful scrutiny, we have seen that the NEP's urban demographic data just don't add up to even a remotely convincing explanation for a Bush victory. The data is clearly inconsistent, incompatible, and results in a conundrum rather than clarity about what happened on November 2, 2004.

There's one more problem that casts doubt on the entire process. The NEP reported a 66 percent increase in voter turnout in the big cities, from 9 million votes in 2000 to 15 million in 2004. This provides the foundation for the increases in Bush urban votes and percentages. *However, the 66 percent vote increase in the urban areas simply can't be true on the basis of actual reports of big city vote totals*, as the data that was available for 13 of the 24 big cities showed nothing close to a 66 percent increase in turnout.

Actual Big City Votes—2000 and 2004

Big City	2000	2004	Change
Baltimore	186,658	213,718	14.50%
Chicago	955,261	1,032,878	8.13%
Denver	198,318	239,945	20.99%
Detroit	300,500	325,961	8.47%
District of Col.	203,894	229,590	12.60%
Los Angles	967,960	1,086,586	12.26%
Milwaukee	165,598	198,907	20.11%
Nashville	209,958	244,306	16.36%
New York	2,182,348	2,438,349	11.73%
Philadelphia	563,180	676,073	20.05%
San Diego	417,388	486,650	16.59%
San Francisco	319,333	351,127	9.96%
San Jose	255,631	283,888	11.05%
TOTAL	6,575,090	7,609,071	15.73%

Chart 1. The cities listed are all "big cities" as defined by the NEP, major urban areas with populations over 500,000. "Turnout" percentages represent the increase in votes for president from 2000 to 2004. They are the actual vote totals from the cities listed. They were obtained from either the city board of elections or the state board of elections.

The total vote for these twelve big cities in 6.57 million in 2000, and 7.61 million in 2004. That represents a 16% increase in turnout.[6] This accounts for 61% of the big city population. The remaining 39% of the big city group would have required over a 100% increase in turnout to realize the big city average of 66% that the NEP claimed. Thus, the explanation of the Bush victory margin through the 66% big city increase evaporates in view of the actual data. There was no 66% increase in urban voting; but there was an increase consistent with the national average, about 16% based on actual voting data from the over 50% sample of big cities as presented above. The net result is this: Take the 9.2 million NEP estimated big city votes in 2000 and apply a 17% increase in turnout for 2004 and you get 10.8 million votes. Subtracting the 10.8 million actual votes from the NEP claims of 15.2 million for the same segment leaves a 4.5 million vote gap.

Or take a different approach. Use the thirteen cities above, which total 61 of the big city population, and generate estimates for big city totals in 2000 and 2004. You get a total of 12.93 million votes in 2004, which is 2.35 million short of the NEP's estimated 15.2 million big city votes.

Either scenario still leaves millions of unaccounted for votes. And we haven't even looked at those counterintuitive results for cities with populations of 50,000 to 500,000. What could this mean? How can we be so sloppy with our vote totals and the election results for our big cities? Why are big city data and results apparently not worthy of investigation and comment? The only way a Bush victory makes sense, given his failure in rural America, is the addition of millions of votes in the urban centers, an impossible phenomenon.

Trying to find a Bush victory in 2004 leads you down a number of dead end streets. What happened to the rural vote? It was less as an overall percent of the national total and this segment provided less actual votes for Bush. What happened in the big cities? White votes were up from 5.0 to 9.0 million in one election; an 80 percent increase in white big city turnout. One thing that we can no longer assume is that the election of 2004 produced a victory for Bush. In fact, the inability to show a logical path to the popular victory argues for a stance of informed scrutiny and intense skepticism.

In the end, if you believe that 4 million new white big city voters showed up in 2004, you can believe the 2004 election results. If you believe that Bush could conjure up those new voters with just the slightest get out the vote activity in big cities, you can believe the 2004 election results. If you acknowledge that Bush *lost* votes in his political base, the rural segment, yet soared to victory on the basis of substantial gains in the urban areas, then you can believe that he was the truly elected president on November 2, 2004.

Those who are elected must be able to demonstrate that they won a majority or plurality of the votes cast. There was no room for that scenario in 2004. In the end, we are left with only the Bush Urban Legend.

NOTES

1. The 2004 National Exit Poll, Edison-Mitofsky, 2004. 2000 National Exit Day Polls, VNS, 2000."Exit polls / voter surveys are taken only minutes after citizens' vote. The results are primary sources from which we can understand the motivations and patterns behind the actual vote. Exit Polls Tell Us: WHO voted for each candidate; WHY voters in your area made critical choices; WHERE geographical differences on candidates and issues were a factor." Edison-Mitofsky, http://www.exit-poll.net/, May 3, 2007

2. Charlie Cook, "GOP Turns Out A Win," *National Journal*, November 9, 2004 http://www.cookpolitical.com/column/2004/110904.php

3. *USA Today*, "Latest Vote, County by County—2000, 2004," November 16, 2004, http://www.usatoday.com/news/politicselections/vote2004/countymap.htm

4. Bill Nichols and Peter Eisler, "President makes peace offer to political rivals," *USA Today*, Posted 11/2/2004, Updated 11/5/2004, http://www.usatoday.com/news/politicselections/vote2004/president.htm

5. Michael Collins, "Zogby - Voters Question Outcome of '04 Election," *Scoop Independent News*, September 25, 2006, http://www.scoop.co.nz/stories/HL0609/S00346.htm

6. Elections for the following city/state election information resource. California: Los Ángeles, San Diego, San Francisco, San Jose Statement of Vote by

Political Division in Counties, California 2000 http://tinyurl.com/2tgaw3 Statement of Vote by Political Division in Counties, California 2004 http://www.ss.ca.gov/elections/sov/2004_general/ssov/pres_general_ssov_all.xls Department of the Registrar-Recorder/County Clerk, County of Los Angeles, 2000. http://rrcc.co.la.ca.us/elect/00110020/rr0020pb.html-ssi

Chicago, Illinois Chicago Board of Elections, Chicago Presidential Results 2000 http://www.chicagoelections.com/wdlevel3.asp?elec_code=120 Chicago Board of Elections, Chicago Presidential Results 2004 http://www.chicagoelections.com/wdlevel3.asp?elec_code=90

Davidson-Nashville, Tennessee Tennessee Secretary of State 2004 Presidential Results http://www.state.tn.us/sos/election/results/2004-11/index.htm Tennessee Secretary of State 2004 Presidential Results http://www.state.tn.us/sos/election/results/2000-11/index.htm

Denver, Colorado David Leip's Presidential Atlas, Presidential Election Returns 2000 and 2004 http://www.uselectionatlas.org/BOTTOM/store_data.php

Detroit, Michigan Department of State, Wayne County Presidential Results 2000 http://miboecfr.nicusa.com/cgi-bin/cfr/precinct_srch_res.cgi Department of State, Wayne County Presidential Results 2004 http://miboecfr.nicusa.com/cgi-bin/cfr/precinct_srch_res.cgi

Election Precinct Result Search (Wayne County, Detroit City), Michigan Department of State, http://miboecfr.nicusa.com/cgi-bin/cfr/precinct_srch.cgi

Milwaukee, Wisconsin City of Milwaukee Elections Commission Presidential Results 2000 - 2004 http://www.city.milwaukee.gov/ElectionResultsArchi15808.htm http://www.city.milwaukee.gov/November720001754.htm

New York, New York David Liep, Presidential Data, New York City http://www.uselectionatlas.org/BOTTOM/store_data.php

Philadelphia, Pennsylvania Pennsylvania Department of State, Elections Information 2000 - 2004 http://www.electionreturns.state.pa.us/ElectionsInformation.aspx?FunctionID=15&ElectionID=2&OfficeID=1#Philadelphia

Washington, DC Presidential Election Returns 2000-2004 Washington, DC Board of Election s 2000 & 2004 General Election Results http://www.dcboee.org/information/elec_2000/general_elec.shtm http://www.dcboee.org/information/elec_2004/pres_general_2004_results.shtm

HOW TO STUFF THE ELECTRONIC BALLOT BOX: "HACKING AND STACKING" IN PIMA COUNTY, ARIZONA

★

DAVID L. GRISCOM

On November 2, 2004, John R. Brakey was the Democratic Cluster Captain for four precincts in Arizona Legislative District (LD) 27, part of the predominately-Hispanic, 80 percent non-Republican Congressional District 7. LD 27 encompasses a part of Pima Country southwest of the city of Tucson. John was new to the job, and part of his duties was to pick up carbon copies of the hand-printed list of voters who had already cast their ballots, a form called the Consecutive Number Register (CNR). In three of John's four precincts, poll workers greeted him with hostility, and in one case they attempted to conceal the existence of several completed CNR pages for which he was requesting copies.

About two hours after the official closing time, he returned to his home polling place, a school located in Precinct 324, to see if he could pick up the final copy of the CNR. To his shock, he walked in on poll workers apparently in the act of altering the document, which should have been completed at the time of the arrival of the last voter. John also observed that the vault to the Diebold optical-scan voting machine was open, instead of being locked shut as it should have been. When he approached to see what they were doing, the poll workers rose to their feet in unison, cursing him and telling him to get out.[1]

The next morning, John caught Greg Palast on *Democracy Now*, urging election sleuths to go to their polling places and pick through the trash for possible evidence of fraud. John did just that. After finding nothing in the trash outside, he walked into the school library where the voting had taken place, where he noticed several boxes. One was unsealed and held 924 "Advice to Voter" slips, which he had seen the poll workers working with the night before. He stuffed these slips into his jacket and left. These slips turned out to be the key to proving what the poll workers had been up to.

From that moment on, figuring out exactly what had just transpired became John's all-consuming passion. He abandoned his job and began working 18-hour days gathering and entering into Excel spreadsheets all the available public records bearing on the voting at Tucson Precinct 324 on Election Day 2004. I soon joined him in the forensic analysis of these records. Eventually it became clear to us that the poll workers at Precinct 324 were making, and causing voters to make, large numbers of errors in the "poll books," which are the public records of Election Day, including the Signature Rosters where the voters are supposed to sign in.

It turned out that the two head poll workers at Precinct 324, the Reverend Benjamin Khan and his wife, had made seven different kinds of errors *exactly eleven times each*. If those errors had been truly random (for example, if they were due to incompetence) then the odds of all seven having happened exactly eleven times each was less than one in 20 million. Therefore, the only possible conclusion was that the Khan team had made those errors deliberately. The only reason we could think of as to why they would do this was to steal votes by stuffing the ballot box according to a well-practiced system involving (1) creation of one of each kind of poll-book "error" about once every hour, and (2) performance of one illegal ballot manipulation corresponding to each of these "errors." Such a system would have had the advantages of spreading out the ballot manipulations throughout the twelve-hour Election Day, as well as leaving behind a record in the poll books that was so confusing that even the likes of Sherlock Holms would have had great difficulty reverse-engineering their scheme. John filed a complaint with the Pima County Attorney's office, but the complaint was eventually dismissed after the Pima County Elections Director reportedly fired the Khans for "incompetence."

How many votes might the Khans have stolen? My most conservative estimate, based on the November 2, 2004 Precinct 324 poll books, is a 6.9 percent net vote shift based on the assumption that the poll workers utilized no more blank ballots than those officially issued to them. However, extra ballots would have been easy enough to obtain, because at that time anyone in Pima Country could request up to two replacement mail-in ballots before the election without returning a spoiled one. (John Brakey's wife had actually ruined hers and was sent another, no questions asked.) At a presentation I made to the American Association for the Advancement of Science in 2007, I inferred a larger shift of 12.8 percent, which I recently corrected to 11.5 percent.[2] This number derives from documentary evidence implying that the poll workers at Precinct 324 handed out twenty-two illicitly obtained blank ballots to voters who signed a roster on Election Day, but whose names do not appear on the CNR; destroyed these ballots (which were presumably for Kerry) after voters had marked them; and then cast nineteen illicit ballots (presumably for Bush) in the names of voters who appeared on the CNR, but who had not signed any roster. Furthermore, the poll workers admitted on the Official Ballot Report and Certificate of Performance that "[It] appears 3 extra ballots—not sure why!"

Early on, John Brakey had realized that election insiders had the motive, means, and opportunity to hack the 1.94w memory cards of the Diebold optical scanners and/or the GEMS central tabulators. He thus reasoned that the Khan team must have been stuffing the ballot box against the possibility of an audit being required, in which case crooked elections officials would have been standing by to "randomly" select precincts like 324 as the only ones to audit. Such a ploy would have created the illusion that the election was honest. John termed this two-pronged attack the "Hack and Stack."[3]

MAIL-IN BALLOTS: AN INVITATION TO THE PERFECT CRIME

Table 1 shows the official results of Election Day 2004 voting for Legislative District 27. Note that the ever-vulnerable mail-in vote exhibits 2.4 percent *fewer* Bush votes than he received in the at-the-precinct voting, while Kerry got 2.7 percent *more*. Thus, at first glance it might seem that the mail-ins had actually been stolen on Kerry's behalf. But things are not always as they seem.

Averages of 63 Precincts of AZ LD 27	Kerry/Dem	Bush/Repub	Other
E2004 At-Precinct Voting	61.9%	37.0%	1.0%
E2004 Early/Mail-In Voting	64.6%	34.6%	0.9%
Party Registration	48.8%	20.6%	30.6%

After nearly two years of assuming I had done all I could by way of exposing election fraud in Pima County, I was inspired to return to the Excel spreadsheets of the 2004 election data compiled by John Brakey for all sixty-three precincts of Arizona LD 27. My idea was to take a deeper look at the relative presidential vote shares in the three permissible forms of voting on Election Day 2004: (a) Provisional, (b) At-the-Precinct, and (c) Mail-In. My operating hypothesis was that the presidential voting patterns may vary from precinct to precinct, but *within the same precinct* the Kerry (and Bush) vote shares (expressed as percentages of the total) should be virtually identical in each of these three voting forms. Stated in another way, the ratios of Kerry's (and Bush's) percentage vote share of form (a) to that of form (b) to that of form (c) should be very close to 1.0 to 1.0 to 1.0 for large enough voting units, provided the election was not hacked in one or two of these three forms. Here is how I went about it.

First, it seemed safe to assume that those provisional ballots actually accepted by the County Registrar of Voters were virtually 100 percent honest, since each was sealed in an envelope with a voter signature and printed name and address on an affidavit affixed to the outside. For such a ballot to be accepted, the recorder must recognize that the signer of the affidavit is registered to vote in that precinct, that he/she appeared at the correct polling place on Election Day to fill out his/her provisional ballot, and that he/she did not vote early (or elsewhere).

I hoped it might be possible to use the provisional ballots as a benchmark for the way people truly voted.[4] The first thing I did was to take the ratios of the presidential vote shares of provisional ballots to the corresponding same-precinct mail-in shares. Figure 1 displays the individual-precinct provisional-ballot-to-mail-in ratios of the Bush shares, while Figure 2 shows the corresponding ratios for the Kerry shares.

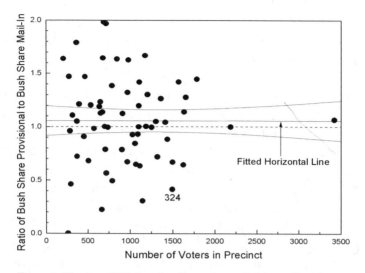

Figure 1. Election-2004 data for 63 precincts of Arizona Legislative District 27: Ratio of Bush's share of the (accepted) Provisional ballots to Bush's official share of the Mail-In ballots for each precinct.

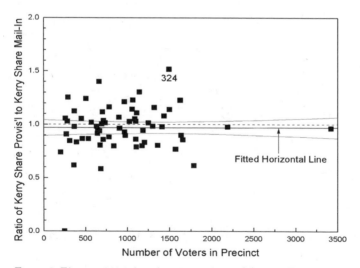

Figure 2. Election-2004 data for 63 precincts of Arizona Legislative District 27: Ratio of Kerry's share of the (accepted) Provisional ballots to Kerry's official share of the Mail-In ballots for each precinct.

Next, I used the mathematical curve-fitting software that came with my graphing program to obtain the continuous horizontal lines in Figures 1 and 2 as the best fits of these data. Lo, each of these fits agreed with my "null hypothesis" that in an honest election these ratios should equal 1.0 (represented by the horizontal dashed line) within the 95 percent confidence limits concomitantly generated by my software (the pair of curved lines above and below the fitted line). Thus, to my surprise, I was forced to conclude that the vast majority of the mail-in ballots were probably not hacked.

But I still wanted to look at the ratios of the at-the-precinct data in comparison to the statistically significant (and now shown to be mostly honest) mail-in data. We see in Figure 3 that Bush's ratio of at-the-precinct vote shares to his (mostly honest) mail-in shares were shifted on average 11.5 percent in his favor, a shift well outside of the 95 percent confidence limits pertaining to the fitted horizontal line.

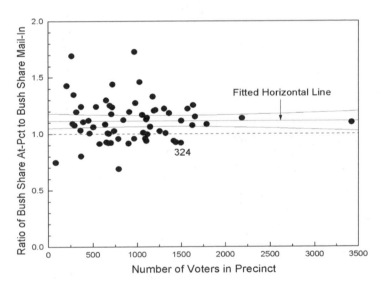

Figure 3. Election-2004 data for 63 precincts of Arizona Legislative District 27: Ratio of Bush's official share of At-the-Precinct ballots to Bush's official share of the Mail-In ballots for each precinct.

In Figure 4, the ratios of Kerry's at-the-precinct vote shares to his (mostly honest) mail-in shares are seen to be shifted an average of 5 percent against him, again outside the 95 percent confidence limits.

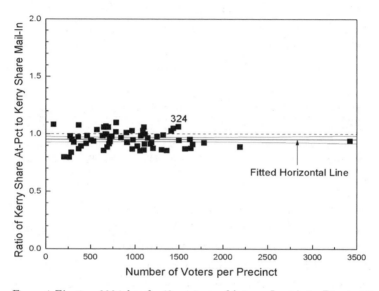

Figure 4. Election-2004 data for 63 precincts of Arizona Legislative District 27: Ratio of Kerry's official share of At-the-Precinct ballots to Kerry's official share of the Mail-In ballots for each precinct.

I believe that these four graphs constitute sufficient proof that the at-the-precinct vote at AZ LD 27 was stolen for Bush by insider implantation of vote-flipping codes in the 1.94w memory cards of the Diebold optical scanners and/or by alteration of the totals in the Diebold GEMS central tabulators by Pima County election officials.

PRECINCT 324: DOING THE NUMBERS ON THE REGISTERED VOTERS WHO EXPRESSED NO PARTY PREFERENCE

A critical reader might well ask: Couldn't the poll workers at John Brakey's Precinct 324 have been stealing votes on Kerry's behalf, given the positions of the Precinct 324 data points labeled in Figures 3 and 4? Well, let's take a closer look at the data. Table 2 breaks out the actual 2004 at-the-precinct and mail-in vote shares of Kerry and Bush in Precinct 324:

Precinct 324 of AZ LD 27	Kerry/Dem	Bush/Repub	Other/NOP
E2004 At-Precinct Voting	56.9%	41.6%	1.6%
E2004 Early/Mail-In Voting	53.6%	45.1%	1.3%
Party Registration	47.1%	21.5%	31.5%

Now let's look at what happens when we subtract the LD-wide-average data shown in Table 1 from the corresponding data in Table 2. In Table 3, we see that Kerry did stunningly *worse* (and Bush correspondingly much better) at Precinct 324 than the average for the entire Legislative District 27. In particular, there was a net mail-in shift of 19.0 percent in Bush's favor (after correction for the lower-than-average Democratic Party registration.)

Difference (Pct 324) - (LD-27 Average)	Kerry/Dem	Bush/Repub	Other/NOP
E2004 At-Precinct Voting	-5.0%	4.5%	0.5%
E2004 Early/Mail-In Voting	-11.0%	10.6%	0.4%
Party Registration	-1.7%	0.8%	2.4%

Let me explain this kind of "vote shift" calculation by using the Precinct 324 at-the-precinct vote shares as the next example. In the first row of Table 3, we see that Kerry had a 5.0 percent *smaller* (negative) at-the-precinct vote share than his LD-27-wide average. We also see that Bush had a 4.5 percent *larger* at-the-precinct share than his LD-27-wide average. To get the "gross shift" of votes from Kerry to Bush, we subtract the number in the Kerry column from the number on the same row in the Bush column. This yields a gross at-the-precinct shift of 9.5 percent in Bush's favor. (Remember, in Table 3 we are measuring all shifts relative to the LD-27-wide average.)

However, if we wish to improve our accuracy, we really ought to correct for the fact that there were 1.7% fewer registered Democrats at Precinct 324 and 0.8% more registered Republicans than was the case for the average LD-27 precinct (third row of Table 3). But for purposes of making any "correction" based on party registration, we have no choice but to first make a "modest assumption," namely, that all registered Democrats voted for Kerry and all registered Republicans voted for Bush (or the numbers of cross-over voters were exactly equal). Then, to make the proposed correction under this assumption, we take the shift of party registration (in this case in Bush's favor) at Precinct 324 relative to the LD-wide average (1.7+0.8 = 2.5%) and subtract it from the gross at-the-precinct Kerry-to-Bush shift relative to the LD-27-wide average (9.5%) to get the net at-the-precinct shift that might be the result of fraud (7.0%).

In the discussion below, I will begin using the terms "red shift" and "blue shift," as well as the acronym "NOP." By a "red shift" I mean a shift favoring Bush (a Kerry loss plus a Bush gain adding to a positive number), and by a "blue shift" I mean one that favors Kerry (a Kerry gain plus a Bush loss adding to a positive number). I will use "NOP" to denote not only the voters who registered as "No Party Preference," but also those very few registered as third-party voters.

Subject to our "modest assumption," one may calculate the percentages of NOP's who cast their votes for each candidate. Consider Bush's Precinct 324 at-the-precinct share of 41.6% in Table 2. If we subtract from this the Republican Party registration of 21.5%, we get 20.1%, which, under our assumption, is the percentage of all voters at Precinct 324 on Election Day 2004 who voted for Bush but were neither Republicans nor Democrats. Therefore, this percentage must have been drawn from the pool of voters that I lump together as NOP. Let's take the ratio of this number to the percentage of all voters (no matter who they voted for) who were registered NOP (or third party), seen from Table 2 to be 31.5%. Expressed as a percentage, 20.1% divided by 31.5% is 64%—an unexpectedly large percentage of NOPs voting for Bush.

Still, the devil's advocate would argue that all red shifts resulted from NOP voters at Precinct 324—and LD-wide—who simply decided to vote for Bush in large numbers. Were the NOPs in John Brakey's predominately-Hispanic precinct rabidly pro-Bush? Not according to the canvasses that John and I carried out a few days before the election, as we encountered very few Bush voters among those NOPs and infrequently voting "turnout" Democrats we spoke to. (Unfortunately, our canvass sheets were lost before we could total them up, so we have no objective pre-polling numbers for that part of Tucson.) Nevertheless, I did retain the results of my own canvass for MoveOn. org of several more-affluent, less-Hispanic, and more-Republican neighborhoods in Arizona Congressional District 8, in the Catalina foothills to the northeast of Precinct 324. Of the 115 individual NOPs and "turnout" Democrats I interviewed there, 95 were certain of, or leaning toward, voting for Kerry, while only six had any intention of voting for Bush.

Let me put these numbers in perspective. I conducted what might be regarded as a statistically significant poll of a predominately upper-middle-class Tucson neighborhood and found that 83% of the NOPs and turnout Democrats intended to vote for Kerry, while only 5% planned to vote for Bush. So, if you should persist in believing that 64% of the at-the-precinct and 75% of the mail-in NOP voters in predominately-Hispanic, less-affluent

Precinct 324 really voted for Bush, there is a bridge in Brooklyn I would like to sell you!

WERE OTHER PRECINCTS AFFECTED IN THE SAME WAY AS PRECINCT 324?

On the basis of the above evidence, I concluded that the mail-in votes for Precinct 324 were hacked. So, the next question becomes: In how many other precincts can the mail-in vote have been hacked? It cannot have been too many, given that Figures 1 and 2 show that the LD-wide average Bush and Kerry shares of the provisional ballots (presumed honest) are equal to their corresponding average shares of the mail-in ballots within 95 percent statistical confidence.

I decided that two of the prime candidates for investigation were the other two precincts (numbers 271 and 235) where John Brakey encountered poll workers behaving peculiarly and/or reacting hostilely to his legitimate presence on Election Day 2004. Tables 4 and 5 show the official results for Precincts 271 and 235, respectively, presented in terms of their differences from the LD-wide averages (exactly analogous to Table 3):

Difference (Pct 271) - (LD-27 Average)	Kerry/Dem	Bush/Repub	Other/NOP
E2004 At-Precinct Voting	1.9%	-1.2%	-0.7%
E2004 Early/Mail-In Voting	-2.6%	2.8%	-0.2%
Party Registration	5.0%	-2.7%	-0.8%

We see in Table 4 a 3.1% gross blue shift in the at-the-precinct voting, and a 5.4% gross red shift in the mail-ins. But when we take into account the net 7.7% party registration advantage enjoyed by the Democrats over the Republicans in Precinct 271, we arrive at the following corrected numbers relative to the average for LD 27: a 4.6% net at-the-precinct *red* shift, and a hefty 13.1% net red shift in the mail-ins.

Now let's look at Precinct 235. In Table 5, we see a 2.3% net red shift in the at-the-precinct voting and a whopping 13.8% net red shift in the mail-ins (both taking into account the tiny 0.2% correction for party registration):

Difference (Pct 235) - (LD-27 Average)	Kerry/Dem	Bush/Repub	Other/NO
E2004 At-Precinct Voting	-1.5%	0.6%	0.9%
E2004 Early/Mail-In Voting	-7.5%	6.1%	1.4%
Party Registration	0.0%	-0.2%	1.7%

Clearly, Pima County officials were hacking the mail-in votes at all three of the precincts where we know (324) or suspect (271 and 235) that poll workers were stacking (stuffing) the ballot box.

SUMMING UP ELECTION DAY 2004 IN ARIZONA LEGISLATIVE DISTRICT 27

Here is my summation of what apparently went down in LD 27 on Election Day 2004. There was a conspiracy comprising insiders with digital access to the 1.94w memory cards in the Diebold AccuVote OS optical scanners and/or to the GEMS central tabulators, and a cadre of colluding poll workers, including the crew headed by Reverend Khan at Precinct 324. Their overall plan was to hack the at-the-precinct vote at all precincts except the ones manned by poll workers whose job it was to stack (stuff) the ballot boxes at those polling places.

With regard to Precinct 324, recall that the net red shift in the at-the-precinct votes was "just" 7.0%, that is, less than John Brakey's and my maximum prediction. But bear in mind all of the red shifts discussed with respect to the LD-27-wide average, and that the LD-wide average at-the-precinct vote was itself a 5.1% red shifted with respect to the LD-wide average mail-in vote, and the mail-in vote was shown to have been (largely) uncorrupted. So, it is logical to arithmetically add the 5.1% red shift of the LD-wide at-the-precinct vote with respect to the putatively-honest LD-wide mail-in vote to the 7.0% net red shift in the Precinct 324 at-the-precinct vote with respect to the LD-wide average at-the-precinct vote to obtain a total Precinct 324 at-the-precinct red shift. This result, 12.1%, is close to the value of 11.5% independently estimated from John's and my study of the Precinct 324 poll books as the amount of vote flipping the Khan team could have accomplished assuming they had at their disposal forty-four illicitly-obtained blank ballots, utilized forty-one of them, and then faked innocent puzzlement over the fact that they had three left over.

In other words, my totally independent "outside-in" calculation of at-the-precinct election theft at Precinct 324 gives the same answer (within standard statistical error), as does John's and my "inside-out" deduction of the maximum vote shift the Khan team could have contrived by running their system—a system that we reverse-engineered in detail by forensic analyses of their own poll books!

In the end, as I reread what I've written, I keep returning to the thought of the 60,000 Americans from various walks of life and ethnic heritages belonging to Arizona Legislative District 27 who turned out in remarkably large numbers on Election Day 2004 to exercise their constitutional right to vote. What happened to these Tucsonans that day is quite likely a microcosm of what was simultaneously happening to Americans all across our country. Not only were these good folks' wills—and their inalienable rights—subverted, but they were never given a clue by the mainstream media as to what was done to them. The words that best describe my feelings leap from the title of Alan Paton's novel: *Cry, the Beloved Country!*

NOTES

1. Mark Crispin Miller, "Fooled Again – The *Real* Case for Election Reform," *Basic Books*, New York, 2007, p 132.

2. David L. Griscom and John R. Brakey, "Forensic Statistical Mechanics Applied to Public Documents Prove Poll-Worker Fraud," presentation by Griscom to the 2007 Annual Meeting of the *American Association for the Advancement of Science*, 2/16/07; http://www.drivehq.com/file/df.aspx/publish/dlgriscom/Election Fraud Research/Griscom_AAAS 2007 Annual Mtg.ppt

3. David L. Griscom, "Sleuthing Stolen Election 2004: John Brakey and the "Hack and Stack," *OpEdNews*, 3/17/07; http://www.opednews.com/articles/opedne_michael__070313_the_long_road_to_dem.htm

4. Forensic analyses involving Provisional-Ballot data are subject to larger statistically uncertainties than the other two forms of voting, owing to the smaller sample sizes: average of only 36 Provisional ballots *officially accepted* per precinct in Arizona LD 27, compared with averages of 502 At-the-Precinct ballots and 411 Mail-Ins. Nevertheless, the results of Figures 1 and 2 acquit my use of the Provisional-Ballot data to prove that the Mail-In tallies were (mostly) uncorrupted.

THE SELLING OF THE TOUCH SCREEN "PAPER TRAIL": FROM NEVADA TO THE EAC

★

MICHAEL RICHARDSON AND BRAD FRIEDMAN
With additional research by John Gideon

An investigation into the improper authorization and use of electronic touch-screen voting in Nevada during the 2004 presidential election has revealed a disturbing tale of misleading public statements, violations of state law, lax or non-existent federal oversight, and a casual wink-and-a-nod relationship between voting machine vendors, elections officials, federal testing bodies, and those who were supposed to be overseeing the entire process.

The public deception concerning Nevada's voting systems began in earnest on December 10, 2003, when current United States Representative and then Nevada Secretary of State Mark Heller held two news conferences, one at the Reno-Tahoe International Airport, and the other in Las Vegas.[1] The press conferences were to announce the choice of Sequoia Voting Systems, Inc. to supply new "paper trail" electronic voting machines to the state of Nevada. However, the announcement was made months before Heller had actually finalized the contract with the California-based voting machine company, and a full year before the equipment would finally be approved by Wyle Laboratory, the designated federal test lab.

"It is a right of every citizen to feel secure that the voting choices they have made are recorded accurately," Heller would say at a press conference several months later, on July 14, 2004, at the National Press Club in Washington, D.C., where he would proudly declare Nevada as "the first state in the nation to complete state certification and federal qualification of the voter-verified paper audit trail printer."[2] But while Heller may have wanted the citizens of Nevada to feel secure in their electoral system, the security and reliability of the systems was, in fact, not his driving concern.

Before electronic voting machines could be approved for use at the national level in 2004, they underwent secret testing at laboratories—known as the "Independent Testing Authorities" (ITA)—which were both selected and paid for by the voting machine companies themselves. Under The National Association of State Election Directors (NASED), which at the time was tasked via provisions in the Help America Vote Act (HAVA) with overseeing the federal testing and standards program, voting systems were qualified only after an "all clear" was officially given in the form of a formal written report from the ITA labs. NASED would then issue a number signifying that the particular machine model or voting system had passed standards testing procedures, and thus had met national standards for use by the public in elections. While not all states require their voting systems be first approved to national standards before they are certified at the state level, Nevada does.

During a lengthy conference call we held with officials with the U.S. Election Assistance Commission (EAC) on December 27, 2006, Executive Director Tom Wilkey explained the "very loose process" for testing voting systems that was in place while he was in charge of voting machine approval for NASED. (Now that standards oversight has been fully moved to the EAC, Wilkey has moved with it, in his position as Executive Director.) "Once a vendor went through an ITA," he explained, "we would assign them a number and put it up on a web, our website, or get it out to the State Director, and that would affirm that this vendor or this system had gone through the process."[3]

That is not, however, what happened in 2004 in Nevada, as Wilkey apparently ignored his own NASED process in order to assign a number to the Sequoia VeriVote system *long before* the ITA procedure and paper work had successfully been completed. Although Wilkey explained on the conference call that there must have been an ITA report before the NASED number was issued, and promised to track down that report, no explanation has ever been given, and apparently no such report exists.

Sequoia's "VeriVote" is a thermal paper-roll attachment printer for use with the company's EDGE DRE voting system. It is similar to the thermal paper-roll systems used for credit card purchases at convenience stores. This type of printer, now used on voting systems in a number of states, is frequently referred to as a "Voter-Verified Paper Audit Trail" (VVPAT) printer. The VVPAT has been at the center of a great deal of controversy because of its frequent failure to perform as promised. Among its many problems are frequent paper jams and difficultly in reading votes. In addition, an independent study done after Cuyahoga County, Ohio's 2006 primary election found that the totals on the "paper trails" frequently did not match the internal ballot tally, which is the one actually used by officials on Election Night, and beyond.

The VeriVote "paper trail" printer was still in development at Sequoia when Heller made the December 2003 announcement about signing the Nevada contract with the company. VeriVote would not see its first scrutiny by a federal ITA lab until April 2004, when it failed testing at the Wyle test laboratory in Huntsville, Alabama. Via discovery documents arising from a lawsuit against Sequoia in Nevada for alleged failure to record votes during the November 2004 general election in Washoe County, plaintiff Patricia Axelrod was able to obtain the confidential Wyle Laboratory test results, which had previously been withheld from the public. These documents revealed a string of failures for the Sequoia VeriVote system at Wyle Laboratory in 2004. However, in his announcement at the National Press Club in July 2004, Heller had declared the new Sequoia EDGE with VeriVote printer to be certified by the state of Nevada. He also claimed it had "passed federal certification with flying colors."[4] But that was not true, as neither state nor national certification had yet been granted.

Voting system certification requires that both the voting machine and the paper record printer to be used with it pass national standards testing as a single unit to ensure that the equipment works on Election Day as expected. While that point is well known among those versed in the testing and certification process, it seems to have escaped the knowledge of EAC Commissioner Donetta Davidson. In the quest to track down the elusive ITA report which would have given either Heller or NASED the go ahead to consider the system as "certified" to national standards, we queried the EAC on what exactly had happened when they assigned an official NASED number to the system, despite a lack of any known approval from the ITA test lab.

"Wasn't that [the VeriVote printer] just put on the existing equipment that had already been tested?" Davidson asked during our conference call, before we explained that complete systems must be tested together as a single unit.[5]

"So let me make sure I understand," the EAC's Communication's Director, Jeannie Layson chimed in skeptically, "We're talking about a *printer*—not a voting system."[6] We then explained that the systems must be tested *together* in order to receive a NASED certification number, which is then used by states to determine whether a system is nationally qualified or not.

"We're talking about a printer," Layson repeated. "We're talking about a . . . a printer, we're not talking about an actual part of the system that tallies votes, collects votes. You're talking about the printer that attaches onto it." Indeed, so was Dean Heller when he told a Reno newspaper in March of 2004 that, "the paper back up . . . is very critical to the election."[7] Yet that same printer, when it failed in Wyle's test lab, caused the voting machine itself to crash, and led to a suspension of testing, according to the reports obtained via litigation. As one report described:

> [T]he printer malfunctioned and began continuously generating blank paper. The DRE Voting machine then locked up and would not allow any further activity. The Sequoia technical representative was present and witnessed the anomaly. The representative directed that EFT [Electrical Fast Transient] testing be suspended pending further analysis.[8]

Additionally, when the VeriVote system was subjected to "Low Temperature Testing," it failed yet again:

> When the 'Cast Vote' button was selected, the DRE locked up and the screen went blank. No further activity was allowed.[9]

Later, during "Reliability Testing," the VeriVote locked up again, and stopped printing, which led to the suspension of testing.[10] Further "Reliability Testing" in May of 2004 resulted in all three test models freezing up, and one of the machines experiencing a paper jam.[11] In the wake of the test failures, the Sequoia representative on hand ordered an end to the testing. On June 17, 2004, the lab tested four machines only to discover paper jams on all four VeriVote printers. Once again, the Sequoia representative ordered an end to the testing.[12]

While the error-prone VeriVote system eventually completed testing at Wyle Labs, the paperwork denoting successful completion of the tests was not finished until December 16, 2004, six weeks *after* the November 2, 2004 general election and *thirteen weeks* after the system had been used in the September primary election. The ITA report was not signed until December 21, 2004, and not filed with the Nevada Secretary of State until January 12, 2005, one day after Ellick C. Hsu, the Deputy Secretary for Elections, wrote to a Sequoia Vice President on behalf of Heller, saying, "I am pleased to inform you that . . . the EDGE Model II with Veri-Vote Printer . . . has been approved for sale and use in the State of Nevada."[13]

Nevada state law [NRS 293B.063] says that "No mechanical voting system may be used in this State unless it meets or exceeds the standards for voting systems established by the Federal Election Commission pursuant to federal law." Certification cannot be given to voting systems until ITA testing has been successfully completed to determine if the system meets federal standards. Nonetheless, Nevada used the Sequoia VeriVote system in two different 2004 elections, without the system having successfully gained ITA approval for compliance with federal standards.

In March 2004, the *Reno Gazette-Journal* reported on concerns surrounding Heller's $9.3 million contract with Sequoia for the unapproved VeriVote printer, and its lack of compliance with national standards for voting equipment. After admitting that there were no such standards for testing at the time, Heller declared, "We'll just do it ourselves. I promised the voters they will have a paper trail, and I'm not going back on that."[14]

The pressure was on. The president of Nevada's State Association of Clerks and Recorders, Alan Glover, was quoted by the *Gazette-Journal* as suggesting that uncertified machines could cast doubts on the election. "If you add something to a machine that is not certified, I think it throws the results of the elections right into the courts. . . . For the purpose of the voters, they do not know whether their vote is going to count or not."[15]

Multiple backup plans had been put in place if the printers weren't either certified or ready in time for the 2004 elections. "We do not know what to tell the voters . . . what piece of equipment they'll be voting on," Glover complained.[16]

Heller's do-it-yourself testing would proceed, however. Documents obtained by Patricia Axelrod during the course of her ongoing litigation against the state show that Heller was aided by Steve V. Freeman, a member of NASED's Voting Systems Board. On May 26, 2004, Freeman wrote a letter indicating his personal approval of the VeriVote system. Freeman's letter minimized the failures of the system and suggested that there were "no significant issues" to disqualify the system for certification under state law. Upon receiving the letter from Freeman, Heller went ahead and mandated VeriVote despite the many problems discovered by the Wyle test lab. Axelrod believes that Freeman's letter became the basis for Heller's use of the flawed Sequoia VeriVote system in Nevada in the face of the frequent test lab failures.[17]

As George W. Bush had been declared the winner of the state's electoral votes by a whisker in 2000, Nevada had become an important swing state for the 2004 campaign. With a fair amount of both pomp and circumstance, Heller had announced his landmark, new system with supposedly "voter verifiable records" at the National Press Club on July 14, 2004. But Heller's comments were not true, because at the time of the announcement, the federal qualification process was *stalled* by the VeriVote failures in the ITA test lab, and NASED had *not* issued a qualification number.

Nevertheless, on July 16, Sequoia followed Heller's lead and issued a press release announcing that the system had "successfully passed federal testing":

> Sequoia Voting Systems today announced it has successfully passed federal testing of the VeriVote printer upgrade to the company's popular AVC Edge touch screen voting system. . . . "We commend the State of Nevada for taking the national lead in the implementation of electronic voting with voter verifiable records," said Sequoia President Tracey Graham. . . . Electronic voting systems

are closely regulated by federal and state officials. Both the hardware and software of electronic voting systems must be tested against more than 500 pages of standards and requirements by federally sanctioned independent testing authorities.

In answer to queries about what happened during the initial certification of the VeriVote system, Sequoia Vice-President Michelle Shafer explained, in a series of emails, that Sequoia had received a letter from Wyle on July 15, 2004 indicating that the testing of the VeriVote was complete. Shafer, however, has declined to provide us with a copy of that letter. While our correspondence with Shafer initially been friendly, when she was asked, in lieu of her providing the letter in question, to simply provide the version number of the system that she claimed had passed testing in July of 2004, she became notably unfriendly:

> Our company is dedicated to improving the conduct of elections for our customers. We do not have the staff or resources to engage in running dialogues with every activist or blogger who contacts us, especially those with an agenda who do not commit to fairness, accuracy, balance and some semblance of journalistic integrity in their postings.[18]

Thus far not a single official document, from the Nevada Secretary of State, from Sequoia, from Wyle Laboratory, from the Election Assistance Commission or from Steve Freeman or Tom Wilkey, has been produced showing that there was any form of official completion of successful testing of the system when Heller made his National Press Club claim. Nonetheless, Heller's announcement of "federal certification" led to a California county, San Bernardino, receiving the go-ahead to try out the same system on an experimental basis that year, even though California law, similar to Nevada's, does not allow for state voting system certification until after federal certification has been granted.

Even worse, EAC Commissioner Davidson and Executive Director Wilkey disputed Heller's claim of "federal certification," flatly dismissing the notion that *any* voting system in America is, or has ever been, "federally certified."

"We didn't certify anything," explained Wilkey during our conference call. "We [NASED] were just trying to make sure that we could get a report that said it would qualify or had the equipment go through to get qualified. So that they—we would assign them a number and we would notify the state this equipment had been qualified by an ITA. It wasn't any formal certification process."

"But what happened over the course of the year," he continued, "is that we had vendors running around saying that they had met the—they got federally certified. Well, they didn't get federally certified. But I guess it sounded better for them to say they were federally certified."

So where did Heller get the idea that his new voting system had "passed federal certification with flying colors," as he said during his July 2004 press conference?

"That was the Secretary of State's decision to use them there," Brian Hancock, the EAC secretariat and liaison to NASED, explained. "Regardless of any federal qualification or NASED qualification or whatever you want—that was completely Nevada's decision and the Secretary of State of Nevada had made that decision on his own."[19]

In October 2004, after the Nevada primary, an email circulated by the EAC to NASED members indicated that there was consternation about Heller's plan to use the uncertified systems in the November general election. At the request of Wilkey, then still at NASED, Brian Hancock rolled into action, articulating Sequoia's position to the Voting Systems Board following an after-hours meeting between a Sequoia representative and EAC Commissioner Donetta Davidson, who was then serving as Colorado's Secretary of State. Buried among hundreds of NASED emails obtained by the non-partisan election watchdog organization Black Box Voting through Freedom of Information Act requests was a copy of a note from Sequoia "integrity support specialist" Lisa Flanagan to Davidson's secretary, Darleen Chacon. With a subject line of "Could you pass this along to Donetta for me?", Flanagan emailed on October 5, 2004 to schedule an after hours meeting with Davidson:

Hi Darleen, I told Donetta I would let her know when I set up a time to meet with Margie Bezjak and a couple of other folks ... would you let her know that I am meeting them at 5:00 PM on Thursday evening (October 7th) at Dewey's....

Both Davidson and Sequoia spokeswoman Michelle Shafer deny that any VeriVote business was discussed at the meeting. According to Shafer, Flanagan's meeting with Davidson, outside of her office at a local Denver watering hole, was an innocent get-together. "Lisa worked in Donetta Davidson's [Arapahoe] County Clerk office," (where Davidson had served as registrar-clerk before becoming Colorado's top elections chief), Shafer explained, inadvertently describing the cozy relationship between elections officials and the voting machine companies where many later go on to work. Flanagan "also worked for Davidson in the Secretary of State's office before she joined Sequoia," Shafer said. "The email is referring to a birthday party or some sort of celebration and Dewey's was just dinner before the party. No business was discussed."[20]

When we queried Davidson during the EAC conference call, she also claimed that it was an innocent, if coincidentally timed event, describing the evening as a ladies night out. "We did that a couple times after I left Arapahoe County...It was just a get-together of people that were friends and knew each other and there were several people there." She also denied that any business was discussed and was quick to add that while Flanagan worked on voter registration issues for Arapahoe, and then for the Secretary of State's office, and then at Sequoia, that "Sequoia wasn't a client of the Secretary of State's office."

But hadn't Colorado been using Sequoia's voting and registration systems at the time?

"Well, Colorado was using Sequoia in, you know, the counties purchased equipment, the voting equipment. All the counties purchased their own equipment, tested it and tested—I mean tested it, set it up and owned it," Davidson recalled. "They purchased their own equipment is really what I'm trying to get to."

But wasn't the Secretary of State's office responsible for granting approval to the counties for use of any given manufacturer's voting systems?

"[What] the state did, at that time," Davidson explained, was simply "look to see if it met the state law. We did not do any testing of the equipment. We went on the Independent Test Authority's reviews." That would, of course, be the same Independent Test Authority that had still failed to give the thumbs up for use of the Sequoia's VeriVote at the time of Davidson's get together with Flanagan.

Flanagan's revolving door status between Davidson's office and Sequoia naturally raises questions about the propriety of contact between the two outside of the public record at a time when Davidson played a key role in determining the company's newest, and arguably most important, product. Flanagan herself is no stranger to questions of conflict of interest. *The Denver Post* reported that Flanagan, as a Sequoia representative, was on the receiving end of a July 14, 2006 email describing the use of Sequoia's new electronic poll book (an Election Day voter check-in device) from the Denver Election Commission operations manager, Matt Crane. Crane is Flanagan's husband. As with the earlier meeting with Davidson, Crane said that Sequoia did not benefit from Flanagan's role in the $85,000 pollbook purchase.[21] The use of the pollbooks in Denver would make national headlines as they failed spectacularly on Election Day 2006, causing lines at polling places for up to eight hours.

Less than a week after Davidson's 2004 meeting with Flanagan, Brian Hancock of the EAC sent Davidson an email requesting "a formal response . . . regarding the...preliminary decision to not qualify the latest version of the Sequoia AVC Edge with the VeriVote printer."[22] This further confirms that the Veri-Vote had still not passed NASED muster a full three months after Heller and Sequoia had specifically claimed that it had. Hancock's request for a response was sent at the behest of the then chair of the NASED Voting Systems Board, Thomas Wilkey. Hancock wrote in the email to Davidson that:

> Sequoia is obviously upset with this decision [to not qualify the VeriVote] since they have spent significant time and money getting the VeriVote to this point, as well as the fact that the VeriVote will be used in Nevada in November.

Shortly thereafter, Sequoia got its way, as just over a week after Hancock's email to Davidson, on October 20, 2004, three months after Heller and Sequoia had claimed that it had been approved, NASED issued a national qualification number for the system. Davidson, who at first had trouble remembering whether she was part of NASED's Voting Systems Board at all, later remembered that she "attended, I think, one or two meetings." She also denied responding to the email from Hancock. "I just didn't have the time," she said, "I did not respond to any of [the emails about the Sequoia VeriVote matter] because I never had the technical ability to do that."[23]

Davidson's lack of understanding of technical and security concerns for voting systems was born out by a state judge in Colorado, who found, in response to a lawsuit filed by the non-partisan election advocate group Voter Action, that the state had failed in its duties to properly certify voting systems.[24] The group had sought decertification of the state's touch-screen voting systems because they said that the man Davidson had appointed to test the systems had been unqualified because he had no formal computer science training. The state testing for the voting systems, the case revealed, amounted to little more than opening the box, checking for documentation, turning the system on and off, and then giving the state's official seal of approval for use in an election. The systems were allowed for use in the 2006 elections nonetheless, since the court determined there would be no time to properly certify alternate voting systems. When the systems went through legitimate certification testing after the election under the new Colorado Secretary of State, Mike Coffman, nearly all of them, including the Sequoia VeriVote system, were decertified when they were found to be prone to error, inaccurate, and easily hackable.

Meanwhile, Nevada voters, unaware of Dean Heller's 2004 ruse, used the systems again to send Heller to the U.S. Congress in 2006.

"The fact of the matter is that we tried to do something," Tom Wilkey said by way of not apologizing for the way NASED had conducted business. "I'm not ashamed of that. I don't think anybody that was involved with that is ashamed of it. As a matter of fact, I think the people that were involved in it try to take great pride in what they tried to do."[25]

Despite Wilkey and Davidson's claims, a new Freedom of Information Act request has now dug out of the EAC cyberfiles the actual story of the rushed approval process to satisfy Sequoia and legitimize Dean Heller's false statements. On October 5, 2004, Brian Hancock emailed the members of the NASED board who issued approval numbers: "Brit is a definitive no on the qualifications for this system with the VeriVote. I need a definitive yes or no answer from you all before I can go back to Tom [Wilkey]. Please respond as soon as possible." Hancock then sent an email to Steve Freeman, who had earlier written Dean Heller's office about VeriVote's "minor hardware problems:"

"Brit is an unequivocal NO on 3.0.134 qualification. It looks like you are a NO also, but with qualifications. Does this sum it up?"

A week later, on October 12, with the 2004 election rapidly approaching, Hancock set up a phone conference with the Voting Systems Board member in question, Brit Williams (the NO vote holdout), Steve Freeman and Wilkey to discuss the "Sequoia issue." Williams sent Hancock and Wilkey a memo the next day outlining his concerns about the VeriVote, saying that the system was "not in compliance" with 1990 Voting System Standards. "However, it is the practice of the ITAs and the Technical Committee to not outright fail a system found to be non-compliant, but rather to advise the vendor of the non-compliance and allow them the opportunity to correct the problem."

On October 15, Hancock sent out another email to the members of NASED, including Davidson, about a "possible solution":

> "Tom requests that you review the attached document and make any comments or suggestions you feel necessary. This may only be the best of an array of very bad solutions to the problem, but perhaps it is a solution which most people can live with at the present time."

The same day, Tom Wilkey sent a memo to Tracey Graham, the president of Sequoia, indicating that Wyle Laboratory was going to cooperate. "Wyle Labs has agreed that this change will need summary review and that they will proceed with such a review in an expedited manner."[26]

On October 18, Freeman raised some "fairly important" concerns about what was being presented to the NASED voting system panel about the "VeriVote issue" in an email addressed to Brian Hancock, other NASED members and Wyle Laboratory, which still had not yet approved the machine. Freeman was concerned that the printer serial number was being printed on voter receipts, preventing a secret ballot. Two days later, on October 20, Hancock got an email from Wyle Laboratory saying that Sequoia had been able to remove the serial number. Not waiting for the final ITA report on all testing, as was the standard NASED practice, Hancock rushed an email to Wilkey. "I'm going to go ahead and send Sequoia their number now. I'll be working out the configuration language for the NASED Qualified List."[27]

"This is a new process, and a brand new day in this whole process," Sequoia spokeswoman Jeannie Layson said on our conference call. "Our program just started this January. None of [the current systems in use in America] were certified by EAC. We have not issued the first certification for a voting system."

All the systems will "have to be brought in and re-certified," Davidson added in. "We want them to bring all the systems in and have them go through the process that we have set up . . . It is such a bigger step than what has been done in the past that that's why we didn't grandfather anything in. You gotta bring it back in, folks."

"I always say," Davidson concluded, "the middle word of our title is 'assistance' . . . And that's what we're here for."

NOTES

1. Ed Vogel. "Sequoia Voting Systems: Voting Machines Chosen," *Las Vegas Review Journal*, Dec. 11, 2003.

2. Dean Heller. "V-PAT Certification News Conference," Office of Secretary of State, July 15, 2004.

3. Tom Wilkey. U.S. Election Assistance Commission Conference Call Phone Interview, December 27, 2006.

4. Dean Heller. July 15, 2004.

5. Donetta Davidson. U.S. Elections Assistance Commission Conference Call Phone Interview, December 27, 2006.

6. Jeannie Layson. U.S. Election Assistance Commission Conference Call Phone Interview, December 27, 2006.

7. Anjeanette Damon. "Board OKs Non-Certified Voting Machines." *Reno Gazette-Journal*, March 9, 2004.

8. Wyle Laboratories. Test Report No. 50932-01, Page 22, April 30, 2004.

9. Wyle Laboratories. Page 23, April 30, 2004.

10. Wyle Laboratories, Page 24, May 3, 2004.

11. Wyle Laboratories, Page 25, May 5, 2004.

12. Wyle Laboratories, Page 28, June 30, 2004.

13. Ellick C. Hsu. "State Certification of AVC EDGE Model II with Veri-Vote Printer: Release 4.3, Build 320," Office of the Secretary of State, January 11, 2005.

14. Anjeanette Damon, March 9, 2004.

15. Anjeanette Damon, March 9, 2004.

16. Anjeanette Damon, March 9, 2004.

17. The Freeman letter is missing from the records of the Nevada Secretary of State. Steve Freeman has confirmed the existence of the letter but declined to provide a copy of it. Sequoia has also confirmed the existence of the letter but declined to provide a copy of it. Patricia Axelrod shared a portion of the letter but declined to produce the full letter because of pending litigation. The EAC has no record of the letter.

18. Michelle Schafer, email correspondence, March 27, 2007.

19. Brian Hancock, U.S. Elections Assistance Conference Call Phone Interview, December 27, 2006.

20. Michelle Schafer, phone interview, February 27, 2007.

21. George Merritt. "City Asked for Pollbook Software," *Denver Post*, December 1, 2006.

22. Brian Hancock, Email Correspondence, October 12, 2004.

23. Donetta Davidson, December 27, 2006.

24. *Conroy v. Dennis*, Denver District Court, 06-CV-6072.

25. Tom Wilkey, December 27, 2006.

26. Tom Wilkey, Memorandum to Sequoia Voting Systems, October 15, 2004.

27. Brian Hancock, Email Correspondence, October 20, 2004.

2006

★

Throughout Bush/Cheney's first six years in power, scrupulous Republicans were largely disinclined to look too deeply into the elections of 2000 and 2004 because they were content with the results, or too intimidated by the party to say otherwise. After 2006, the Democrats were the complacent ones, since they were now victorious, and therefore saw no need to fret about the Bush regime's election fraud—despite the many races that were stolen from the party, even in what was, for them, the best of years.

Of course, the silence of those lambs expressed not genuine contentment, but the same old tense refusal to confront explosive truths; for the Democrats were well aware that certain, if not many, of their candidates had illegitimately "lost." As Jonathan Simon and Bruce O'Dell reveal in "Landslide Denied," on the basis of a close comparative analysis of all the exit polls available for the 2006 election, the Republicans had given themselves a 3.9 percent advantage in tight races nationwide—a boost just under the margin of error, and therefore unlikely to raise eyebrows. That the GOP had thus to fix the memory cards some weeks, or even months, before Election Day would help explain their "thumpin'" by the Democrats, as circumstances shifted radically late in the game, with scandals such as Foleygate, bad news such as Bob Woodward's *State of Denial*, and an extraordinary national turn-out making that near—4 percent inadequate, except in districts where the fraud and dirty tricks were just enough to stem the Democratic tide.

DuPage County, Illinois, was one such place. There, Democrat Tammy Duckworth faced Peter Roskam of the GOP in a race for the vacated House seat held for over thirty years by the grandiloquent rightist Henry Hyde. Although the district was historically Republican, Duckworth was apparently a shoo-in by Election Day. A Rotarian with an M.A. in International Relations, and a Major in the National Guard who had lost both legs in Iraq, Duckworth polled at 54 percent a week before Election Day, with Roskam far behind at 40 percent. As Jean Kaczmarek explains in painful detail, Roskam's "victory" was enabled by a staggering combination of election fraud and vote suppression, including the manipulation of Diebold's op-scan machines; and such Republican malfeasance was rewarded, or abetted, by the Democratic Party, which ordered Duckworth to concede with half the votes uncounted.

LANDSLIDE DENIED: EXIT POLLS VS. THE VOTE COUNT IN 2006

★

JONATHAN SIMON AND BRUCE O'DELL

INTRODUCTION: PRE-ELECTION CONCERN, ELECTION DAY RELIEF, ALARMING REALITY

There was an unprecedented level of concern approaching the 2006 election (E2006) about the vulnerability of the vote counting process to manipulation. With questions about the integrity of the 2000, 2002 and 2004 elections remaining unresolved, and with e-voting having proliferated nationwide, the alarm had spread from computer experts to the media and the public at large.

For many observers, however, the results on Election Day 2006 permitted a great sigh of relief—not because control of Congress shifted from Republican to Democrat, but because it appeared that the public will had been translated more or less accurately into electoral results. There was therefore a rush to conclude that the vote counting process had been fair and the concerns of election integrity proponents overblown.

Unfortunately, the evidence forces us to a very different and disturbing conclusion: that there was gross vote count manipulation that had a great impact on the results of E2006, significantly decreasing the magnitude of what would have been, accurately tabulated, a Democratic landslide of epic proportions. Because much of this manipulation appears to have been computer-based, and therefore invisible to the legions of at-the-poll observers, the public was informed of the usual "isolated incidents and glitches" but remains unaware of the far greater story: The electoral machinery and vote counting systems of the United States did not honestly and accurately translate the public will, and certainly cannot be counted on to do so in the future.

THE EVIDENTIARY BASIS

Our analysis of the distortions introduced into the E2006 vote count relies heavily on the official exit polls undertaken by Edison Media Research and Mitofsky International (Edison/Mitofsky) on behalf of a consortium of major media outlets known as the National Election Pool (NEP). In presenting exit poll-based evidence of vote count corruption, we are all too aware of the campaign that has been waged to discredit the reliability of exit polls as a measure of voter intent. Our analysis is not, however, based on a broad assumption of exit poll reliability. Rather we maintain that the national exit poll for E2006 contains within it specific questions that serve as intrinsic and objective yardsticks by which the representative validity of the poll's sample can be established, from which our conclusions flow directly.

For the purposes of this analysis, our primary attention is directed to the exit poll in which respondents were asked for whom they cast their vote for the House of Representatives.[1] Although only four House races (in the single-district states) were polled as individual races, an additional nationwide sample of more than 10,000 voters was drawn, the results representing the aggregate vote for the House in E2006.[2] The sample was weighted according to a variety of demographics prior to public posting, and had a margin of error of +/- 1%.[3]

When we compare the results of this national exit poll with the total vote count for all House races we find that once again, as in the 2004 Election (E2004), there is a very significant exit poll-vote count discrepancy. The exit poll indicates a Democratic victory margin of nearly 4%, *or* 3 million votes, greater than the margin recorded by the vote counting machinery. This is far outside the margin of error of the poll, and has less than a one in 10,000 likelihood of occurring as a matter of chance.

THE EXIT POLLS AND THE VOTE COUNT

In E2004, the only nontrivial argument against the validity of the exit polls—other than the mere assumption that the vote counts *must* be correct—turned out to be the hypothesis, never supported by evidence, that Republicans had been more reluctant to respond and that therefore Democrats were "oversampled." In E2006, the claim was once again made that the exit polls were "off" because Democrats were oversampled.[4] Indeed, this claim of sampling bias is by now accepted with something of a "so what else is new?" shrug. The 2006 exit poll, however, contains *intrinsic yardsticks* that directly refute this familiar and convenient claim. But before turning to the yardstick questions themselves, we need to clarify certain aspects of exit polling data presentation that have often proven confusing.

Any informed discussion of exit polling must distinguish among three separate categories of data:

1. **"Raw" data,** which comprises the actual responses to the questionnaires simply tallied up; this data is never publicly released and, in any case, makes no claim to accurately represent the electorate and cannot be usefully compared with vote counts.
2. **"Weighted" data,** in which the raw data has been weighted or stratified on the basis of numerous

demographic and voting pattern variables to reflect with great accuracy the composition and characteristics of the electorate.

3. **"Forced" or "Adjusted" data**, in which the pollster *overrides* previous weighting in order to make the "Who did you vote for?" result in a given race match the vote count for that race, however it distorts the demographics of the sample (that's why they call it "forcing").

Because the NEP envisions the post-election purpose of its exit polls as being limited to facilitating academic dissection of the election's dynamics and demographics (e.g., "How did the 18-25 age group vote?" or "How did voters especially concerned with the economy vote?"), the NEP methodology calls for "correcting" or "adjusting" its exit polls to congruence with the actual vote percentages after the polls close and actual returns become available. Exit polls are "corrected" on the ironclad assumption that the vote counts are valid. This becomes the supreme truth, relative to which all else is measured, and therefore it is assumed that polls that match these vote counts will present the most accurate information about the demographics and voting patterns of the electorate. A *distorted* electorate in the adjusted poll is therefore a powerful indicator of an invalid vote count.

We examined both "weighted" and "adjusted" exit polls of the nationwide vote for the House of Representatives as published by the NEP. On Election Night, November 7, 2006, at 7:07 p.m., CNN.com posted a national exit poll that was demographically weighted but not yet adjusted to congruence with the vote counts.[5] We call this the **Weighted National Poll**. At various intervals over the next eighteen hours, as polls closed and official tabulations became available, the results presented in the Weighted National Poll were progressively "corrected" to match the official vote totals, culminating in a fully adjusted national exit poll posted on CNN.com at 1 p.m. on November 8, 2006. We call this the **Adjusted National Poll**. We will make reference to both polls in the analysis that follows.

The 2006 national vote for the House, as captured by the Weighted National Poll, was 55.0% Democratic and 43.5% Republican—an 11.5% Democratic margin. By 1:00 p.m. on November 8, the Adjusted National Poll reported the overall vote for the House as 52.6% Democratic and 45.0% Republican, just a 7.6% margin.[6] This 7.6% Democratic margin of course matched the tabulated vote count, but was 3.9% smaller than that recorded by the Weighted National Poll the night before. This was a net difference of 3 million fewer votes for the Democrats.

DID THE 2006 EXIT POLL OVERSAMPLE DEMOCRATS? CROSS-TABS ANSWER THIS QUESTION

The national exit poll administered by Edison/Mitofsky for the NEP is not, as some may imagine, a simple "Who did you vote for?" questionnaire. It poses some 40 to 50 additional questions pertaining to demographic, political preference, and state-of-mind variables. Voters are asked, for example, about such characteristics as race, gender, income, age, and also about such things as church attendance, party identification, ideology, approval of various public figures, importance of various issues to their vote, and when they made up their minds about whom to vote for.

When the poll is posted, these characteristics are presented in a format known as "cross-tabs," in which the voting choice of respondents in each subgroup is shown. For example, respondents were asked whether they thought the United States was "going in the right direction." In the Weighted National Poll, the cross-tab for this characteristic (see below) shows us that 40% said "Yes" and 56% said "No"; and further that, of the 40% subgroup who said "Yes," 21% voted Democrat and 78% voted Republican for the House of Representatives, while, of the 56% who said "No," 80%

voted Democrat and 18% voted Republican. We also see that this question is quite highly correlated with voting preference, with fully four-fifths of the "pessimists" voting Democratic:

IS U.S. GOING IN RIGHT DIRECTION?

TOTAL	Democrat	Republican
Yes (40%)	21%	78%
No (56%)	80%	18%

Cross-tabs vary greatly in the degree to which the characteristic is correlated with voting preference. The more strongly correlated, the more important the cross-tab becomes in assessing the poll's validity as an indicator of the vote.

Prior to public posting, the exit poll data is weighted according to a variety of demographics, in such a way that the resulting cross-tabs closely mirror the expected, independently measurable characteristics of the electorate as a whole. The cross-tabs, in turn, tell us about the sample, giving us detailed information about its composition and "representativeness." This information is of critical importance to our analysis, because among the many questions asked of respondents are several that enable us to tell whether the sample is valid or *politically biased* in one direction or another. These are the "intrinsic yardsticks" to which we have made reference.

Among the most salient yardstick questions were the following:

- Job Approval of President Bush
- Job Approval of Congress
- Vote for President in 2004

With respect to each of these yardsticks, the composition of the sample can be compared to measures taken of the voting population as a whole, giving us a very good indication of the validity of the sample. Examining these cross-tabs for the Weighted National Poll—the 7:07 p.m. poll that was written off by the media as a "typical oversampling of Democrats"—this is what we found:

- Approval of President Bush: 42%
- Approval of Congress: 36%
- Vote for President in 2004: Bush 47%, Kerry 45%

When we compare these numbers with what we know about the electorate as a whole going into E2006, we can see at once that the poll that told us that the Democratic margin was 3 million votes greater than the computers toted up was not by any stretch of the imagination an oversampling of Democrats. Let's take each yardstick in turn.

PRESIDENTIAL APPROVAL RATING

We can compare the 42% approval of President Bush in the Weighted National Poll with any or all of the host of tracking polls measuring this critical political variable in the weeks and days leading up to the election. It is important when comparing approval ratings to make sure that we compare apples with apples, since the question can be posed in different ways leading to predictably different results. The principal formats of the approval measure are either simply "Do you approve or disapprove . . .?" or "Do you strongly approve, somewhat approve, somewhat disapprove, or strongly disapprove. . . ?" We can call these the *two-point* and *four-point* formats respectively. By repeatedly posing the question in both formats on the same days, it has been determined that the four-point format consistently yields an approval rating 3%-4% higher than the two-point format.[7]

Bearing this in mind and comparing the Weighted National Poll respondents' approval of President Bush with that registered by the electorate going into the election, we find very close parity. PollingReport.com catalogued thirty-three national polls of presidential approval taken between October 1 and Election Day using the two-point format, with an average (mean) approval rating of 37.6%.[8] This translates to a 41% approval rating in the four-point format used for the Weighted National Poll. A direct comparison is also possible with the Rasmussen tracking poll, which unlike the other tracking polls, uses the four-point format. The Rasmussen approval rating for October 2006 was also 41%, with 57%.[9] Thus, the 42% approval of President Bush in the Weighted National Poll matches the figure established for the electorate as a whole going into the election; in fact it is 1% "over par." As Bush approval correlates very strongly with voting preference (see below), an oversampling of Democrats would unavoidably have been reflected in a lower rating. The rating at or above the established level thus provides the first confirmation of the validity of the Weighted National Poll.

HOW GEORGE W. BUSH IS HANDLING HIS JOB

TOTAL	Democrat	Republican
Approve (42%)	15%	84%
Disapprove (58%)	83%	15%

CONGRESSIONAL APPROVAL RATING

As with the presidential approval yardstick, comparison between the 36% of the Weighted National Poll sample that approved of how Congress was handling its job and the value established for the electorate in numerous tracking polls corroborates the Weighted National Poll's validity. The mean of the seventeen national polls catalogued by PollingReport.com measuring approval of Congress between October 1 and Election Day (all employing the two-point format) was 27.5% approval.[10] Translating to the four-point format used for the exit poll yields a comparable approval rating of 31%, a full 5% *below* the congressional approval given by the Weighted National Poll respondents. As with the presidential rating, approval of what was at that point a Republican Congress correlates strongly with voting preference (see below). We would have expected an oversampling of Democrats to give a *lower* approval rating to Congress than did the electorate it was supposedly misrepresenting. Instead the Weighted National Poll yielded a significantly *higher* congressional approval rating—indicative, if anything, of an oversampling of Republicans.

HOW CONGRESS IS HANDLING ITS JOB

TOTAL	Democrat	Republican
Strongly Approve (5%)	29%	70%
Somewhat Approve (31%)	25%	73%
Somewhat Disapprove (32%)	62%	37%

VOTE FOR PRESIDENT IN 2004

Edison/Mitofksy asked all respondents how they had voted in the 2004 presidential election. The Weighted National Poll sample included 45% who said they had voted for Kerry and 47% who said they had voted for Bush (8% indicated they had not voted or voted for another candidate). This Bush margin of +2% closely approximates the +2.8% margin that Bush enjoyed in the official popular vote count for E2004.

VOTE FOR PRESIDENT IN 2004

TOTAL	Democrat	Republican
Kerry (45%)	93%	6%
Bush (47%)	17%	82%

While poll respondents have often shown some tendency to indicate they voted for the sitting president when questioned at the time of the next presidential election (i.e., four years out), Bush's historically low approval rating, coupled with his high relevance to this off-year election, and the shorter time span since the vote in question, make such a generic "winner's shift" singularly un-likely in E2006.

And while we present the reported 2.8 percent Bush margin in 2004 at face value, it will not escape notice that the distortions in vote tabulation that we establish in this essay were also alleged in 2004, were evidenced by the 2004 exit polls, and were demon-strably achievable given the electronic voting systems deployed at that time. We note that, if upon retrospective evaluation the unadjusted 2004 exit polls prove as accurate as the 2006 exit polls appear to be, and their 2.5 percent margin for Kerry in 2004 is taken as the appropriate baseline, a correctly weighted sample in 2006 would have included even more Kerry voters and even fewer Bush voters than Edison/Mitofsky's Weighted National Poll, with a substantial consequent up-tick in the Democratic margin beyond the 3 million votes thus far unaccounted for.

These critical comparisons between measures taken of the Weighted National Poll sample and established benchmarks are presented together in the chart immediately below:

COMPARISON OF 2006 WEIGHTED NATIONAL POLL (WNP) TO ESTABLISHED BENCHMARKS

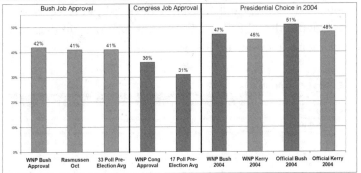

The Weighted National Poll sample, as can be seen below, is 80% White, 10% African-American, and 8% Latino in composition, with Whites splitting their vote evenly between the parties while

Latinos and particularly Blacks voted overwhelmingly Democratic.

VOTE BY RACE

TOTAL	Democrat	Republican
White (80%)	49%	49%
African-American (10%)	88%	12%
Latino (8%)	72%	26%
Asian (1%)	65%	35%
Other (2%)	59%	36%

We can compare these demographics with an established measure of the electorate published by the University of Michigan Center for Political Studies. *The ANES Guide To Public Opinion and Electoral Behavior* is a longitudinal study of many aspects of the American electorate, including racial composition.[11] The chart below presents the *ANES* results for the past six biennial national elections:[12]

	'94	'96	'98	'00	'02	'04
White :	78	72	74	74	75	70
Black :	12	14	12	13	12	16
Asian :	2	2	1	3	2	3
Native American:	3	5	3	3	2	4
Hispanic :	6	8	9	7	8	8
Other :	-	-	-	-	2	-

As can be seen by comparing the chart above, in *none* of the past six elections was White participation as high or Black participation as low as represented in the Weighted National Poll.[13] The average White proportion of the electorate was 74%, 6% below the exit poll's representation of Whites, while the average Black proportion was 13%, 3% above the exit poll's representation of Blacks. The relative under-representation of every strong Democratic constituency in this cross-tab, in favor of the least Democratic voting bloc, hardly jibes with the "Invalid: Oversampled Democrats" label cheerfully pasted on the Weighted National Poll.

VOTE BY PARTY ID

Though Vote By Party ID generally fluctuates relatively modestly from one election to the next, it is, not surprisingly, sensitive to the dynamics of atypical turnout battles. While we will address the E2006 turnout dynamics more fully in a later section, for the present we will simply note that a Democratic turnout romp was generally acknowledged in 2006, Republican voters having a number of late-breaking reasons for staying home.

In the Weighted National Poll, Democratic voters comprised 39 percent of the sample to 35 percent for the Republicans, as shown below:

VOTE BY PARTY ID

TOTAL	Democrat	Republican
Democrat (39%)	93%	6%
Republican (35%)	9%	90%
Independent (26%)	58%	38%

Only twenty states register their voters by party, so there is no direct comparison to be made to actual registration figures. But the *ANES Guide* once again proves useful. The chart below records party identification amongst the electorate as a whole on a seven-point scale, but the comparison is convincing.[14]

	'94	'96	'98	'00	'02	'04
Strong Democrat :	15	18	19	19	17	17
Weak Democrat :	19	19	18	15	17	16
Independent Democrat :	13	14	14	15	15	17
Independent Independent:	11	9	11	12	8	10
Independent Republican :	12	12	11	13	13	12
Weak Republican :	15	15	16	12	16	12
Strong Republican :	15	12	10	12	14	16
Apolitical :	1	1	2	1	1	0

In each of the past six biennial national elections through 2004, self-identified Democrats have outnumbered Republicans. The margins for 1994, 1996, 1998, 2000, 2002, and 2004 have been +4%, +10%, +11%, +10%, +4%, and +5% respectively. If Independent leaners are included, the Democratic margin increases every year to +5%, +12%, +14%, +12%, +6%, and +10% respectively. These numbers confirm a consistent plurality of self-identified Democratic voters from election to election.[15] The 4% Democratic plurality in the Weighted National Poll sample is seen to be at the extreme *low* end of the margins recorded since 1994, matching only the 4% Democratic margins recorded in the major *Republican* victories of 1994 and 2002. But E2006 was a major *Democratic* victory and, as will be seen, a likely *turnout landslide.*

While it would probably insult the intelligence of the media analysts who proclaimed that the E2006 Weighted National Poll was "off" because it had oversampled Democrats to even suggest the possibility that one or more of them took the 39–35 percent

Democratic ID margin in the poll to be indicative of Democratic oversampling—such misinterpretation quickly spreading among, and taking on the full authority of, the election night punditry—it is very difficult to comprehend by what other measure the election night analysts, and all who followed their lead, might have reached that manifestly erroneous, though obviously comforting, conclusion.

In short, there is no measure anywhere in the Weighted National Poll—in which the Democratic margin nationwide was some 3 million votes greater than tabulated by the machines—that indicates an oversampling of Democrats. Any departures from norms, trends, and expectations indicate just the opposite: a poll that likely undersampled Democratic voters and so, at 11.5 percent, *understated* the Democratic victory margin.

THE ADJUSTED NATIONAL POLL: MAKING THE VOTE-COUNT MATCH

In the wake of our primary analysis of the validity of the Weighted National Poll, consideration of the Adjusted National Poll is something of an afterthought, though it does serve to further reinforce our conclusions.

As we described earlier, in the "adjusted" or "corrected" poll, the pollster overrides all previous weighting to make the "Who did you vote for?" result in a given race (or set of races) match the vote count for that race, however it distorts the demographics of the sample. In the Adjusted National Poll, which appeared the day after the election and remains posted (with a few further updates not affecting this analysis) on CNN.com, Edison/Mitofsky was faced with the task of matching the tabulated aggregate results for the set of House races nationwide. This translated to reducing the Democratic margin from 11.5 percent to 7.6 percent by giving less weight to the respondents who said they had voted for a Democratic candidate, and more weight to the respondents who said they had voted Republican. Of course this process, referred to as "forcing," also affects the response to every question on the questionnaire, including the demographic and political preference questions we have been considering.

The most significant effect was upon "Vote for President in 2004." In order to match the results of the official tally, the Adjusted National Poll was forced to depict an electorate that voted for Bush over Kerry *by a 6 percent margin* in 2004, more than twice the "actual" margin of 2.8 percent, taken charitably at face value for the purposes of this analysis.

VOTE FOR PRESIDENT IN 2004

TOTAL	Democrat	Republican
Kerry (43%)	92%	7%
Bush (49%)	15%	83%

As might be expected, other yardsticks were also affected: Bush approval increases to 43%; congressional approval to 37%; and party ID shifts to an implausible 38% Democratic, 36% Republican.

There were, as we identified earlier, indications that the Weighted National Poll itself may have undersampled voters who had cast their votes for the Democratic House candidates.[16] The Adjusted National Poll compounds such distortions in order to present an electorate cut to fit the official vote totals. If such an adjusted poll yields inaccurate and distorted information about the demographics and voting patterns of the electorate, then very basic logic tells us that the vote count it was forced to match is itself invalid. This, of course, corroborates the story told by the Weighted National Poll, as well as by the pre-election polls, as shown in the graph below: [17]

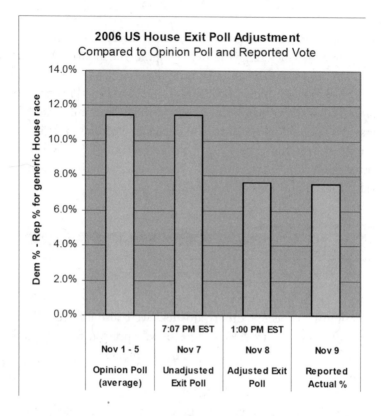

See Appendix 1 for detailed tabular presentation of the above data.

PLAUSIBLE EXPLANATIONS?

Since, as we have seen, the Weighted National Poll's inclusion of Democratic voters (or, better put, voters with characteristics making them likely to vote Democratic) either jibes with or falls somewhat short of established benchmarks for the electorate, there are only two possible explanations for the dramatic disparity between it and the official vote count: either Republicans unexpectedly turned out in droves and routed the Democrats in the E2006 turnout battle, or the official vote count is dramatically "off."

To our knowledge, no one has contended the former, and with good reason: there are a plethora of measures, including individual precinct tallies and additional polling data that we will examine in the next section, that confirm the obvious—the Democrats were the runaway winners of the 2006 get out the vote battle. Indeed it is generally acknowledged that Republican voters stayed home in droves, dismayed and turned-off by a late-breaking run of scandals, bad news, and missteps.[18] Hence, it must be the reported nationwide vote tally that is inaccurate. Although this is, to put it mildly, an unwelcome finding, it is unfortunately consonant with the many specific incidents of vote-switching and mistabulation reported in 2006, with an apparent competitive-contest targeting pattern, and with a host of other evidence and analysis that has emerged about electronic voting technology as deployed in the United States.[19]

SO WHY DID THE REPUBLICANS LOSE?

It will no doubt be objected that if such substantial manipulation of the vote count is possible, why would it stop short of bringing about a general electoral victory? While we would naturally like to credit the heightened scrutiny engendered by the untiring efforts of election integrity groups, an awakening media, and a more informed and vigilant public, an alternative, more chilling explanation has emerged—that the mechanics of manipulation (software modules, primarily) had to be deployed before late-breaking pre-election developments greatly expanded the gap that such manipulation would have been calibrated to cover.[20]

To quantify the extraordinary effect of the various "October surprises," we reference below the *Cook Political Report* National Tracking Poll's Generic Congressional Ballot, ordinarily a rather stable measure:[21]

GENERIC CONGRESSIONAL BALLOT

(Most Likely Voters)

Date	This Poll
Sample Size/MoE	807/3.5%

MLV	Dem	Rep
Oct. 26-29	61	35
Oct. 19-22	57	35
Oct. 5-8	50	41
Sept. 27-30	51	35
Sept. 21-24	49	41

Thus, the Democratic margin among most likely voters increased from 9 percent (50% – 41%) to 26 percent (61%– 35%) during the month of October, an enormous 17 percent jump occurring after the vote-shifting mechanisms were, or could be, deployed.

It should be noted that among the various tracking polls, there were some that did not pick up the dramatic trend reflected in the Cook poll. Indeed, Cook's own parallel tracking poll of all registered voters (not screened for likelihood of turnout) found only a modest gain of 2 percent in the Democratic margin over the same period. This is indicative of the phenomenon to which we have already made reference: what most boosted the Democrats during the month of October was an extraordinary gain in the relative *motivation and likelihood of turning out* among their voters. It supports our belief that it was primarily the exceptional turnout differential, understandably missed by exit polls calibrated to historical turnout patterns, that would have given the Democrats an even greater victory than the 11.5 percent reflected by the Weighted National Poll, in an honestly and accurately counted election.

IMPLICATIONS

The 2006 Election gave the Democrats control of both houses of Congress, by margins of thirty-one seats (233 – 202) in the House and two seats (51 – 49) in the Senate. The Democrats won twenty House races and four Senate races by margins of 6 percent of the vote or less.[22] The odds are very good that the outcomes of most if not all of these races would have been reversed a month earlier—post-deployment of vote shifting mechanisms but pre-October surprises—before the resulting dramatic movement to the Democrats as reflected in the 17 percent Generic Ballot jump. The ballpark *sans*-October Surprise numbers: 222R – 213D in the House and 53R – 47D in the Senate.

Absent a very Blue October, which came too late to be countered by deployment of additional vote-shifting mechanisms, we can conclude that, with the assistance of the vote-shifting mechanisms already deployed, the Republicans would almost certainly have maintained control of both houses of Congress. This should be a rather sobering observation for Democrats looking ahead to their electoral future and assessing to what extent the system is broken as they contemplate the various legislative proposals for reform.[23]

CONCLUSION

There is a remarkable degree of consensus among computer scientists,[24] security professionals,[25] government agencies,[26] and independent analysts[27] that U.S. electronic vote tallying technology is vulnerable both to unintentional programming errors,[28] and to deliberate manipulation—certainly by foul-play-minded insiders at voting equipment vendors, but also by other individuals with access to voting equipment hardware or software.[29]

We have arrived at a system of "faith-based" voting where we are simply asked to trust the integrity of the count produced by the secret-software machines that tally our votes, without effective check mechanisms. In the context of yet another election replete with reported problems with vote tallying, the continuing mismatch between the preferences expressed by voters as captured in national exit polls and the official vote tally as reported to the public is beyond disturbing.[30] It is a bright red flag that no one who values a democratic America can in good conscience ignore.

False elections bequeath to all Americans—right, left, and center—nothing less sinister than an illusory identity and the living of a national lie. Our biennial elections, far more than the endless parade of opinion polls, define America—both in terms of who occupies its seats of power, and as the single snapshot that becomes the enduring national self-portrait that all Americans carry in their mental wallets for at least the biennium, and more often for an era. It is also, needless to say, the portrait we send abroad.

While the reported results of the 2006 election were certainly well-received by the Democratic Party and were ballpark-consistent with public expectations of a Democratic victory, the unadjusted 2006 exit poll data indicates that what has been cast as a typical midterm setback for a struggling president in his second term was something rather more remarkable—a landslide repudiation of historic proportions.

We believe that the demographic validity of the Weighted National Poll in 2006 is the clearest possible warning that the ever-growing catalog of reported vulnerabilities in America's electronic vote counting systems are not only *possible* to exploit, *they are actually being exploited*. To those who would rush to find "innocent" explanations on an ad hoc basis for the cascade of mathematical evidence that continues to emerge, we ask what purpose is served and what comfort is given by relying on a series of implausible alibis to dispel concerns and head off effective reform?

The vulnerability is manifest; the stakes are enormous; the incentive is obvious; the evidence is strong and persistent. Any system so clearly at risk of interference and gross manipulation cannot and must not be trusted to tally the votes in any future elections.

APPENDIX 1 — US HOUSE EXIT POLL DATA

1. National Generic US House Exit Poll summary

US House Exit Poll 2006	Opinion Poll (average) Nov 1 - 5	Unadjusted Exit Poll Nov 7 7:07 PM EST	Adjusted Exit Poll Nov 8 1:00 PM EST	Reported Actual % Nov 9	Reported Actual Vote Nov 9
	7 polls**	Sample size 10,207	Sample size 13,251		
Total Democrat vote for US House*	55.0%	55.0%	52.6%	52.7%	40,323,525
Total Republican vote for US House	43.5%	43.5%	45.0%	45.1%	34,565,872
Total Other Parties vote for US House		1.5%	2.4%	2.2%	1,694,392
Total US House					76,583,789
*CBSnews.com, 11/9/06 + additional sources for unopposed candidates					
Democrat - Republican spread (%)	11.5%	11.5%	7.6%	7.6%	
Variance: Exit Poll - Actual [%]	3.9%	3.9%	0.0%		
Democrat - Republican spread (count)		8,807,136	5,820,368	5,820,368	
Variance: Exit Poll - Actual (count)		2,986,768	0		
Variance from actual					
Democrat	2.3%	2.3%	-0.1%		
Republican	-1.6%	-1.6%	-0.1%		
Other	-2.2%	-0.7%	0.2%		

2. Exit Poll Screen Captures

Exit poll screen capture files will be posted at http://www.electiondefensealliance.org/ExitPollData after the release of this report.

NOTES

1. Edison/Mitofsky exit polls for the Senate races also present alarming discrepancies and will be treated in a separate paper. The special significance of the House vote is that, unlike the Senate vote, it offers a nationwide aggregate view.

2. The sample size was roughly equal to that used to measure the national popular vote in presidential elections. At-precinct interviews were supplemented by phone interviews where needed to sample early and absentee voters.

3. We note with interest and raised brows that the NEP is now giving the MOE for their national sample as +/-3 % (Exit Polling by Edison Media Research: Subscriber FAQ, http://www.exit-poll.net/faq.html#a15). This is rather curious, as their published Methods Statement in 2004 assigns to a sample of

the same size and mode of sampling the expected MOE of +/-1%. Perhaps the NEP intends its new methodology statement to apply to its anticipated effort in 2008 and is planning to reduce the national sample size by 75% for that election; we hope not. It of course makes no sense, as applied to E2004 or E2006, that state polls in the 2000-respondent range should yield a MOE of +/-4%, as stated, while a national poll of more than *five times* that sample size should come in at +/-3%. It would certainly be useful in quelling any controversy that has arisen or might arise from exit poll-vote count disparities far outside the poll's MOE, but it is, to our knowledge, not the way that statistics and mathematics work.

4. See for example David Bauder, "ABC Captures Election-Night Ratings Race," *Associated Press*, November 8, 2006. Oddly enough, "oversampling" of Democrats has become a chronic ailment of exit polls since the proliferation of e-voting, no matter how diligently the nonpartisan collection of experts at the peak of their profession strives to prevent it. Of course the weighting process itself is undertaken to bring the sample into close conformity with the known and estimated characteristics of the electorate, including partisanship; so the fact that more of a given party's adherents were actually sampled, while it would be reflected in the unpublished raw data, would not in fact bias or affect the validity of the published *weighted* poll. *That is the whole point of weighting*, in light of which the hand-wringing about Democratic oversampling strikes us as misunderstanding at best, and quite possibly intended misdirection.

5. The 7:07 p.m. poll reported a 10,207 sample size and, in accordance with NEP methodology, the raw data had been weighted to closely match the demographics of the electorate.

6. Analysts noticing the substantial increase in "respondents" between the Weighted (10,207) and Adjusted (13,251) National Polls may understandably but erroneously conclude that the shift between the two polls is the result of a late influx of Republican-leaning respondents. This is not the way it works. Since these are both weighted polls, each is in effect "tuned" to a profile of the electorate assumed to be valid—the Weighted National Poll to a set of established demographic variables and the Adjusted National Poll to the vote count once it is tabulated. The published number of respondents is *irrelevant* to this process and has significance only as a guide to the poll's margin of error. 10,000+ respondents is a *huge* sample (cf. the 500 – 1500 range of most tracking polls), and obviously an ample basis on which to perform the demographic weighting manifest in the Weighted National Poll.

7. Rasussen Reports, "Polling Methodology: Job Approval Ratings," July 23, 2006, http://www.rasmussenreports.com/public_content/politics/polling_methodology_job_approval_ratings As Rasmussen notes, the 3%-4% upwards

adjustment in the four-point format impounds the virtual elimination of the "Not Sure" response obtained with greater frequency in the two-point format.

8. PollingReport.com, "President Bush: Overall Job Rating in Recent National Polls," http://www.pollingreport.com/BushJob.htm Typical of the national polls included are Gallup, AP-Ipsos, *Newsweek*, Fox/Opinion Dynamics, CBS/*New York Times*, NBC/*Wall Street Journal*, and ABC/*Washington Post*. The median approval rating is 37.4 percent, indistinguishable from the mean, and there is no discernible trend up or down over the October 1 – November 7 period.

9. Rasmussen Reports, "President Bush Job Approval," January 29, 2008, http://www.rasmussenreports.com/public_content/politics/political_updates/president_bush_job_approval The rating combines "strong" and "somewhat" approve and is the average of Rasmussen's daily tracking polls conducted throughout the month.

10. PollingReport.com, "Congress: Job Rating in Recent National Polls," http://www.pollingreport.com/CongJob.htm

11. The American National Election Studies; see www.electionstudies.org. Produced and distributed by the University of Michigan, Center for Political Studies; based on work supported by the National Science Foundation and a number of other sponsors.

12. The full chart, dating to 1948, may be referenced at The American National Election Studies, "Race of Respondent 1948-2004," November 27, 2005, http://www.electionstudies.org/nesguide/toptable/tab1a_3.htm

13. Asian and Native American voters, also strong Democratic constituencies, likewise seem to be significantly under-represented in the Weighted National Poll. The ANES results for 2006 are due to be published later this year. In *E2004* the Weighted National Poll was 77% White and 11% Black, as opposed to the ANES proportions of 70% and 16% respectively. It was this disproportionately White sample—supposedly short on "reluctant" Bush responders, but in reality overstocked with White voters who favored Bush by a margin of 11% and understocked with Black voters who favored Kerry by a margin of 80%!—that gave Kerry a 2.5% *victory* in the nationwide popular vote.

14. The full chart, dating to 1952, may be referenced at The American National Election Studies, "Party Identification 7-point Scale," November 27, 2005, http://www.electionstudies.org/nesguide/toptable/tab2a_1.htm

15. It is worth noting that among the most suspicious demographic distortions of the Adjusted National Poll in *E2004* was the Party ID cross-tab which indicated an electorate *evenly* divided between self-identified Democrats and Republicans, at 37 percent apiece. Not only was this supposed parity unprecedented, but it flew in the face of near-universal observational indications of

a major Democratic turnout victory in 2004: not only in Ohio but nationwide, long lines and hours-long waits were recorded at inner-city and traditionally Democratic precincts, while literally no such lines were observed and no such complaints recorded in traditionally Republican voting areas (see EIRS data at Voteprotect.org, "Election Incident Report System: All Election Incidents," 2004, https://voteprotect.org/index.php?display=EIRMapNation&tab=ED04).

16. To the extent that weighting is based on prior turnout patterns, a significant shift in the turnout dynamic, as was apparent in E2006, would be one cause for this undersampling. A second and more disturbing cause: "actual" results from recent elections, which themselves have been vulnerable to and distorted by electronic mistabulation, fed into the weighting algorithms.

17. The 11.5% Democratic margin in the Weighted National Poll was strictly congruent with the 11.5% average margin of the seven major national public opinion polls conducted immediately prior to the election. Indeed, this 11.5% pre-election margin was drawn down substantially by the appearance of three election-week "outlier" polls, which strangely came in at 7%, 6%, and 4% respectively. To put this in perspective, excluding these three polls, 30 of the 31 other major national polls published from the beginning of October up to the election showed the Democratic margin to be in double-digits, and the single exception came in at 9%. Real Clear Politics, "Generic Congressional Ballot," http://www.realclearpolitics.com/epolls/2006/house/us/generic_con-gressional_ballot-22.html It is also worth noting that most pre-election polls shift, in the month before the election, to a "likely-voter cutoff model" (LCVM) that excludes *entirely* any voters not highly likely (on the basis of a battery of screening questions) to cast ballots; that is, it excludes *entirely* voters with a 25% or even 50% likelihood of voting. Since these are disproportionately transients and first-time voters, the less educated and affluent, it is also a correspondingly Democratic constituency that is disproportionately excluded. Ideally these voters should be down-weighted to their estimated probability of voting, *but that probability is not 0%*. By excluding them entirely, these pre-election polls build in a pro-Republican bias of about 2-5 percent, which *anomalously* in 2006 appears to have been offset by the significantly greater enthusiasm for voting on the part of the Democrats, reflected in an elevated LCVM failure rate among Republicans responding negatively or ambivalently to the battery question about their intention to vote in E2006. Dr. Steven Freeman, visiting professor at the University of Pennsylvania's Center for Organizational Dynamics, has examined this phenomenon in great detail. Of course, one of the reasons for the recent shift to the LVCM—a methodology that pollsters will generally admit is distorted but which they maintain nonetheless "gets it right"—is that pollsters are *not* paid for methodological purity, *they are paid to get it right*. From the

pollster's standpoint, getting it right is the measure of their success whether the election is honest or the fix is in. The reality is that distorted vote counts and a distorted but "successful" pre-election polling methodology wind up corroborating and validating each other, *with only the exit polls (drawn from actual voters) seeming out of step.*

18. Indeed, once on-going analysis fully quantifies the extent of the Democrats' turnout victory, it will be time to recalculate upward the magnitude of the vote miscount in 2006.

19. For evidence for targeting of competitive races in 2006 see "Fingerprints of Election Theft" at http://www.electiondefensealliance.org/fingerprints_election_theft

20. The powerful impact of the succession of lurid scandals (Foley, Haggard, Sherwood, et al) is clear from the Weighted National Poll responses in which voters were asked about the importance of "corruption/ethics:" 41% responded "extremely important" and another 33% "very important," *the highest response of all the "importance" questions,* outstripping even the importance of "terrorism." Iraq, another source of late-breaking negatives for the GOP, also scored high on the importance scale (36% extremely, with this category breaking for the Democrats 61% –38%).

21. The Cook Political Report, "Question 6: Poll To Be Released," http://www.cookpolitical.com/poll/ballot.php

22. In the House: four races by 1%, four races by 2%, one race by 3%, 5 races by 4%, one race by 5% five races by 6%, one race by 7%, five races by 8%, two races by 9%; in the Senate: two races by 1%, one race by 3%, one race by 6%, one race by 8%.

23. If we are correct in our assessment that the limitations on vote shifting were more temporal than spatial—that is, had more to do with timing of deployment than with the potential size of the shift—then only extraordinary and unanticipated eleventh-hour pre-election surges *a la* E2006 will suffice to overcome future foul play. However, whatever quantitative limits may apply to electronic vote shifting, *it should obviously not be necessary to enjoy super-majority support in order to eke out electoral victories.*

24. For instance Association for Computing Machinery U.S. Public Policy Committee (USACM) Technology Policy Weblog, http://www.acm.org/usacm/weblog/index.php?cat=6

25. See the credentials of the interdisciplinary Brennan Center Task Force membership at Brennan Center for Justice, "About the Voting System Security Task Force," http://www.brennancenter.org/page/-/d/download_file_39281.pdf

26. United States Government Accountability Office, "Elections: Federal Efforts to Improve Security and Reliability of Electronic Voting Are Under

Way, but Key Activities Need to Be Completed," September 2005, http://www.gao.gov/new.items/d05956.pdf

27. See Harri Hursti, "Diebold Tsx Evaluation: Security Alert May 11, 2006, Critical Security Issues with Diebold Tsx," Black Box Voting, http://www.blackboxvoting.org/BBVtsxstudy.pdf ; Harri Hursti, "Diebold Tsx Evaluation: Security Alert May 22, 2006, Supplemental Report, Additional Observations," Black Box Voting, http://www.blackboxvoting.org/BBVtsxstudy-supp.pdf; Harri Hursti, "Black Box Report: Security Alert July 4, 2005, Critical Security Issues with Diebold Optical Scan Design," Black Box Voting, http://www.blackboxvoting.org/BBVreport.pdf

28. Credible reports of voting equipment malfunctions are all too common; one good starting point is VotersUnite.org, "Malfunctions and Miscounts, Sorted by Vote," http://www.votersunite.org/info/messupsbyvendor.asp

29. For example see, The Brennan Center Task Force On Voting System Security, "The Machinery of Democracy: Protecting Elections in an Electronic World," 2006, www.brennancenter.org/dynamic/subpages/download_file_36340.pdf

30. Election 2006 incidents at VotersUnite.org, "Election Problem Log - 2004 to Date," http://www.votersunite.org/electionproblems.asp

THE FATE OF TAMMY DUCKWORTH: FIGHTING FOR DEMOCRACY IN DUPAGE COUNTY, ILLINOIS

★

JEAN KACZMAREK

It was 10 o'clock on the evening of November 7, 2006. I had been awake since 4:15 that morning watching polls and hopping between precincts. Now all I wanted to do was park my car. I circled the Drury Lane conference center before finding a space, then tried to freshen up with lipstick, powder and a hairbrush before heading for the door, a black binder under my arm.

Inside was more than the gathering spot for Democrats in DuPage County, Illinois. It was also the finish line for the election to the open Illinois 6th Congressional District slot, which had been created by the retirement of longtime Republican representative Henry Hyde. Local journalist Eric Krol of the *Daily Herald* referred to it as "the nation's most-watched congressional contest." The contenders to replace Hyde were Peter Roskam on the Republican side, and Tammy Duckworth for the Democrats. Roskam was a state senator, and a stay-the-course supporter of President Bush. Major Duckworth was a former staff supervisor at Rotary International, held a Master of Arts degree in international affairs, and was a National Guard officer who had lost both her legs when the helicopter she was piloting was attacked in Iraq in 2004. She fit the "Fighting Dems" strategy of Rahm

Emanuel, who was placing Iraq War veterans into races across the country against Republicans, most of whom had never served in the military.

DuPage County, a western neighbor of Cook County, had been a Republican stronghold for decades. However, shifting demographics had created a new playing field. The Republican voters were aging, dying off or moving to escape the high property taxes and bleak winters. The Democrats, on the other hand, were younger, more diverse, and had relocated from Cook County and other metropolitan areas. In addition, DuPage had the highest growth of Latinos of any county in Illinois. With each election, Democrats were showing a steady gain in vote share, which was indicated by a Zogby/Reuter's poll taken on November 1, just six days before the election, which showed Duckworth leading Roskam 54 percent to 40 percent.

On Election Night, the Drury Lane ballroom was packed with candidates and their families, local Democratic leaders, and election workers rejuvenated after weeks of exhausting pavement pounding. They all expected a historic victory, and there was a roar of cheering and applause when it was reported that Democrats had won the House.

While everyone else was excited about an expected Duckworth victory, I, along with my colleague Melisa Urda, were focused instead on a seemingly dull county government office fifteen miles away in Wheaton. For the previous eighteen months, Melisa and I had been investigating this office, which was home to the DuPage County Election Commission. Among our discoveries were:

- Public records being destroyed without compliance to the Illinois Local Records Act.
- A small, local company with partisan ties had been given carte blanche to all things electronic in DuPage's electoral process—the software, the

machines, the tabulation room, the voter registration database and the election night hosting.

- Public records and election equipment had been stored in a warehouse owned by the brother of the Commission's chairman.
- Cronyism was pervasive, with vendors making generous contributions to local officials.
- Tens of thousands of voters had been purged from the registration database.
- Suspiciously large voter turnout in many elections, affecting the outcomes of both local and state races.
- The Illinois Election Code was questionably interpreted and selectively followed.

While Bev Harris of Black Box Voting fame had declared that DuPage County was among the worst places to vote in America, few among the packed conference center crowd understood what was happening behind the scenes and how it would impact that night's election results.

To understand the DuPage County Election Commission, it is helpful to first understand DuPage County. Current Illinois State Senator—and former DuPage County Republican Chairman—Kirk Dillard liked to brag that DuPage was most Republican county in Illinois. One city, Wheaton, is home to the well-known Christian undergraduate school, Wheaton College. The alma mater of Reverend Billy Graham, the school is just half a mile away from Milton Township Precinct 21, which would report a miraculous 106 percent voter turnout in the 2006 midterm election. Although once considered quite conservative, the school now attracts a mixture of evangelicals, both left and right. It also boasts the J. Dennis Hastert Center for Economics, Government and Public Policy, in honor of the 1964 alumnus and former Speaker of the House.

In the 1960 presidential election, where John Kennedy narrowly defeated Richard Nixon, neighboring Cook County had gained notoriety for Chicago Mayor Richard J. Daley's "impossible" 89 percent "get out the vote" turnout, which was widely reported as giving the election to JFK. However, one would be hard-pressed to find a single news article on that year's 93 percent voter turnout in DuPage County in support of Nixon.

My first encounter with the Election Commission was in the spring of 2005, when I gave a public statement before it. Melisa and I had already been actively working on state and national election reform, and we were enraged to have discovered voter suppression, problems with electronic voting, and exit polls that did not match the outcome in the 2004 presidential election. At the time, I knew nothing about the DuPage County Election Commission. I didn't know the names of the commissioners or high-ranking staff members. I had to use Map Quest to even find where it was located.

The Commission's boardroom is just what you would expect for a municipal office. Non-descript color scheme. Government-issue office furniture. American flag hanging in the corner. Large table in the middle for the commissioners to conduct their meetings. What I didn't expect, however, were Diebold vendors seated and joking with commissioners and staff members before the public was herded into the room. My education on local government had begun.

Around the table were the six people who held the keys to the kingdom: Chairman Dean Westrom, Commissioners Charlotte Mushow and Jeanne McNamara, Executive Director Robert T. Saar, Assistant Executive Director Doreen Nelson, and the Commission's outside attorney, Patrick Bond.

My statement before the Commission was on Jeffrey Dean, the consultant hired by Diebold to program its 1.96 software for the opti-scan voting systems used in DuPage County, as well as thirty other states, in 2004. Dean, among other things, had twenty-three convictions for computer-related fraud. Ironically, while thousands of convicted felons were disenfranchised from voting nationwide, a felon had programmed the software for millions of Americans to use on Election Day.

I have given several speeches during the course of my life. Yet my statement before the Election Commission was the first time I had created a sensation with my words. My temperature rose, my eyes watered and I trembled. From what I was later told, the Diebold vendors sitting fifteen feet away from me were fuming. Later when Robert Kennedy, Jr. asked me on his *Ring of Fire* radio program how the Election Commission had responded to my statement about Jeffrey Dean, I replied that they responded by buying more Diebold.

Meanwhile, Melisa had been in contact with Bev Harris, who had faxed FOIA (Freedom of Information Act) requests to every jurisdiction in the country, including DuPage County, asking for public records pertaining to the 2004 election. However, the county had never responded. Three months later, when Harris called seeking a response, she was astonished to learn that some of the materials from the election had been destroyed. She had been told that the records had been "retained statutorily for 60 days," though, according to the Federal Election Code, all public records from federal elections must be retained for a minimum of twenty-two months. Destroying these records prematurely is a felony.

Several months later, we sent a FOIA request to the Election Commission for the same records. We were particularly interested in seeing the poll tapes—the print-outs from the optiscan machines, which resemble grocery store receipts. Poll tapes, sometimes referred to as results slips, can provide a quick audit to compare with the official totals. They also contain the signatures of the election judges at each polling place. This comparison verifies the accuracy of vote counts. This time, we were told that the poll tapes had not been destroyed after all, but were "sealed" and "exempt from disclosure."

Soon after, Melisa discovered numerous payments to a company called "Accurate Document Destruction" in the Commission's line-item expenditures. We alerted the media, local and state authorities that the Commission was destroying election records. We also sent letters to the Election Commission and their attorneys demanding that they halt the destruction of public records. In June 2006, the Illinois Local Records Commission presented a request to the Illinois Attorney General's office on our behalf seeking an opinion to clarify if the Illinois Local Records Act included elections records. That same month, I contacted DuPage Chief Judge Ann Jorgensen; as chief judge, Jorgensen had signed off on audits of line-item expenditures, including the payments to Accurate Document Destruction. In August, I traveled to Springfield to make a public statement before the Illinois Local Records Commission, requesting that they alert the authorities regarding the destruction of the records. While they complied with my request, the destruction still continued. To date, 194 ninety-six gallon toters of material have been destroyed since we began our efforts. No certificate of disposal has ever been filed.

As of this writing, the Illinois Attorney General's office still has not rendered an opinion on the Illinois Local Records Act. My requests to that office that they have the Election Commission's records preserved in the meantime, or to provide a reason why this is not necessary, have been ignored. As a result, we still don't know what was destroyed in the Election Commission's backrooms.

In the summer of 2006, Melisa had become intrigued with a vendor for the Election Commission called Robis Elections, Inc. Located in downtown Wheaton, Robis had sold the Election Commission wireless hand-held devices called AskEDs, which are used in polling places to assist in verifying voter registration. Robis' website showed that the company was divided into two branches—Robis Elections and Robis Marketing. Robis Marketing had developed websites for local companies, churches and the Election Commission. Robis' president, David Davoust, was author of a book called *Creating Effective Ministry Websites*. We wondered how Davoust had made the leap from designing Christian websites to working with elections. Curiously, this fit a national pattern of fundamentalists owning and operating electronic voting companies. In addition, top officials in many of these firms did not hide their Republican sympathies.

Eventually, we learned that Robis was involved in the programming of voting machine software, and also had full access to the voter registration database through its AskEd devices. It appeared that our vote counting process was in the hands of a private company with partisan affiliations.

In the fall of 2005, I predicted that Peter Roskam would "win" the 6th Congressional District by 2 percent. The reason for my prediction was simple: 2 percent isn't large enough to raise a red flag, yet it fell just outside the margin for a recount. Since the advent of electronic voting, two percent margins have become a cliché nationwide.

That prediction began to solidify when we learned that the Election Commission was in the market for touch screen voting systems. They accepted proposals for the Hart Intercivic e-Slate, ES&S iVotronic and the Diebold TSx touch screen systems. At the Illinois State Board of Elections board meeting in December 2005, it was obvious that the Diebold TSx was the Commission's choice, as Executive Director Robert Saar had spent the entire day with Mark Radke, director of marketing for Diebold's Election Systems. Saar urged the Board to make an immediate certification. Because ES&S and Hart touch screens had not yet been certified, this gave the Election Commission a "legitimate" reason to choose Diebold. The Board passed a conditional certification by a 6-2 margin.

• • •

Slowly, Melisa and I were getting our message out via speeches and the occasional newspaper article, touching the nerves of people belonging to both political parties. We also captured the attention of vendors who had been denied contracts, disgruntled employees and insiders. We were asked to meet with whistle-blowers in stairwells and in basements. During our most memorable clandestine meeting, we were shown fifty years of DuPage County voter registration and turnout statistics. The numbers showed what appeared to be a historic record of partisan election administration. For example, in the eighteen months between the 2002 General Election and the 2004 primaries, voter registration had increased 106,000—nearly 12 percent of DuPage's entire population. Yet between the primaries and the 2004 election, nearly 84,000 names had been purged from the voter registration database. (New registrations decreased the overall number to 66,000.) When I learned that business reply mail was typically used when attempting to contact voters before removing them from voter lists, I looked at the Commission's line-item expenditures. There it was—payment for business reply postage and bulk mail for $90,000 in August 2004. I checked out election cycles for similar bulk mail payments: nothing of significance showed up for 2000, 2002 or 2006.

In addition, the Election Commission had hired Frank Salvato as a consultant for "voter outreach" in both 2003 and 2004. Salvato was a right-wing operative with no previous experience in voter registration. Executive Director Saar refused to release any specific information on Salvato, but according to media quotes, was quite satisfied with his work. With a drop in voter registration of over 66,000 in the months leading up to the 2004 election, one can only suspect Salvato's work and the county's voter purge were timed to enhance the GOP's prospects in the 2004 presidential election.

In the weeks leading up to the 2006 election, Melisa and I tried to offset the problems we anticipated. Melisa created detailed forms for poll watchers to list machine malfunctions, serial numbers and just about everything imaginable that could go wrong on Election Day. With a degree in biochemistry, she was in her element laying the groundwork for the science of evidence. We distributed these forms to political parties, groups and individuals, hoping to cover anticipated hot spots.

At the same time, the Election Commission had hired both a public relations firm and a media consultant to promote both the accuracy of the electronic machines and trust in the electoral process. In addition, they sent out slick color postcards alerting voters to early voting sites. What wasn't mentioned on these postcards was that the only method available during early voting would be the Diebold TSx touch screens, and that many of these machines had been left at polling places, which included shopping malls, a church, and a country club, for a full three weeks before the election. Thus, if anyone wanted to tinker with them, they had ample opportunity. The postcard also did not mentioned that none of the votes cast on the touch screens in early voting would be hand-audited.

However, there was something very important written on the postcards that flew right past most voters. To the left of the voter's name and address was printed their precinct location and address. Traditionally, the Election Commission had sent out distinctive color postcards several weeks before Election Day, which included a registration information wallet card. However, these cards were never sent in 2006, which meant that the early voting cards were the only source for most people to figure out where they were supposed to go to vote on Election Day. This would not have been a concern had the location of most polling places remained the same, but the Election Commission, confident that the public would be voting early in droves, moved and combined the number of polling places. As a result, some places now had four precincts instead of two, while other polling places were abolished altogether. When asked if notices would be placed on old polling sites on Election Day directing people to the new locales, the Election Commission said no.

On Election Day, I arrived at my precinct at 5:15 in the morning for poll watching. The janitor unlocked the door, and there before my very eyes, was the touch screen machine set up the previous day. A Princeton University study had recently released a video showing how a Diebold touch screen could be opened with a filing cabinet key. If a key wasn't handy, a nail file could do the same job in about ten seconds. It was also reported that a single memory card placed into a single machine could spread an undetectable vote-flipping virus. Executive Director Saar assured the media that this wasn't the case with the Diebold machines in DuPage because they were the TSx, not touch screens, and that any flaws in the accuracy and security of the touch screens did not apply to these machines. However, the only difference between the two machines is that the TSx has a printer attached to it.

As I went from precinct to precinct that day, I encountered numerous problems. Poll watchers reported that voters were facing registration issues, that some touch screens hadn't been set up on time, that some weren't functioning at all, that printers were jamming, and that poll tapes weren't available in many locations. In addition, one poll watcher reported that a touch screen machine in Naperville had pre-selected Republican Judy Baar Topinka in the gubernatorial race.

I was present for the closing of a polling place in Lombard. Before the touch screens, closing out a precinct had been relatively quick. In 2004, I had been done by 7:45 pm, with a copy of the poll tape in hand. That was not the case this night, as precinct judges hunched over the touch screen machine for over an hour, trying to figure what to do, before giving up. Since no poll tapes were printed, the judges couldn't sign off on the results. They were then told via cell phone to bring the machine to the Election Commission office. The machine's battery kicked in when it was unplugged, so that the machine was still live with a lit screen and the memory card still inserted as it was transported.

There were closing problems like that all over DuPage County. I would learn the next day from an observer that eighty memory cards had not been returned to the tabulation room properly. Memory cards are electronic ballot boxes; leaving them behind is a grave breach in the chain of custody. Two-dozen memory cards stayed out all night long. When the cards were retrieved the next day, with a police escort no less, some were found unlocked or outside their protective pouches.

Duckworth began her concession speech at 11:15 pm on election night. At that point, Robis had reported that she was behind by 5 percent. While we had expected the Democrats to surrender without a ruckus, we didn't expect it to come this early, as only 50 percent of the vote had been counted. Several days later, a reliable source said that Chicago Mayor Richard Daley had called Roskam at 10:45 to congratulate him and was surprised to learn that Duckworth had not yet conceded. Daley then called Duckworth, saying words to the effect of, "we've gotta work with this guy," so she should concede. Illinois Army National Guard Major Tammy Duckworth had had her legs cut off again.

By morning, the margin in the race had tightened to 2 percent.*

---

* All the information presented in this essay, with substantial documentation and evidence, has been presented to the DuPage County Ethics Commission, the DuPage County State's Attorney's office, the Illinois Secretary of State's office, the Illinois Attorney General's office and the U.S. Attorney's office/Northern Illinois District. To date, no action has been taken.

TOWARD 2008

★

The bad elections covered in this book, from Florida in 2000 to DuPage County in 2006, were not anomalies or aberrations, but typical examples of the new Republican crusade against U.S. democracy. That effort is ongoing nationwide, and scoring victories on every front, because the subject is taboo, with Democrats, journalists and principled Republicans refusing even to acknowledge it, much less talk about it. Such silence is especially perverse, as we are now just months away from yet another presidential race—one that the Republican machine is readier than ever to subvert.

The fierce persistence of that anti-democratic drive has been apparent in Ohio, where the Republican Party certainly did not lay low after "delivering" the state in the 2004 election (a feat entailing the pre-emption, alteration, fabrication or destruction of at least half a million votes). The party's record since that infamous Election Day is, or should be, no less infamous, as Bob Fitrakis makes clear in his startling survey of the GOP's continuing depredations (or "high jinks," as the press might call them). Certainly the next election in Ohio should be monitored exquisitely, and its official outcome studied just as carefully; for, as of this writing, the Republican election personnel throughout the state are warring openly against all efforts to reform the voting system there. Such administrators wield great power in their respective counties, and, as Fitrakis points out, break laws and resist court orders with impunity, openly defying the reformist secretary of state.

Things are much worse at the national level; for, in Washington today, there are no authorities inclined to make the voting system work. As Paul Lehto observes, we must confront the devastating implications of *Bush v. Gore*, whereby the Supreme Court did not just arbitrarily elect a single president, but radically expanded its prerogative to nullify elections from now on.

As Lehto notes, this wild stroke of judicial activism complements the anti-democratic character of Congress, which largely functions now as an incumbency machine, whose members have no interest in reforming an election system that almost always benefits themselves. We can't begin to fight that power, Lehto contends, without our full rededication to America's first principles: a mass commitment just as radical today as it was when this nation was conceived against the British Empire.

The alternative, as Nancy Tobi argues, is to keep on trying to patch up our disastrous voting system with various high-tech bells and whistles which won't do anything but further complicate a process that should have been rejected in the first place. Tobi offers an invaluable critique of an election reform movement that has favored technocratic fixes over fundamental democratic principles of openness and fairness. Her essay reminds us that all electronic vote-counts are opaque, and therefore unacceptable; and it also offers the beginnings of a history of the Help America Vote Act—a law conceived by criminals intent on fattening the coffers of the GOP (and, of course, whole-heartedly supported by most Democrats).

With a reform movement fixated on machinery, U.S. democracy is at grave risk, and not just because e-voting is itself an anti-democratic practice, granting ultimate control of our elections to a caste of partisan technicians. The over-focus on those iffy gadgets also has distracted us from the far graver threat posed by the state itself, which evidently seeks to disenfranchise the majority before Election Day, making such machines irrelevant. As Steve Rosenfeld reports, the Jim Crow-type laws lately passed in many states have mighty champions not only on the Supreme Court, but even in the Department of Justice, whose civic function now is not to guard our voting rights but to suppress them.

In short, the government is working to pre-empt the votes of the majority, in order to ensure perennial "victory" by a partisan minority—an effort cast, and possibly imagined, as a strong defensive move against the threat of (Democratic) "voter fraud." That there's no evidence of any such real threat suggests that the Republican crusade against democracy may finally be as pathological as Bush & Co.'s "war on terror" (which the Democrats also support, although, of course, we never voted for it).

"AS OHIO GOES ..."

★

BOB FITRAKIS

More than three years after George W. Bush's highly implausible 2004 victory, Ohio's top election officials finally conceded that the state's vote counts were "vulnerable" to manipulation and theft. "Critical security failures" are embedded throughout Ohio's electronic voting systems, and those failures "could impact the integrity of elections in the Buckeye State," Ohio Secretary of State Jennifer Brunner said on December 14, 2007. She noted that "the tools needed to compromise an accurate vote count could be as simple as tampering with the paper audit trail connector or using a magnet and a personal digital assistant."[1]

Ohio was riddled with a staggering array of irregularities, apparent fraud and clear illegalities on Election Day 2004. Many of the problems were focused on electronic voting machines, whose lack of official accountability and a reliable paper trail had been an issue since the bitterly contested election of 2000. On Election Day, the *Free Press* (www.freepress.org) put out a news account alleging missing voting machines in inner city polling sites in Columbus.[2] In addition, *Free Press* reporters and election observers flooded the organization's website with scores of irregularities from throughout the state. After the election, the Columbus Institute for Contemporary Journalism (CICJ), publisher of the

Free Press, organized public hearings in order to solicit testimony from voters. While the mainstream media would later echo former Ohio Secretary of State J. Kenneth Blackwell's mantra that not a single irregularity had occurred in the election, the CICJ hearings produced the largest know body of evidence on election irregularities in Ohio history:

- In various polling stations in Democrat-rich inner city precincts in Youngstown and Columbus, voters who pushed touch screens for Kerry saw Bush's name light up. In addition, voting procedures regularly broke down in inner city and campus areas known to be heavily Democratic.
- A voting machine in Mahoning County recorded a negative 25 million votes for Kerry. The problem was allegedly fixed.
- In Gahanna Ward 1B, at a fundamentalist church, a so-called "electronic transfer glitch" gave Bush 4258 votes when only 638 people had actually voted at the polling place. The tally was allegedly corrected, but remains infamous as the "loaves and fishes" vote count.
- In Franklin County, dozens of voters swore under oath that their vote for Kerry faded away on the DRE without a paper trail.
- In Miami County, at 1:43 am the morning after Election Day, with the county's central tabulator reporting 100 percent of the vote, 19,000 more votes mysteriously arrived; 13,000 were for Bush at the same percentage as prior to the additional votes, a virtual statistical impossibility.
- In Cleveland, large, entirely implausible vote totals turned up for obscure third party candidates in traditional Democratic African-American wards. Vote counts in neighboring wards showed virtually

no votes for those candidates, with 90 percent going instead for Kerry.[3]

As we can see, the wide range of discrepancies in both electronic and paper balloting systems leaned almost uniformly toward the Bush camp. For example, 14.6 percent of Ohio's ballots were cast on computerized devices that left no paper trail, but nearly all votes were counted on computerized central tabulators. With more than 5.7 million votes cast in a state yielding an official margin for Bush of less than 119,000 votes, a skewed vote count on those machines alone could have made the difference in Bush's reelection.[4]

The most widely publicized problems came when predominantly African-American precincts turned up suspiciously short of voting machines. As a result, many inner-city voters had to wait three hours on average, and occasionally up to seven hours, to vote, according to election officials and the sworn testimony of local residents. The wait at liberal Kenyon College, located in Knox County, Ohio, was eleven hours, while voters at a nearby conservative Bible school were able to vote in a few minutes.[5]

In a series of visits to Ohio after the election, the Reverend Jesse Jackson rallied an African-American community that felt it had been deprived of its vote. Calling it "a bigger deal than Selma," Jackson likened what had happened to the deprivation of black voting rights in the nineteenth century Jim Crow south.[6] To try and get to the bottom of it all, he enlisted the support of Congressman John Conyers and Representative Stephanie Tubbs Jones. Conyers, the ranking Democrat on the House Judiciary Committee, convened two Congressional forums, one in Washington and one in Columbus, where activists delivered thousands of public records and hundreds of sworn voter affidavits documenting the election irregularities. These became the basis of Conyers' report, "Preserving Democracy: What Went Wrong in Ohio, Status Report of the House Judiciary Committee Democratic Staff."

At the same time, on December 13, 2004, an Ohio legal team filed two election challenge lawsuits, *Moss v. Bush*, and *Moss v. Moyer*, to try and overturn the Bush victory. At the federal courthouse that same morning in Columbus, suits were also filed on behalf of the Green and Libertarian Party candidates, demanding that the Ohio electors not be seated until a full investigation of both the balloting and the recount was conducted. On January 3, 2005, Reverend Jackson hosted a rally in downtown Columbus at which Representative Tubbs Jones announced that she would formally question the seating of the Ohio Electoral delegation. The next day, a busload of activists left from Columbus for an overnight "Winter Freedom Ride" to Washington D.C. As they arrived the next morning, the burgeoning "Election Protection" coalition staged a media briefing at the National Press Club, generating major global media coverage, including ABC's *Nightline*. Throughout that day and the next, Reverend Jackson, with this author and others in tow, lobbied Congress, providing in-depth briefings for key Democratic leaders, including Senator Hillary Clinton.

On January 6, 2005, at a morning rally across from the White House, Reverend Jackson announced that Senator Barbara Boxer would join Representative Tubbs Jones in questioning the seating of the Republican delegation from Ohio to the Electoral College. By invoking an 1877 law, Tubbs-Jones and Boxer stopped Congressional ratification of the 2004 Electoral College vote by challenging the Ohio results. A handful of progressive Democrats in the House and Boxer in the Senate forced the Republican-dominated Congress to hear two hours of protest about how the 2004 presidential vote had been replete with efforts to disenfranchise Democratic voters and suppress turnout. While the national news media, particularly the major television networks, exercised a virtual blackout on the challenge, those tuned it to C-SPAN, public radio and the Internet saw the emergence of a new generation of Democratic leaders willing to fight for progressive causes, starting with the most fundamental tenet of American Democracy, the right to vote.

The *Moss v. Bush* lawsuit challenging Ohio's 2004 presidential race was withdrawn after Bush's inauguration in 2005. The contesters had stated that Ohio Secretary of State J. Kenneth Blackwell, Karl C. Rove, Richard B. Cheney and George W. Bush "were properly noticed for depositions" and "failed to appear for their depositions." Blackwell argued he did not have to testify because he was "a public official." His office also labeled the deposition notices a form of "harassment." Without his testimony, and the ability to examine actual election records in a more detailed manner, *Moss v. Bush* had little chance of proving what had really happened on November 2, 2004.[7]

However, on March 21, 2005, Blackwell finally testified about the controversial 2004 election before the House Committee on Administration, chaired by then Representative Bob Ney. "While much has been written by the conspiracy theorists, I would like to point out that there has only been one complaint filed by the HAVA process," Blackwell said, referring to the Help America Vote Act, which was enacted by Congress after Florida's 2000 election debacle. "I am interested in clean, fair and transparent elections."

"We had the most successful election on a punch card system ever," he continued. "It's silly on its face to say there was systematic attempt to disenfranchise blacks in Franklin County ... We have to work very hard to make sure our system is fraud proof ... and that's what I found so offensive, that charges were made against the system by folks who didn't have the decency to check the facts ..."[8]

Also testifying was an obscure Republican political operative serving as general counsel to a newly formed "voting rights" group, the American Center for Voting Rights (ACVR). Mark F. "Thor" Hearne told the Congressional committee that one of the reasons for the problems in Ohio was that the NAACP was bribing people with crack cocaine in order to entice them to register to vote. Hearne based his "testimony" on a lawsuit filed against the NAACP in Wood County, Ohio "alleging fraudulent voter registration under the Ohio Corrupt Practices Act." He also wrote a letter to the U.S. Department of Justice in March 2005 claiming there was "substantial evidence to suggest potential criminal wrongdoing by organizations such as Americans Coming Together (ACT), ACORN and the NAACP—Project Vote." Hearne turned out to be the former national general counsel for Bush-Cheney '04, and had no history of working in a voting rights organization.[9]

The Republican state legislature used this "voter fraud" spin to introduce the draconian Ohio House Bill 3, which became law in time for the 2006 elections. While HB 3's most publicized provision required voters to show ID before casting a ballot, it also opened voter registration activists to criminal prosecution, exempted electronic voting machines from public scrutiny, quintupled the cost of citizen-requested statewide recounts, and made it illegal to challenge a presidential vote count or any federal election result in Ohio. In addition, HB 3 reduced voter rolls by ordering county boards of elections to send cards to registered voters every two years. If a card came back as undelivered, the voter was forced to rely on a provisional ballot.

As the League of Women Voters put it in a letter to Republican legislative leaders, "Its [HB 3's] purported purpose of preventing voting fraud is based on the fallacy that there was widespread fraud perpetrated by voters in Ohio. In fact, the fraud was committed against Ohio voters by inadequate preparation that suppressed the votes of those whose registrations were not recorded correctly, those who could not wait for hours to vote or those whose votes were not counted because of misdirection or mishandling."[10]

• • •

In June 2005, the Democratic National Committee released an "investigative" report, "Democracy at Risk: The 2004 Election in Ohio." Although the report conceded that the African-American vote was suppressed, it downplayed the extent, stating that African-American voters waited an average of fifty-two minutes in line, compared to eighteen minutes on average for white voters.[11] In addition, the report said nothing about precinct-by-precinct illegalities—including unguarded ballots and election machine tampering—an unexplained bogus Homeland Security alert in Warren County Ohio, or the firing of a whistle-blowing election board official. It also ignored the discrepancies between exit polls and the highly improbable and virtually impossible vote total that gave George W. Bush a second term. In response to the report, John Tanner, Chief of the Voting Section of the U.S. Department of Justice, issued a June 29, 2005 letter denying that there was any suppression of black votes in Ohio.

However, a report released by the Government Accountability Office in September 2005 demonstrated the fragility of the system on which the election of 2004 had been decided. Representative Conyers had asked the GAO to investigate electronic voting machines as they were used during the 2004 presidential election, and the organization's final report stated, among other issues, that:

- Some electronic voting machines "did not encrypt cast ballots or system audit logs, and it was possible to alter both without being detected."
- "It was possible to alter the files that define how a ballot looks and works so that the votes for one candidate could be recorded for a different candidate." Numerous sworn statements and affidavits assert that this did happen in Ohio in 2004.
- "Vendors installed uncertified versions of voting system software at the local level."

- Access to the voting network was easily compromised because not all digital recording electronic voting systems (DREs) had supervisory functions that were password-protected, so access to one machine provided access to the whole network.
- Access to the voting network was also compromised by repeated use of the same user IDs combined with easily guessed passwords.
- The locks protecting access to the system were easily picked and keys were simple to copy.
- Problems with the security protocols and background screening practices for vendor personnel.
- One DRE model was shown to have been networked in such a rudimentary fashion that a power failure on one machine would cause the entire network to fail.[12]

Another example of a "fragile" electronic voting system occurred a month before the report was released, during the August 2005 special election for a Cincinnati-area Congressional seat, when outspoken Iraqi War vet, Democrat Paul Hackett, lost to Republican Jean Schmidt amidst a bizarre Election Day glitch. At 9:00 pm on election night, Hackett and Schmidt were in a virtual dead heat, with Schmidt leading by less than 900 votes, when election officials announced a mysterious "computer glitch" that delayed reports from Clermont County, which accounted for roughly a quarter of all the ballots cast in the district. When things were finally "fixed," Clermont gave Schmidt a 5000-vote margin over Hackett. The official explanation from Clermont County voting officials was that there was too much moisture from humidity in the optiscan voting machines, causing them to malfunction.[13]

In Ohio's 2005 general election, four reform measures backed by Reform Ohio Now, a well-funded bi-partisan statewide effort meant to bring some semblance of reliability back to the state's vote count, were on the ballot: Issue Two, which proposed early voting by mail or in person; Issue Three, which involved campaign finance reform; Issue Four, which meant to end gerrymandering by establishing a non-partisan commission to set Congressional and legislative districts; and Issue Five, which proposed taking administration of Ohio's elections away from the Secretary of State, and giving control to a nine-member non-partisan commission.

Also on the ballot was Issue One, which proposed state programs to create high-tech jobs and industry in Ohio. *The Columbus Dispatch's* headline the Sunday before Election Day announced "3 issues on way to passage," referring to Issues One, Two and Three. The *Dispatch* had based its conclusions on a poll of 1,872 registered Ohio voters. The results turned out to be dead-on accurate for Issue One.[14]

The Sunday *Dispatch* also carried another headline: "44 counties will break in new voting machines," adding that forty-one of those counties "will be using new electronic touch screens from Diebold Election System."[15]

On November 6, two days before the election, a *Dispatch* poll showed Issue Two passing by a vote of 59% to 33%, with 8% undecided, an even broader margin than that predicted for Issue One. But on Election Day, the official vote count showed Issue Two going down to defeat by the margin of 63.5%-36.5%. The official results also showed Issue Three going down to defeat in perhaps the most astonishing reversal in Ohio history, claiming just 33% of the vote. For this to have happened, Issue Three's polled support had to drop 28 points, with an apparent 100 percent opposition from those who had previously been undecided. The reversals on both Issues Two and Three were statistically staggering, to say the least.

As in 2004, there were several instances of chaos during the 2005 election. In inner city, heavily Democratic precincts in Montgomery County, the *Dayton Daily News* reported that "Vote count goes on all night: Errors, unfamiliarity with computerized voting at heart of problem." Among other things, 186 memory cards from the e-voting machines went missing, prompting election workers in some cases to search for them with flashlights, before all were allegedly found.[16] The *Daily News* also reported that, "Some machines began registering votes for the wrong item when voters touched the screen correctly. Those machines had lost their calibration during shipping or installation and had to be recalibrated."[17] Steve Harsman, the Director of the Montgomery County Board of Elections, told the *Daily News* that the recalibration could be done on site, but poll workers had never performed the task before.

In Lucas County, Board of Election's Director Jill Kelly explained that her staff could not complete the vote count for thirteen hours because poll workers "were not adequately trained to run the new machines." The *Toledo Blade* found that despite an $87,568 federal grant to the Lucas County Board of Elections for "voter education and poll worker training," only $1,718.65 had been spent from the grant. The *Blade* also reported that ten days after the 2005 election, "Fourteen touch-screen voting machines have sat unattended in the central hallway at the University of Toledo Scott Park Campus."[18]

The AP reported additional irregularities. In Wood County, election results were not posted until 6:23 a.m. the following morning after workers at four polling places accidentally selected the wrong option on voting machines, preventing the machine's memory cards from being automatically uploaded. In five counties—Brown, Crawford, Jackson, Jefferson and Marion—which were using Diebold machines, there were problems with the counting of absentee ballots as a result of "the width of the ballot."[19]

In addition, many counties used roving employees assigned to pick up memory cards from voting machines. In Lucas County, these "rovers" traveled "to multiple locations before delivering the cards to the election office at Governmental Center." The polls closed at 7:30 p.m., but "[t]he final memory cards were delivered to the Board of Elections office just before midnight," according to WTOL Channel 11 News in Toledo.[20]

Electronic voting machines malfunctioned again in Ohio's 2006 primary, as Secretary of State Blackwell grabbed the GOP nomination for governor. In Franklin and Delaware Counties, election officials had to "shut down and recalibrate [machines] throughout the day," according to the *Columbus Dispatch*. Electronic and mechanical breakdowns delayed poll openings in Cuyahoga County. The *Cleveland Plain Dealer* also reported that, "Cuyahoga County election workers continued to count votes Wednesday, with about 85 percent of the votes cast on the touch-screen machines counted by 11:15 a.m. But 70 memory cards—with results from 200 precincts—were missing."[21]

With electronic voting machines in place, Ohio's 2006 vote count included a higher percentage of uncounted ballots than in 2004. It also included—missed by the media due to Democratic victories—a statistically impossible swing in favor of the Republicans. The final *Columbus Dispatch* poll before Election Day had predicted that the Democratic gubernatorial candidate, Ted Strickland, would defeat Blackwell by 36%. In the end, Strickland won by 24 %, an unexplained loss of 12% of the vote. Additionally, the *Dispatch* predicted that Democratic Senate candidate Sherrod Brown would defeat Republican Mike DeWine by 24%. Brown wound up besting DeWine by 12%, like Strickland, coincidentally losing 12% from his final pre-election poll results.

Just prior to the scheduled September 3, 2006 destruction date for the 2004 presidential ballots, Ohio election protection activists won a landmark court battle to preserve the election records in *King Lincoln Bronzeville Neighborhood Association et. al. v. J. Kenneth Blackwell*. Finally, the 2004 votes in Ohio would be accurately counted. In addition, the election of a Democratic and pro-election reform Secretary of State, Jennifer Brunner, had heartened the voting rights community. In a bold first act, Brunner forced the resignations of the entire Cuyahoga County Board of Elections after two board members were convicted for rigging the 2004 recount.

While things looked promising initially, that promise disappeared quickly when voting rights activists learned of the illegal destruction of the federally protected 2004 election materials by fifty-six of Ohio's eighty-eight counties. In all, 1.6 million cast and uncast 2004 ballots were destroyed.[22]

Every county had a unique excuse for the destruction. Hancock County said it had "received verbal directions" from then Secretary of State Blackwell's office that unused and soiled ballots "did not have to be retained and these items were destroyed." But any election audit requires a complete set of used and unused ballots to ensure that the unused ballots weren't stuffed illegally into the ballot box. Putnam County apparently understood this all too clearly, which is why they informed Brunner that, "all unused ballots were destroyed for security purposes." Clermont County "could not locate" the unused ballots, according to Mike Keeley, Director of the county's Board of Elections. Butler County could not provide its "2004 General Election Ballot Pages," because "our staff unintentionally discarded boxes containing Ballot Pages as requested in Directive 2007-07 due to unclear and misinterpreted instructions," said Butler BOE Director Betty McGary. (For complex reasons having to do with Ohio's precinct ballot rotation law, the ballots from Butler County could not be recounted with the Ballot Pages missing.) Holmes County BOE Director Lisa Welch wrote Brunner that, "a shelving unit collapsed in the Board of Elections storeroom on the morning of Friday, April 7, 2006. That shelving unit held the voted ballots, stubs, soiled and defaced ballot envelopes, and ballot accounting charts from the 2004 General Election. The shelves and stored items collapsed onto a side table holding a working coffee maker. The carafe on the coffee maker was full at the time of the incident. Many of the stored items had to be destroyed due to the broken glass and hot coffee."

Allen County "labeled all voted ballots and placed [them] in our vault for the required 22 months of storage," said Keith Cunningham, director of the country's Board of Elections. However, Cunningham told the Secretary of State that in the ". . . latter part of 2004 and into 2005 . . . [we] began to experience problems with storm water migrating and subsequently penetrating our primary storage areas including our vault." He later told *Free Press* reporter Paddy Shaffer that the vault had been flooding for "six years," and he had to put the 2004 presidential ballots on the floor because he needed the shelf space. "As a result of these events," Cunningham said, "much of what was stored in our vault, including the 2004 general election ballots, were compromised by water damage and subsequently destroyed on or about August 20, 2006. Pursuant to the recommendations of the Allen County Health Department the boxes displaying mold or mildew were set aside to be discarded. Unfortunately, the contractor hired to remove the damaged boxes also accidentally removed the undamaged boxes as well."

Guernsey County's ballots suffered a similar twisted fate. According to BOE Director Jacqueline Newhart, "The unused ballots as well as the punch card ballot pages were destroyed in error" because "the county maintenance worker, when collecting trash, picked up the boxes" that contained them. In Mahoning County, the Board of Elections blamed environmentalists for inadvertently destroying the ballots. Apparently the "Mahoning County Green Team picked up all recyclables in the storage room for disposal pursuant to the retention schedule," according to BOE Director Thomas McCabe. As a result, some 115, 936 ballots "were accidentally disposed of on Friday, March 23 of 2007." Down in Hamilton County (Cincinnati), home of the Taft family dynasty, both the used and unused ballots were "inadvertently shredded between January 19th and 26th of '06."

Perhaps the most egregious case of ballot destruction, and

the easiest to criminally prosecute, was in the aforementioned Montgomery County. Researcher Richard Hayes Phillips reported in the *Free Press* that, "... the Board was eager to destroy them [the ballots]. The employees who handled the ballots for me brought up the subject themselves." In addition, BOE Director Steve Harsman said that, "We literally ran out of space to prepare, stage, and retain material for these elections. It was imperative that we process the 2004 materials for destruction under the guidelines of the 22-month retention. Therefore, all materials were properly destroyed in a timely manner and we were unable to comply [to the court order saying that the records should be preserved] due to these circumstances. We did not receive formal notice from the courts prior to preparing the certification of destruction." Thus Harsman admitted to openly defying a federal court order and destroying evidence because he wasn't notified "prior to preparing the certification of destruction."

Finally, there was the case of Warren County. On Election Day 2004, the board of elections in Warren County had declared a Level 10 Homeland Security alert for which neither the Homeland Security Agency nor the FBI has any documentation or explanation. The alert served as cover for moving the vote count to an isolated warehouse, away from the media. Eventually, Bush emerged from Warren County with a huge majority, far in excess of what he had received there in 2000. To this day, some twenty-two thousand officially unused ballots from Warren County are still missing. Warren County Board of Elections Director Michael E. Moore wrote Brunner, stating that, in complete defiance of the law, "They were not accidentally destroyed. They were destroyed pursuant to standard practices that had been used by the Board of Elections for many years in Warren County regarding unused punch card ballots." He added that, "The unused ballots were destroyed 60 days after the 2004 election." Warren, along with neighboring Clermont and Butler counties, provided Bush with more than his entire 118,775 margin of victory in Ohio in 2004. As a result, these three counties had been singled out for allegations of fraud in the election contest case *Moss v. Bush.* However, the destruction of ballots meant that the allegations of fraud were never tested in court, since, as with much of what happened in Ohio in 2004, the evidence had been destroyed.[23]

NOTES

1. Ohio Secretary of State, "Study: Voting Systems Vulnerable," press release, http://www.sos.state.oh.us/News/Read.aspx?ID=233

2. Bob Fitrakis, "Is there inner-city election suppression in Franklin County, Ohio?" *Columbus Free Press,* November 2, 2004, http://www.freepress.org/departments/display/19/2004/1159

3. U.S.Congress, Status Report of the House Judiciary Committee Democratic Staff, "Preserving Democracy: What Went Wrong In Chicago," January 5, 2005, http://www.truthout.org/Conyersreport.pdf. Also published as *What Went Wrong In Ohio: The Conyers Report on the 2004 Presidential Election,* (Chicago: Academy Chicago Publishers, 2005).

4. Ohio Secretary of State, 2004 Official Election Results, http://www.sos.state.oh.us/sos/ElectionsVoter/Results2004.aspx

5. Bob Fitrakis, Steve Rosenfeld and Harvey Wasserman, "The "Crime of November 2": The human side of how Bush stole Ohio, and why Congress must investigate rather than ratify the Electoral College (Part Two of Two)," *Columbus Free Press,* January 5, 2005, http://www.freepress.org/departments/display/19/2005/1067

6. Bob Fitrakis, Steve Rosenfeld and Harvey Wasserman, "Ohio Electoral Fight Becomes 'Biggest Deal Since Selma' as GOP Stonewalls," *Columbus Free Press,* December 22, 2004, http://www.freepress.org/departments/display/19/2004/1015

7. Bob Fitrakis, Steve Rosenfeld and Harvey Wasserman, "Ohio GOP election officials ducking notices of deposition as Kerry enters stolen vote fray," *Columbus Free Press,* December 8, 2004, http://www.freepress.org/departments/display/19/2004/1046

8. Steve Rosenfeld, Bob Fitrakis, and Harvey Wasserman, "As Blackwell Says, Ohio's in 2004 was a National Model," *Columbus Free Press,* March 24, 2005, http://freepress.org/departments/display/19/2005/1208

9. Bob Fitrakis, "Fake voting rights activists and groups linked to White House," *Columbus Free Press,* December 30, 2005, http://www.freepress.org/col-

umns.php?strFunc=display&strID=1289&strYear=2005&strAuthor=3

10. Ibid

11. The Democratic Party, "Democracy At Risk: The 2004 Election in Ohio,"June 2005, http://www.democrats.org/a/2005/06/democracy_at_ri.php

12. U.S. Government Accountability Office, "Federal Efforts to Improve Security and Reliability of Electronic Voting Systems Are Under Way, but Key Activities Need to Be Completed," September 2005, http://www.gao.gov/new.items/d05956.pdf

13. Bob Fitrakis and Harvey Wasserman, "Did the GOP steal another Ohio Election?" *Columbus Free Press*, August 5, 2005, http://www.freepress.org/departments/display/19/2005/1398

14. Darrel Rowland, "3 issues on way to passage, poll finds," *Columbus Dispatch*, November 6, 2005, http://www.dispatch.com/live/contentbe/dispatch/2005/11/06/20051106-A1-01.html

15. *Columbus Dispatch*, "44 counties will break in new voting machines," November 6, 2005, http://www.dispatch.com/live/contentbe/dispatch/2005/11/06/20051106-A1-03.html

16. Bob Fitrakis and Harvey Wasserman, "Has American Democracy Died an Electronic Death in Ohio 2005's Referenda Defeats?" *Columbus Free Press*, November 11, 2005, http://freepress.org/departments/display/19/2005/1559

17. Robert C. Koehler, "Poll Shock: Off by 40 points, newspaper's predictions may be disturbingly accurate," *Tribune Media Services*, November 24, 2005.

18. Bob Fitrakis and Harvey Wasserman, "Ohio's Diebold Debacle: New machines call election results into question," *Columbus Free Press*, November 24, 2005, http://freepress.org/departments/display/19/2005/1593

19. Ibid.

20. *Toledo Blade*, "Ohio's Election Problems Not Limited to Lucas County," December 21, 2005, http://www.wtol.com/Global/story.asp?s=4104855

21. *Cleveland Plain Dealer*, "Cuyahoga election results delayed until at least Friday," May 04, 2006.

22. Bob Fitrakis and Harvey Wasserman, "The criminal cover-up of Ohio's stolen 2004 election sinks to the fraudulent, the absurd, the pathetic," *Columbus Free Press*, August 2, 2007, http://www.freepress.org/departments/display/19/2007/2730

23. Ibid. All the above quotes are from official public records archived on freepress.org and at the Ohio Secretary of State's office, http://www.freepress.org/departments/display/19/2007/2730

BUSH V GORE
AND THE SUPREME COURT
AS ELECTION TERMINATOR

★

PAUL LEHTO

*"[I]t is proper to take alarm at the first experiment on our
liberties. We hold this prudent jealousy to be the first duty
of Citizens [. . .] not [to] wait till usurped power ha[s]
strengthened itself [. . .] in precedents."*—James Madison[1]

*"The great check imposed upon Executive power was a
popular mode of election; and the true object of jealousy,
which ought to attract the attention of the people of every
State, is any circumstance tending to diminish or destroy
that check."*—Senator Uriah Tracy[2]

The unmistakable theme of patriots throughout history, as evidenced by the two quotes above, is that "jealousy" is the first duty of all citizens. Put another way, the first duty of citizens is not to be fooled, much less "fooled again," as Mark Crispin Miller aptly titled his previous book on elections. Not only is this duty repeated throughout the writings of the American Revolution, it is also repeated in many state constitutions where, amidst all the expected provisions limiting the powers of government in the name of freedom, there sticks out what can only be considered stark warnings to future citizens, warnings that have identical themes and similar wordings, which can be closely paraphrased as: "Frequent recurrence to fundamental principles and rights is necessary to the preservation of liberty and free government." In other words, if we don't regularly invoke the "tools of democracy" (our fundamental rights and principles), the founders of our states and our nation predicted that freedom, liberty and democracy would perish.[3]

Indeed, even the famous African-American abolitionist Frederick Douglass, so very conscious of the compromise made at the founding of our country, provided a ringing defense of the most powerful and concentrated source of these rights and principles: the Declaration of Independence:

> "I have said that the Declaration of Independence is the ring-bolt to the chain of your nation's destiny; so, indeed, I regard it. The principles contained in that instrument are saving principles. Stand by those principles, be true to them on all occasions, in all places, against all foes, and at whatever cost."

The inalienable right upon which elections as well as the Declaration of Independence is based is the right to "alter or abolish" the government, which includes the ability to change the representatives who hold their power by delegation at will. Thus, there's no excuse for not having proper elections in which our ability to "kick the bums out" is absolutely not subject to question. This is most important when we need to remove a criminal regime from power. Because the secret vote counting that undeniably occurs with computerized voting of all types leaves us utterly insecure in our right and ability to remove a criminal (cheating) regime if and when We the People desire to, as of today, we can no longer say that we are a free people.

Since the very reason our government was instituted was to guarantee us free elections, our politicians today ought to be falling over themselves trying to return power and control over elections to the people—that is, if they truly practiced democracy, which means "people-rule." Government "of the people, by the people and for the people" is not just rhetoric, but reality when things are done right. Years ago, I had a minor supporting role as an attorney in a death penalty case, representing the defendant. Twelve people randomly selected from the populace literally decided life and death, ultimately sparing the defendant's life. That's rule by the people in the judicial branch—the jury system. Elections, by contrast, are rule by the people in the executive and legislative branches.

When thinking of election law, we must consider not only statutes, but case law, fundamental rights and principles, inalienable rights, and canons of statutory construction before we can know what the law will be held to mean where it truly counts: in court. Consequently, an intelligent reading of the Help America Vote Act (HAVA), which Congress passed in 2002, is not a completely accurate guide to what our election law is without heavy consideration of the constitutional equal protection holding of *Bush v. Gore*, the case that halted the recount in 2000 and handed the election to George W. Bush. It should be unnecessary to say that we are all on the most complete form of notice conceivable that the U.S. Supreme Court can, will, and has intervened to terminate a presidential election and decide the election itself. This fact alone exposes the mistaken conventional wisdom that *Bush v. Gore* is "not a precedent" to be a delusional self-deception to the extent such conventional "wisdom" leads us to believe that *Bush v. Gore* won't strike again, albeit in a slightly different form.

Fundamentally, the incentives are not set up correctly for election law to "work" because if the incumbents, who by definition make up election law, really foul things up, the election will be unconstitutional and/or void, as we saw in *Bush v. Gore*. Here again, we have ample notice this can and will happen, and the fact that lower courts don't have the political courage of the Supreme Court of the United States misses the mark entirely, because lower court judges are often elected through secret vote counting procedures and would fear to overturn them, but the unelected Supreme Court of the United States and the higher federal appellate courts suffer no similar limitations. It should be apparent, then, that an entirely new incumbent-protection strategy emerges for federal courts especially: agree that election activists make a great deal of good points, declare the election (or perhaps just the recount or "audit") invalid, void or unconstitutional, and thereby deprive We the People of the only method to remove an incumbent regime: a valid election. Given the time-honored strategy of running out the clock, especially in regards to an presidential election (as seen in 2000), it should not come as a surprise that I would assert that election law itself is often a rigged game every bit as or more insidious than corrupted vote counts themselves, especially since election law can parade as justice.

Moreover, successful election cheaters (by winning elections) get to set or influence future election law. Thus, in order to truly appreciate the legal pickle we are in with regards to our elections, we should imagine what things would be like if bank robbers somehow became bank officials or got to set future bank vault security policy, just like successful election stealers get to become election officials and/or influence or set election security policy. In this context, when election officials or their supporters complain about us not "trusting" them, one should point out that our country is not based on trust, but rather on checks and balances as distinct forms of *distrustful* oversight and supervision. Willie Sutton famously explained that he robbed banks because "that's where the money is." Similarly, people cheat in elections because that's where the power is.

OVER-RIDING IMPORTANCE OF ELECTION LAW

By "constitutionalizing" elections as equal protection issues, *Bush v. Gore* greatly expanded the territory in which the Supreme Court has an un-appealable final decree on what our elections mean, simply because the Supreme Court always has the un-appealable final decree on what the U.S. Constitution means. *Bush v. Gore* also expanded the Supreme Court's role in presidential elections by emphasizing the "unique federal concerns" of the presidency, supposedly justifying the Court in ignoring both jurisdictional and procedural doctrines that should have normally barred Supreme Court review or caused it to defer to the Florida Supreme Court, as pointed out in the dissents. The conventional wisdom that this case is "not a precedent" is the opposite of reassuring: If a case is not precedent, then that literally means that even if exactly the same facts came up again, the Court would be free to decide entirely differently.

One likely issue to justify Court intervention and an option to decide either way would be the California initiative that would purport to split the state's electoral votes along the lines of the victor in each congressional district, rather than "winner take all" as in the rest of the country. As a recent *Hastings Constitutional Law Quarterly* article concluded, whether the term "Legislature" in the Constitution (referring to the method of selecting presidential electors for the Electoral College) can be read to include deciding the method of selection of electors **by initiative** is something that reasonable minds can disagree on, and a *"Supreme Court decision either way is both plausible and defensible."*[4] However, this very plausibility and defensibility means that if the initiative were to pass, the U.S. Supreme Court has an *option* to decide the 2008 presidential election either way, and be more (seemingly) justified in doing so than they were in their *Bush v. Gore* election intervention of 2000. This option works out just the same if the Federal Circuit courts decide the issue to the liking of the U.S. Supreme Court. In that event, the Supreme Court can decline to grant *certiorari*, and then most likely various newspapers around the country will salute the Court's noble "abstention" from politics when in fact the Court simply liked the result already obtained in the lower courts and thus left it undisturbed.

ELECTION TERMINATION EXPANDS FURTHER: TO THE ORIGINAL VOTE COUNT

As if not to be outdone by the Supreme Court, in a June 6, 2006 special election in California's 50th Congressional District, the House of Representatives actually terminated an election not during the recount, but during the very *first* count. In the infamous "CA-50" race, which was conducted to replace Randy "Duke" Cunningham, had who resigned in November 2005 after pleading guilty to bribery, wire fraud, mail fraud, and tax evasion charges, the Democrat, Francine Busby, led in many pre-election polls. However, on election night, using non-transparent optical scan counting systems, the Republican, Brian Bilbray, was reported to hold a narrow lead. A week later, on June 13, with over 65,000 ballots still uncounted and no result yet certified, the House, without objection, swore in Brian Bilbray as a Congressman.[5]

According to a case filed in state court when two voters that attorney Ken Karan and I represented contested the election by asking for a recount, Bilbray claimed that the premature swearing-in caused "exclusive jurisdiction" to transfer to the House of Representatives, depriving the California courts of any jurisdiction to investigate, recount or otherwise do anything about the election. According to Bilbray's lawyers, the "Qualifications Clause" of Article I, Section 5 of the Constitution meant that only Congress could review the qualifications of its own members, including that of election, after a swearing-in, even if it happened before the vote counts were completed.

The direct implication of Bilbray's legal arguments of "no jurisdiction" in California was that every action in the state after

June 13, 2006 was void, and that there was nothing the people of the 50ᵗʰ District could do, other than to ask the House of Representatives to reconsider their decision. Thus, the election had been legally terminated of significance or effect before all the votes had been counted.

HOW HAVA AND *BUSH V. GORE* ELIMINATED THE VOTER INTENT STANDARD

In 2002, Congress funded the virtual elimination of "neutral and transparent" balloting procedures via the Help America Vote Act. HAVA mandated for "uniform and nondiscriminatory vote counting" procedures that reflected the *Bush v. Gore* case holdings. Although HAVA purported to grandfather-in paper ballot systems—a point that helped obtain key votes for its passage in Congress—this alleged preservation of paper ballots, as we see in a 6ᵗʰ Circuit case, *Stewart v. Blackwell*, is an illusion at best. In that case, all voting systems that didn't give "notice" of undervotes to the voter (paper ballots cannot talk, and thus cannot give "notice") were held unconstitutional, while touch screen DREs and precinct-notice "optical scans" where upheld.[6]

The "voter intent standard" declares that if the voter's intent is apparent, the vote should count despite whatever technicalities may arise. This is a reflection of the special sovereign status that the act of voting holds. As the Massachusetts Supreme Court said back in 1996, "The voters are the owners of our government, and our rule that we seek to discern the voter's intention and to give it effect reflects the proper relation between government and those to whom it is responsible."[7] As Gore's brief before the U.S. Supreme Court in *Bush v. Gore* noted, the "voter intent" standard was the universal standard *prior to* the adoption of voting machines in the United States. In contrast, the final ruling in *Bush v. Gore* called voter intent merely "a starting point" and imposed the requirement of detailed uniform "objective" rules. The whole idea, however, is not to allow technicalities to disfranchise the voter if intent can be determined. The law nowadays, by requiring as HAVA does "uniform nondiscriminatory" rules for vote counting, makes this "sovereignty-of-the-voter" standard obsolete. In its place, voters must now *comply* with rules, instead of being *listened* to, as was true in the voter intent standard that has been used during most of this country's history. Moving from government listening to voters to voter compliance is a *tectonic shift* in the relationship between voters and their government. We the People are in charge when we are voting (unlike the rest of the year, when we are subjects who have to obey the laws), and this is the critical difference that makes election secrecy unjustifiable, and distinguishes it from whatever justifiable secrecy might exist in other cases, such as in national security.

DEFENDING DEMOCRACY TODAY

Thinking of *Bush v. Gore*, "Loser Take All" might fairly be considered to mean democracy as well. But we do have nonviolent recourse, which, over the centuries, has shown itself to work pretty well. The inalienable rights of the Declaration of Independence have proved successful for abolitionists, suffragists, and for the modern Civil Rights movement, specifically because they were incapable, by definition, of destruction by any "mortal power" or government, as Hamilton put it. That these rights are "self-evident" means we don't have to prove anything to anybody. Thus, we can take a cue from Thomas Jefferson and play the ultimate power card with regards to voting: inalienable rights. Though the situation seems complicated, it's amenable to asking simple but powerfully clarifying questions like "Whose Country is this?" and "What's the government's primary job?" As the owners of this country, our employees/public servants cannot legitimately hide the vote counts from us. As Justice Brandeis said of transparency: "Sunshine is the best disinfectant."

NOTES

1. James Madison, "Memorial and Remonstrance against Religious Assessments," June 1785, http://press-pubs.uchicago.edu/founders/documents/amendI_religions43.html

2. "Debate on Amendment XII to U.S. Constitution," December 1803, http://presspubs.uchicago.edu/founders/documents/amendXIIs5.html

3. See, e.g. Wash. Const. Art. I, § 32; see Also Arizona Const. Art II, sec. 1; Illinois Const., Art. I, § 23; Massachusetts ALM Constitution Pt. 1, Art. XVIII; New Hampshire RSA Const. Part 1, Art. 38; North Carolina N.C. Const. art. I, § 35; West Virginia W. Va. Const. Art. III, § 20

4. Hasen, Rick L., "When "Legislature" May Mean More Than "Legislature:" Initiated Electoral College Reform And The Ghost Of Bush v. Gore," *Hastings Constitutional Law Quarterly*, April 2008.

5. Collins, Michael, "Congressional Election Nullified—Nobody Noticed," Scoop Independent News, August 25, 2006, http://www.scoop.co.nz/stories/HL0608/S00316.htm

6. United States Court of Appeals for the 6th Circuit, Eric Stewart, et al v. J. Kenneth Blackwell, et al http://www.ca6.uscourts.gov/opinions.pdf/06a0143p-06.pdf

7. Ford Fessenden and Christopher Drew, "Counting the Vote: The Legal Precedent; For Texas and Other States, A Bump Is Sometimes a Vote," *New York Times*, November 23, 2000.

THE PERILS OF
NAIVE REFORM:
A SECOND LOOK AT
FEDERAL ELECTION LAW

★

NANCY TOBI

Watching federal election reform efforts in twenty-first century America is a lot like watching a high tech magic show. The audience suspends disbelief while the wizards on stage pull rabbits out of their hats. In the same vein, Americans believe in the magic of election reform because we are, at heart, an idealistic people. We believe in the democratic dream of life, liberty, and the pursuit of happiness, and even with roughly 80 percent of the nation's votes counted in secret by private corporations, idealistic activists are still eager to accept election reform illusions over the challenging reality of corporate controlled elections.[1]

However, the stakes in election reform are high, and therefore we cannot afford to be fooled by the magician's act. Bad election reform legislation can destroy our democracy, as evidenced by the disastrous 2002 Help America Vote Act (HAVA). HAVA "reformed" the very meaning of *our right to vote,* turning it instead into the opportunity to *verify a voting machine's vote.*

To restore and protect the American Republic, election reform must flow from the guiding principles of democracy. We don't need magic to "solve" our election crisis, as we already have the solutions. We just need the will to implement them.

LOBBYIST ALCHEMY AND ELECTION REFORM

In 1995, House Majority Leader Tom DeLay and Republican strategist Grover Norquist launched the "K Street Project." Named for the Capitol Hill street that housed several lobbying firms, the project gave lobbyists direct access to Washington lawmakers through weekly policy and strategy meetings. The most infamous K Street lobbyist was Jack Abramoff, who worked for the firm Greenberg Traurig. Abramoff, now in prison, took money from his Native American clients and laundered it to congressional representatives in return for legislative and policy favors aligned with the project's political agenda.

The K Street project also influenced the most sweeping election reform ever enacted: the Help America Vote Act (HAVA). In addition to delivering a multi-billion dollar payoff to the electronic voting industry, including Greenberg Traurig's client, Diebold Election Systems, HAVA also, among other things:[2]

- Required every state in the nation to implement electronic voter registration databases
- Mandated accessible voting equipment, specifically recommending computerized touch screen machines
- Created the Election Assistance Commission (EAC), which is made up of four presidential appointees with broad and ever-expanding powers over the nation's election systems

Post-HAVA elections have delivered one disaster after another, from e-voting machine crashes, unequal distribution of expensive computerized equipment, registration database complications and abuse, electoral lawsuits, and the voting industry's complete and utter failure to deliver a quality product.[3]

RISE OF THE MACHINE

The media painted the contested 2000 election as a problem of butterfly ballots and pregnant chads, incessantly playing video clips of Florida election officials staring at computer punch cards trying to discern the "intent" of the voter.[4] Americans were told that *paper ballots* had caused the chaos in Florida, and that HAVA would fix the problem. As part of the "fix," nearly $3 billion was distributed to the states to buy electronic voter registration databases and computerized voting machines. Consequently, the number of votes counted by computers went from 40% in 2000, to 70% in 2004, to 80% in 2006.[5] This change was cataclysmic for election systems, and officials have continued to this day to struggle with the transformation of familiar and manageable low-tech elections to the complex high-tech theatre wrought by HAVA.

The destabilizing effect on America's mechanism of democracy has been substantial. In addition to causing shortages of poll workers, who, with an average age of seventy-two years, are averse to the complexities of e-voting, today's "techno-elections" have harmed the ability of public officials to independently administer elections without the support of the e-voting industry.[6] As a result, corporate voting company employees have become part of the election process, assisting poll workers in the use of voting equipment, administering "fixes" when the equipment malfunctions, and keeping vote data and election results in "black box" secret vaults, far from public scrutiny. A Republican House attorney involved in the drafting of HAVA once remarked to me that, "They are trying to complexify our elections to the point where citizens have no idea what is going on."

ELECTION REFORM ALCHEMY: FROM "RIGHT TO VOTE" TO "OPPORTUNITY TO VERIFY A VOTING MACHINE"

The cornerstone of HAVA are elections that are designed to adhere to technology, rather than voter needs. Nowhere is this better exemplified than in the now normative vocabulary of election reform: "verifiable voting." HAVA states that a voting system must "permit the voter to verify (in a private and independent manner) the votes selected by the voter on the ballot before the ballot is cast and counted."[7] However, if a voter marks an "X" next to a candidate's name on a paper ballot, they don't need to "verify" their choice; a voter only needs to "verify" his vote when it has been marked and/or counted by a computer. In HAVA alchemy, our Constitutional *right to vote* has been transformed into the *opportunity to verify a voting machine's vote*. As a result, many election reformers now believe that giving voters the opportunity to verify voting machines, and election officials the opportunity to audit those machines, equates to the right to vote. Indeed, the verifiable voting movement has spawned an entire cottage industry of election reform-minded computer scientists and statisticians who devise elaborate protocols to support the "verifiability" and "auditability" of technology-based elections. The net result is that verifiable voting is turning voters and election officials into quality control agents for the e-voting industry. The problem is further exacerbated when computerized voting systems are privately owned and controlled by corporations claiming proprietary trade secrecy for the software counting our votes. Despite the inherently false premise of verifiable voting, it has become the clarion call for twenty-first century election reform, as Congress, the Election Assistance Commission, and activists have all jumped on board.

In addition, many reformers would willingly exchange touch screen voting machines for optical scanners using voter marked paper ballots. But optical scan technology, like touch screens, keeps the count secret. Although they use real paper ballots, optical scanners, with their proprietary, black box computer counts, turn public votes into privatized election data. Corporate controlled, trade secret optical scanners, like their touch screen brothers, fail the test for democratic elections.

THE MAGICAL BREW OF HAVA'S ELECTION ASSISTANCE COMMISSION

In 2007, the HAVA-created EAC released its vision for America's elections: the "Voluntary Voting System Guidelines" (VVSG).[8] The recommendations in the 2007 VVSG (which was a complete rewrite of the guidelines from 2005) include "software independent" voting systems (dual systems so the same software doesn't mark *and* count the ballot), and even goes so far as to suggest completely *paperless* verifiable systems, where one computer will check (verify) another. In the EAC paperless verifiable voting scheme, the voter is so incidental as to completely disappear, as the ultimate goal is to enable and promulgate technology-based voting systems. Accordingly, the EAC's principal recommendation addressing voter needs is for large print signage reminding voters to verify their voting machine's vote.

The EAC's power is further amplified in the uncomfortable confluence of the Commission and federal law. A 2007 version of the controversial election reform proposal known as HR 811, aka the Holt Bill (and its companion bills in the Senate, sponsored by Senators Nelson and Feinstein) is a perfect example of this.[9] Hidden within sixty-two pages of convoluted language, HR 811 mandates new, complex and expensive technology for every polling jurisdiction in the nation. This odd provision did not come out of nowhere, however: it came straight out of the EAC's 2005 VVSG.

With the industry designing its voting systems to EAC specifications, and Congress putting those specifications into federal law, instead of publicly owned, observable elections, we are getting complex, corporate-owned, voting computers controlled by private interests.

RESTORING DEMOCRACY IN AMERICA: PAPER BALLOTS

Democratic elections demand that we ask, for each proffered election reform, does it enable citizen oversight? Does it enable checks and balances? None of the corporate-controlled, privatized reforms meet these standards. With black box technologies and claims of trade secrecy, it is a stretch to say they can even provide verifiable voting, although that is the illusion under which they are sold to the American public.

In contrast, hand counted paper ballot elections offer an observable, reliable, accurate, and secure election system. Some say that moving from technology-based elections to hand count elections is going backwards, but this method is in fact best when considered in the context of democratic elections. In hand count elections, people manage the process, the paper, the numbers, and the people. With the right methodology and management in place, election costs come down as integrity goes up. With a two to four person team, you have built-in double checks on every count, every tally mark, every contest, every ballot. This is a self-authenticating system; combined with accessible hand recounts, there is no need for the complex and expensive audit protocols suggested for computerized elections.

Many election officials are afraid that if they give up their machines, they won't have enough help to count the ballots, or they will have the "wrong" kind of people. But our communities are filled with the "right" kind of people. We just need to reach out to them.

Every city and town has community organizations: church groups, rotary clubs and neighborhood watch groups are just a few that come to mind. Walter Holland, an election official in Lyndeborough, New Hampshire, reflects on this kind of community outreach:

"All of these [hand counters] are local volunteers, they are neighbors in our community, and it's important that they handle the votes of their neighbors, because it's sacred. It's an important thing to be able to vote in a democracy, and you handle each one of those votes with care, and you count it as best you can."[10]

While New Hampshire has a high percentage of ballots counted by computerized optical scanners, it still retains a stubborn tradition of grassroots democracy, with community members volunteering to help out at the polls, often refusing financial compensation. In addition, New Hampshire's publicly observable manual recounts are accessible and financially feasible. The official *New Hampshire Election Procedure Manual* states that:

> Anyone can come and watch the casting of ballots and the counting of ballots and see for himself or herself whether the election is conducted in accordance with the law . . . The public trust in elections, sometimes referred to as the legitimacy of elections, relies in part on elections being conducted in the open. [11]

Activists observing the community-based nature of New Hampshire elections have often remarked that "maybe democracy really does work in New Hampshire!" And truly, when ballots are hand counted, democracy *is* working, and becomes an integrated facet of community life. The only thing that can dispel the alchemy of transforming democratic elections into technological electoral illusion is a good solid dose of reality. Community based, hand counted paper ballot elections are about as real as you can get.

NOTES

1.Election Data Services, "69 Million Voters Will Use Optical Scan Ballots in 2006," 2006 Voting Equipment Study, February 6, 2006,
http://www.electiondataservices.com/EDSInc_VEStudy2006.pdf

2.Help America Vote Act of 2002 Public Law 107-252, http://www.fec.gov/hava/hava.htm

3. Wolf, Richard, "Legal Voters Thrown off Rolls," *USA Today*, January 2, 2008, http://www.usatoday.com/printedition/news/20080102/1a_lede02.art.htm

4. Jackson, Brooks,"Hanging Chads' often viewed by courts as sign of voter intent", CNN, November 16, 2000, http://archives.cnn.com/2000/ALLPOLI-TICS/stories/11/16/recount.chads/

5. Brace, Kimball, "2004 Election Day Survey: A Summary of Findings," September 7, 2005, Election Data Services, http://www.electiondataservices.com/home.htm.

6. Drinkard, Jim, "Panel Cites Poll Workers' Age as Problem, *USA Today*, August 9, 2004.

7. Help America Vote Act of 2002 Public Law 107-252, Section 301, http://www.fec.gov/hava/hava.htm

8. Unites States Election Assistance Commission. "TGDC Recommended Guidelines." http://www.eac.gov/vvsg

9. Election Defense Alliance, HR 811 Resource Page, http://www.election-defensealliance.org/hr_811_holt_bill_resource_page

10. Democracy for New Hampshire, "We're Counting the Votes Video: Lyndeborough, New Hampshire 2004 Part I and II", Online Video, November 2004, http://www.youtube.com/watch?v=SxZ0jCoH2BQ and http://www.youtube.com/watch?v=95GRMhotMOQ

11. New Hampshire Department of State, New Hampshire Election Procedure Manual 2006-2007, http://www.sos.nh.gov/FINALpercent20EPM-percent208-30-2006.pdf

THE DEPARTMENT
OF JUSTICE
WHISTLES "DIXIE"

★

STEVEN ROSENFELD

Jim Crow has returned to American elections, only in the twenty-first century, instead of men in white robes or a barrel-chested sheriff menacingly patrolling voting precincts, we are more likely to see a lawyer carrying a folder filled with briefing papers and proposed legislation about "voter fraud" and other measures to supposedly protect the sanctity of the vote.

Since the 2004 election, activist lawyers with ties to the Republican Party and its presidential campaigns, Republican legislators, and even the Supreme Court—in a largely unnoticed ruling in 2006—have been aggressively regulating most aspects of the voting process. Collectively, these efforts are undoing the gains of the civil right's era that brought voting rights to minorities and the poor, groups that tend to support Democrats.

In addition, the Department of Justice (DOJ), which for decades had fought to ensure that all eligible citizens could vote, now encourages states to take steps in the opposite direction. Political appointees who advocate for stringent requirements before ballots are cast and votes are counted have driven much of the DOJ's Voting Section's recent agenda. As a result, the Department has pushed states to purge voter lists, and to adopt newly restrictive voter ID and provisional ballot laws. In addition, during most of George W. Bush's tenure, the DOJ has stopped enforcing federal laws designed to aid registration, such as the requirement that state welfare offices offer public aid recipients the opportunity to register to vote.

The Department's political appointees have also pressured federal prosecutors to pursue "voter fraud" cases against the Bush administration's perceived opponents, such as ACORN (Association of Community Organizations for Reform Now), which conduct mass registration drives among populations that tend to vote Democratic. Two former federal prosecutors have said they believe that they lost their positions for refusing to pursue these cases.[1]

The proponents of this renewed impetus to police voters comes from a powerful and well-connected wing of the Republican Party that believes steps are needed to protect elections from Democratic-leaning groups that are fabricating voter registrations en masse and impersonating voters. Royal Masset, the former political director of the Republican Party of Texas, said in 2007 that is an "article of religious faith that voter fraud is causing us to lose elections." While Masset himself didn't agree with that assertion, he did believe "that requiring photo IDs could cause enough of a drop off in legitimate Democratic voting to add 3 percent to the Republican vote."[2]

While voter fraud and voter suppression have a long history in American politics, registration abuses and instances of people voting more than once are rare today, as federal officials convicted only twenty-four people of illegal voting between 2002 and 2005. Moreover, modern voter fraud, when it occurs, has involved partisans from both parties, although it is rarely on a scale that overturns elections. In contrast, new voter registration restrictions, such as requiring voters to show a government-issued photo ID, are of a scale that can affect election outcomes. The Brennan Center for Justice at New York University Law

School has found that 25% of adult African-Americans, 15% of adults earning below $35,000 annually, and 18% of seniors over sixty-five do not possess government-issued photo ID.[3] While various studies—such as a 2006 Election Assistance Commission report by Tova Andrea Wang and Job Serebrov, and a 2007 study by Lorraine Minnite of Barnard College—have found modern claims of a voter fraud "crisis" to be unfounded, that has not stopped states from adopting remedies that impose burdens across their electorate and on voter registration organizations.

"Across the country, voter identification laws have become a partisan mess," Loyola University Law Professor Richard Hasen said in an Oct. 24, 2006 *Slate.com* column, speaking of one such remedy. "Republican-dominated legislatures have been enacting voter identification laws in the name of preventing fraud, and Democrats have opposed such laws in the name of protecting potentially disenfranchised voters."[4] Hasen was commenting on a little-noticed 2006 Supreme Court ruling, *Purcell v. Gonzales*, which upheld Arizona's new voter ID law. The court unanimously affirmed the state's 2004 law, writing that, "Voter fraud drives honest citizens out of the democratic process and breeds distrust of our government. Voters who fear their legitimate votes will be outweighed by fraudulent ones will feel disenfranchised."

Hasen said that while the ruling "seem[ed] reasonable enough" at first glance, it actually was deeply troubling, as the Court never investigated if there was evidence of widespread voter fraud, and never examined "how onerous are such [voter ID] laws." Instead, it adopted the Republican rhetoric on the issue "without any proof whatsoever." Hasen then quoted Harvard University History Professor Alexander Keyssar on the Court's rationale. "FEEL disenfranchised? Is that the same as 'being disenfranchised?' So if I might 'feel' disenfranchised, I have a right to make it harder for you to vote? What on Earth is going on here?"

"WHAT ON EARTH IS GOING ON HERE?"

"These things have become partisan," Democratic California Representative Juanita Millender-McDonald replied at a March 2005 congressional field hearing when asked why she and others in Congress had come to Ohio to investigate the 2004 election. "Images are so critical, especially when the stakes are high and stakes are high in presidential elections," the now-deceased congresswoman continued, referring to the lingering memory of thousands of African-Americans waiting for hours outside in a cold rain to vote the previous November in Ohio's inner cities. Many elected Democrats and voting rights attorneys saw the delays as intentional voter suppression resulting from partisan election administration. To some, it stirred memories of the segregated south.

Cleveland Democratic Congresswoman Stephanie Tubbs Jones, who six weeks earlier had stood with California Democratic Senator Barbara Boxer to contest Ohio's 2004 Electoral College votes, was also present at the hearing, and had several testy exchanges with Ohio's Republican Secretary of State Kenneth Blackwell over his administration of the election. One particular exchange concerned how Blackwell had spent millions of dollars for advertisements that neglected to tell Ohioans where else they could go to vote if they were delayed at their own polling place—a small but telling example of election administration with partisan implications:

> **Ms. Tubbs Jones:** In this ad you said, "Vote your precinct," but you never told them that if they couldn't vote in precinct, they could go to the Board of Elections and vote. Did you, sir?
> **Secretary Blackwell:** I sure didn't.
> **Ms. Tubbs Jones:** Excuse me?
> **Secretary Blackwell:** Can't you hear? I said I sure didn't.[5]

But while Democrats like Tubbs Jones were looking back at 2004, Republicans were looking ahead at shaping the future electorate to their advantage. The hearing was notable because it signaled the start of a renewed Republican campaign to highlight "voter fraud" as an issue needing legislative redress. The assertions and responses that unfolded that day would be heard in many states in 2005 and 2006 as GOP-majority legislatures "dealt" with the issue. Ohio Republican Representative Kevin DeWine spoke of a proposed voter ID law—which would later pass—and suggested that the Legislature's concern was not whether the law would pass, but how tough it should be. The state also added strict new rules for mass voter registration drives early in 2005, which were overturned in federal court in February 2008, and later passed a bill facilitating Election Day challenges to individual voters. Ohio Republican State Senator Jeff Jacobson said that these laws were needed to stop "fraudulent registrations" because national groups "are paid to come in and end up registering Mickey Mouse . . . The millions of dollars that poured in, in an attempt to influence Ohio, is not normal."[6]

What Jacobson said was true, though lacking in context. Groups like ACORN and Americans Coming Together had registered millions of new voters in battleground states before the 2004 election, and some of ACORN's staff—i.e. temporary workers—had filed a handful of registration forms with fabricated names. ACORN discovered the error, alerted the authorities and prosecutions ensued. While those mistakes were cited by politicians like Jacobson as evidence of a national voter fraud crisis, others, such as Norman Robbins, a Case Western University professor and co-coordinator of the Greater Cleveland Voter Coalition, urged the House panel to look at the facts and keep the issue in perspective:

"We desperately need research on all of the issues raised today," he said. "For instance, what are the real causes and effects of the long lines? How many voters were actually disenfranchised? How long did they take to vote? That would be one set of questions. Does showing an ID increase the reliability of the vote or does it disenfranchise people? Those are answerable questions. How many people truly have been convicted of election fraud? What do we really know about this in terms of cases and conditions."[7]

To answer those questions, the committee chairman, Republican Bob Ney—who has since been convicted and jailed on bribery charges—turned to a long-time Republican operative, Mark "Thor" Hearne, who introduced himself as an "advocate of voter rights and an attorney experienced in election law." Hearne, a lawyer based in St. Louis, certainly was experienced. In 2000, he had worked for the Bush campaign in Florida during the presidential recount. He was also the Vice President of Election Education for the Republican National Lawyers Association, which helps the party train partisan poll monitors. In 2004, he became counsel to the Bush-Cheney campaign, where he "worked with White House presidential advisor Karl Rove and the Republican National Committee to identify potential voting fraud in battleground states . . . and oversaw more than 65 different lawsuits that concerned the outcome of the election."[8] After 2004, "with encouragement from Rove and the White House, Hearne founded the American Center for Voting Rights (ACVR), which represented itself as a nonpartisan watchdog group looking for voting fraud." The group would go on to urge federal and state officials to prosecute voter fraud, adopt tougher voter ID laws and purge voter rolls. It would also file legal briefs in voter ID cases, urging tighter regulations.

Hearne presented the panel with a report suggesting that fraudulent registrations were threatening U.S. elections. The report listed problems in Ohio cities with sizeable African-

American populations—the state's Democratic strongholds. Nationally, ACVR would use the same approach to identify other voter fraud "hot spots."

A NATIONAL PATTERN

Though the facts were slim, Republicans across the country acted as if a voter fraud crisis was rampant. As a result, Republican-controlled legislatures in Georgia, Indiana, Missouri, Pennsylvania and Wisconsin passed new voter ID requirements after the 2004 election, although gubernatorial vetoes or court orders nullified these laws in every state except for Indiana. (In January 2008, the Supreme Court heard a challenge to Indiana's voter ID law.) Meanwhile, two states with Republican-majority legislatures—Florida and Ohio—made voter registration drives more difficult by raising penalties for errors on registration forms, as well as shortening the timeline for organizers to submit these forms—which prevents these groups from checking the registrations for accuracy and completeness. Litigation and court rulings reversed those laws before the 2006 election, but not before the League of Women Voters was forced to halt registration drives in Florida for the first time in the group's 75-year history. In Ohio, where ACORN was registering approximately 5,000 new voters per week, those efforts were suspended during the litigation, meaning an estimated 30,000 people were not given the opportunity to register.

Since 2004, five other states have imposed new restrictions on voter registration drives— Colorado, Georgia, Maryland, New Mexico and Missouri—according to research by Project Vote, which has worked with the Brennan Center for Justice to challenge these laws. To date, these laws still remain on the books in Missouri and New Mexico. "It's no secret who these restrictions affect," wrote Michael Slater, Project Vote's deputy director, in the October 2007 issue of *The National Voter*, a publication of the League of Women Voters. "In 2004, 15 percent of all African-American and Latino voters were registered to vote as a result of an organized drive; an African-American or Latino voter was 65 percent more likely to have been registered to vote by an organized drive than a White voter. In the final analysis, spurious allegations of voter fraud give rise to yet more roadblocks on the path to full participation in political life for historically disadvantaged Americans."[9]

These state-level responses to voter fraud did not occur in a vacuum. Since the creation of the Civil Rights Division of the Justice Department a half-century ago, the federal government has had great power and influence over how states implement voting rights. But by early 2005, the same mindset shared by GOP legislators in Ohio and other states, and by vote fraud activists like Hearne, could also be found among the Bush administration's senior appointees overseeing voting rights at the DOJ.

Just four days before the 2004 election, the Department's civil rights chief, Assistant Attorney General Alex Acosta, wrote to a federal judge in Cincinnati who was deciding whether to allow the Ohio Republican Party to challenge the credentials of 23,000 mostly African-American voters. Acosta supported the voter challenges, saying an order to block them could undermine the enforcement of state and federal voting laws. The challenges, Acosta wrote, "help strike a balance between ballot access and ballot integrity."[10] The voter challenges were allowed to go forward, although the final judicial ruling came too late for Ohio's Republican Party to deploy thousands of party members to local precincts to challenge voter credentials.

Another sign of the Department's shift from its historic mission of enfranchising voters to a new "selective enforcement" mindset could also be seen by 2005 when a coalition of voting rights groups failed to convince the Department to enforce the law that requiring states to offer welfare recipients the opportunity to register to vote. "In January 2005, we had a 10-year report, which documented the 59 percent decline [in registrations] from 1995 through 2004," said Scott Novakowski of the center-left think tank Demos. He added that many states, including Arizona, Connecticut, Florida, Massachusetts, Missouri, Montana, New Jersey, Pennsylvania and Tennessee, were ignoring the registration requirements for welfare recipients. "John Conyers [now the House Judiciary Committee chairman] and 29 other representatives asked Attorney General Alberto Gonzales to look into this, and there was no response."[11]

The political stakes in registering low-income voters are enormous. The Election Assistance Commission's biennial voter registration report for 2005-2006 found that while 16.6 million new registration applications were received by state motor vehicles agencies, only 527,752 applications came from public assistance offices—a 50 percent drop from 2003-2004.[12] As a result, in early 2005, voting rights groups met with the DOJ's top Voting Section officials—including Hans Von Spakovsky, counsel to the assistant attorney general overseeing the Voting Section, and Voting Section Chief Joseph Rich—to discuss enforcing the public assistance requirement. Von Spakovsky, like ACVR's Hearne, had worked for Bush in Florida during the 2000 recount and was among a handful of GOP appointees who were established "vote fraud" activists. Rich, a Civil Rights Division attorney for thirty-seven years, had been chief of the Voting Section for six years when he resigned in April 2005, citing politicization of voting rights enforcement.

Rich recalled the meeting about the voter registration requirements, saying that Von Spakovsky—who had become his de facto boss—decided to ignore that part of the law, and instead focus on one line in the statute that allowed the Justice Department to pressure states to purge voter rolls. "Four months before I left, in 2005, Von Spakovsky held a meeting where he said he wanted to start an initiative for states we want to purge . . . Their priority was to purge, not to register voters . . . To me, it was a very clear view of the Republican agenda . . . to make it harder to vote: purge voters and don't register voters."[13]

THE BUSH ADMINISTRATION VOTING SECTION

Rich was one of a number of career attorneys at the DOJ Voting Section who resigned because pressure from the Bush administration had altered the agency's historic civil rights mission. Between 2005 and 2007, 55 percent of the attorneys in the Voting Section left, according to a report by NYU's Brennan Center and the Lawyers' Committee for Civil Rights Under Law, which cited, among other things, a "partisan hiring process," "altered performance evaluations" and "political retaliation on the job."[14] The shift in enforcement philosophy did not go unnoticed. In July 2006, *The Boston Globe* reported that the Civil Rights Division had turned away from hiring lawyers with civil rights movement backgrounds. Of the nineteen attorneys hired since 2003, *The Globe* reported, eleven were members of the conservative Federalist Society, Republican National Lawyers Association, or had volunteered for Bush-Cheney campaigns.[15] Moreover, the Voting Section had virtually stopped filing suits on behalf of minority voters. Wade Henderson, president of the Leadership Conference on Civil Rights, told the House Judiciary Committee on March 22, 2007 that, "The Voting Section did not file any cases on behalf of African-American voters during a five-year period between 2001 and 2006," adding that, "no cases have been brought on behalf of Native American voters for the entire administration." While the Justice Department had all but stopped filing lawsuits on behalf of Native and African-Americans, the Voting Section had more than doubled the number of lawsuits seeking to enforce the providing of bilingual ballots and election materials in Latino and Asian communities, constituencies that were seen as likely Republican swing votes, particularly after the GOP made electoral gains among Latinos in 2004.

That the administration's appointees overseeing voting rights would politicize the Voting Section should have surprised no one. Early in Bush's first term, conservative publications like the *National Journal* were clamoring for wholesale changes in the Civil Rights Division. "There may be no part of the federal government where liberalism is more deeply entrenched," the *Journal's* John Miller wrote on May 6, 2002.[16] "Keeping ineligible voters off registration lists is the first step in limiting fraud," wrote Von Spakovsky in a 1997 Georgia Public Policy Foundation article, where he described various scenarios where he believed Democratic partisans were "sending imposters to vote, to request absentee ballots, or to otherwise generate fraudulent votes."[17] In July 2001, Von Spakovsky began his testimony on "election reform" before the Senate Rules Committee by stating that, "One of the biggest threats to voter rights and election integrity today is the condition of our voter registration rolls. Many jurisdictions now have more registered names on their voter rolls than they have voting age population within their borders. This is an invitation to fraud and chaos since the many invalid and multiple registrations that exist can serve as a source pool for fraud."

According to a Brennan Center and Lawyers' Committee for Civil Rights Under Law report, there were four "connected pieces of strategy" to politicize the enforcement of voting rights by the Department of Justice from 2004 through 2007: "fomenting fear of voter fraud;" "dismantling the infrastructure of Justice;" "restricting registration and voting;" and "politically motivated prosecutions."[18] According to the report, from 2003 to 2005, the Voting Rights Section:

- Sent Maryland a letter before the 2004 presidential election saying that the state could reject voter registrations that did not match information on other state databases. That "no-vote, no-match" standard has been criticized as being too strict, due to typos and data-entry errors.

- Pre-cleared congressional redistricting in Texas in mid-decade, instead of waiting for the once-a-decade census report, as has been the standard practice. The Department must approve election law changes in states and counties under jurisdiction of the Voting Rights Act. The Texas redistricting case was seen as leading to the election of four Republican House candidates in 2004. In 2006, the Supreme Court issued a decision upholding parts of that redistricting plan.
- Argued that individual citizens have no right to private action—or the ability to sue to seek redress—under HAVA. That right has been a key component of the Voting Rights Act of 1965, leading citizens to file numerous suits such as one in 2006 by African-American voters in Columbus, Ohio, whose precincts did not receive the same per capita number of voting machines as nearby white suburbs.
- Pre-cleared a new Georgia photo ID law, even though the section's career attorneys recommended rejecting it. The courts later nullified the law, comparing it to imposing a "poll tax" due to costs associated with obtaining the required government photo ID. The state has since modified the law, relaxing the ID standard.
- Issued an opinion saying provisional ballots could not be given to people who lacked ID. The ballots were created by HAVA to ensure that people who are not on voter rolls could vote, though registrations of those voters must be verified before counting the ballots. The section also said it was okay to cast but not count provisional ballots.
- Tried to pressure the Election Assistance Commission to change its decision on Arizona's voter

ID law, which requires residents to provide proof of
U.S. citizenship when registering to vote. Arizona
wanted the EAC to add the citizenship requirement
to a national voter registration form. The EAC did
not grant Arizona's request, despite supporting e-
mails from Von Spakofsky.

• Filed the first of a half-dozen lawsuits forcing states
to purge voter rolls. Only Missouri fought the suit,
which it later won, though the Justice Department
is appealing that ruling. U.S. District Court Judge
Nanette K. Laughrey wrote in her decision that, "It
is . . . telling that the United States has not shown
that any Missouri resident was denied his or her right
to vote as a result of the deficiencies alleged by the
United States. Nor has the United States shown that
any voter fraud has occurred." New Jersey, Indiana,
and Maine were also sued by the Department and
reached consent decrees—settlements—that included
voter purges.

These actions were all part of a growing crescendo of enforcement
actions with political overtones leading up to the 2006 election.

TURNING TOWARD 2008

As the country approaches the 2008 election, it is an open question how the GOP's ballot security strategies will affect voting in
the battleground states. As in any election, there are a handful of
unknowns that could have a major impact. The Supreme Court,
for example, will decide whether Indiana's voter ID law, seen as
one of the country's toughest, places an unconstitutional burden
on low-income people and minority voters. Meanwhile, in states
where immigration is a hot-button issue, Arizona's efforts to add a
proof of citizenship requirement to the national voter registration

form will be closely watched. Under that state's Proposition 200, which passed in 2004, residents must show proof of citizenship before registering to vote or receiving public assistance. Maricopa County, where Phoenix is located, is now rejecting 30 percent of all new registrations due to inadequate proof of citizenship, according to Jeff Blum of USAction. Since Proposition 200 was implemented in 2005, more than 32,000 voter registrations have been rejected.[19] Meanwhile, in January 2008, the Texas Legislature began consideration of a new voter ID law.

Similarly, efforts by states to comply with HAVA by creating statewide voter lists pose an entirely new set of election administration issues. Since 2000, most states have been struggling to transition to a new generation of electronic voting systems. These paperless systems have been criticized for being unreliable, potentially inaccurate, and accessible to hackers. While some states have moved to restrict the use of these machines, the creation of statewide voter databases—a part of these systems—has not been as widely scrutinized. In some states, officials have instituted strict name-matching requirements to verify the accuracy of voter registrations. Whether typos or other data entry errors will mistakenly remove legal voters—as was the case in California in 2005—remains to be seen, although Florida recently joined a handful of states, including Washington, where litigation rolled back strict name-matching standards that were disenfranchising legal voters.

Another large unknown concerns voter purges. In April 2007, the Justice Department sent letters to the top election administrators in ten states—Iowa, Massachusetts, Mississippi, Nebraska, North Carolina, Rhode Island, South Dakota, Texas, Utah and Vermont—to pressure them to purge their voter rolls. Former Voting Section attorneys and others said the statistics cited by the Justice Department in the purge letter were flawed and did not confirm that those states had more voter registrations than eligible voters, as the department alleged. "That data does not say what they purport it says," said David Becker, senior voting rights counsel for People for the American Way and a former Voting Section senior trial attorney, after reviewing the data cited in the Justice Department's letter. "This stuff disenfranchises voters . . . There are eligible voters who will be removed. There is no evidence that rolls need to be cleaned up to this degree. This will make things more chaotic on Election Day. People will be given provisional ballots that won't get counted."[20]

Looking toward the 2008 election, it appears the purges—as well as the new voter ID laws, restrictions on registration drives and stricter rules for counting provisional ballots—could be a new and legal way to accomplish a longstanding GOP electoral tactic: thinning the ranks of likely Democratic voters. In numerous elections dating back to the 1960s, the Republican Party has tried to challenge new voter registrations to accomplish this goal, although since 1981 federal courts have blocked some of those efforts as illegal electioneering.

"Until the mid-1960s, the political entity most closely associated with efforts to disenfranchise people of color was the southern wing of the Democratic Party," wrote Rice University Sociology Professor Chandler DavidsonChandler Davidson and several graduate students in a paper titled, "Republican Ballot Security Programs: Vote Protection or Minority Voter Suppression—Or Both?" However, the passage of civil rights laws in the early 1960s prompted some Republicans to appeal to southern Democrats who supported the Jim Crow system. Part of that political sea change was that the Republican Party adopted some of the voter suppression tactics used by southern Democrats. Indeed, the debate and remedies framed by the GOP's contemporary "voter fraud" activists comes from this same political lineage:

"There are several noteworthy characteristics of these programs. They focus on minority precincts almost exclusively. There is often only the flimsiest evidence that voter fraud is likely to be perpetrated in such precincts. In addition to encouraging the presence of sometimes intimidating Republican poll watchers or challengers who may slow down voting lines and embarrass potential voters by asking them humiliating questions, these programs have sometimes posted people in official-looking uniforms with badges and side arms who question voters about their citizenship or their registration. In addition, warning signs may be posted near the polls, or radio ads may be targeted to minority listeners containing dire threats of prison terms for people who are not properly registered—messages that seem designed to put minority voters on the defensive."[21]

Will this history of vote suppression tactics repeat itself during the 2008 presidential election? While the Democrats are not saints when it comes to voter suppression—recall how John Kerry's supporters disqualified signatories to Ralph Nader's presidential petitions in 2004—they do not have the same kind of vote suppression apparatus in place as the Republicans do. Indeed, it appears that Republicans are already following Chandler Davidson's inventory by seeking to regulate the voting process well before the 2008 election. The tactics that can be implemented well before the voting begins—stricter voter ID laws, voter purges, registration drive curbs, tougher provisional ballot laws and easing rules for voter challenges—are already underway in several states.

NOTES

1. Manu Raju, "Attorney Probe Deepens," *The Hill*, January 22, 2008.

2. Kristen Mack, "In Trying to Win, has Dewhurst Lost a Friend?" *Houston Chronicle*, May 17, 2007.

3. The Brennan Center for Justice at NYU Law School, "Analysis and Reports: Voter Fraud Resources," http://www.truthaboutfraud.org/analysis_reports/

4. Richard Hasen, "Election Deform: The Supreme Court Messes Up Election Law. Again," Slate.com, October 26, 2006, http://www.slate.com/id/2152116/

5. House Committee on Administration field hearing, Columbus, Ohio, 109th Cong., *Congressional Record*, March 21, 2005.

6. Ibid.

7. Ibid.

8. Murray Waas, "The Scales of Justice," *National Journal*, May 31, 2007.

9. Michael Slater, "Voter Fraud?" *The National Voter*, October 2007.

10. Greg Gordon, "Ex-Justice official accused of aiding scheme to scratch minority voters," *McClatchy Newspapers*, June 25, 2007.

11. Author interview.

12. U.S. Election Assistance Commission, "The Impact of the National Voter Registration Act of 1993 on the Administration of Elections for Federal Office 2005-2006," June 30, 2007.

13. Author interview.

14. The Brennan Center for Justice at NYU Law School and Lawyers Committee for Civil Rights Under Law, "*Using Justice To Suppress The Vote*," Powerpoint presentation at The National Press Club, Washington, D.C., June 7, 2007.

15. Charlie Savage, "Civil Rights Hiring Shifted in Bush Era," *Boston Globe*, July 23, 2006.

16. John J. Miller, "Fort Liberalism: Can Justice's civil rights division be Bushified?" *National Journal*, May 6, 2002.

17. Hans A. Von Spakovsky, "Voter Fraud: Protecting the Integrity of Our Democratic System," Issue Brief, Georgia Public Policy Foundation, Inc., 1997.

18. The Brennan Center for Justice at NYU Law School and Lawyers Committee for Civil Rights Under Law, ibid.

19. Author interview.

20. Author interview.

21. Chandler Davidson, Tanya Dunlap, Gale Kenny, Benjamin Wise, "Republican Ballot Security Programs: Vote Protection or Minority Voter Suppression – Or Both: A Report to the Center for Minority Voting Rights and Protection," September 2004.

A 12-STEP PROGRAM
TO SAVE U.S. DEMOCRACY

★

MARK CRISPIN MILLER

Certainly the outlook for democracy seems pretty bleak—and how could it be otherwise? The surest way to make a problem worse is to pretend it isn't there, which is exactly what our press and politicians have been doing; and the rest is, unfortunately, history. But history can be changed, as We the People have continually learned, from our refusal of colonial subjection, to our (partial) establishment as a democratic republic, to the abolition of slavery, to the enfranchisement of women, to the end of formal segregation and the passage of the Voting Rights Act. After that, our progress seemed to stop, and it must now resume: for history *can* be changed, and for the better, but only through our own unbreakable commitment to, and action for, enlightened policies for the renewal of our democracy. Based squarely on America's first principles, such policies would not be wholly new, however revolutionary they must sound in these bad, backward times. As it was certain policies that got us into this horrific situation, certain other policies can get us out.

The fact is that We the People are in lousy shape, and must get straight as soon as possible. For we are all addicted to the horse race—and we can't win, because it's fixed. And so, before we end up losing everything, we need to pull ourselves together, face the music, and then take all necessary steps to change the tune.

1. Repeal the Help America Vote Act (HAVA)
This step will inevitably follow an in-depth investigation of how HAVA came to be.

2. Replace *all* electronic voting with hand-counted paper ballots (HCPB)
Although politicians and the press dismiss this idea as utopian, the people would support it just as overwhelmingly as national health care, strong environmental measures, withdrawal from Iraq, and other sane ideas.

3. Get rid of computerized voter rolls
It isn't just the e-voting machines that are obstructing our self-government. According to *USA Today*, thousands of Americans have had their names mysteriously purged from the electronic databases now used nationwide as records of our registration.

4. Keep all private vendors out of our elections
With their commercial interests, trade secrets and unaccountable proceedings, private companies should have no role in the essential process of republican self-government.

5. Make it illegal for the TV networks to declare who won before the vote-count is complete
Certainly the corporate press will scream about its First Amendment Rights, but they don't have the right to interfere with our elections. When they declare a winner before even know if the election was legitimate, they pre-define all audits, recounts and even first counts of the vote as the mere desperate measures of "sore losers."

6. Set up an exit polling system, publicly supported, to keep the vote-counts honest
Only in America are exit poll results not meant to help us gauge

the accuracy of the official count. Here are they are meant only to allow the media to make its calls.

7. Get rid of voter registration rules, by allowing every citizen to register, at any post office, on his/her 18th birthday

Either we believe in universal suffrage or we don't.

8. Ban all state requirements for state-issued ID's at the polls

As the Supreme Court smiles on such Jim Crow devices, we need a law, or Constitutional amendment, to forbid them.

9. Put all polling places under video surveillance, to spot voter fraud, monitor election personnel, and track the turnout

We're under surveillance everywhere else, so why not?

10. Have Election Day declared a federal holiday, requiring all employers to allow their workers time to vote

No citizens of the United States should ever lost the right to vote because they have to go to work.

11. Make it illegal for Secretaries of State to co-chair political campaigns (or otherwise assist or favor them)

Katherine Harris wore both those hats in Florida in 2000, and, four years later, so did Ken Blackwell in Ohio and Jan Brewer in Arizona. Such Republicans should not have been allowed to do it, nor should any Democrats.

12. Make election fraud a major felony, with life imprison-men—and disenfranchisement—for all repeat offenders

"Three strikes and you're out" would certainly befit so serious a crime against democracy.

CONTRIBUTORS

★

Larisa Alexandrovna is the managing editor of Investigative News for *The Raw Story* (rawstory.com), and contributes opinion and columns to online publications such as Alternet. She is also a blogger at *The Huffington Post* and at her own journalism blog, at-Largely (www.atlargely.com).

Michael Collins reports and comments on U.S. elections, voting rights, and broader social justice concerns. His March 2007 series, "Fried Federal Prosecutors and Election Fraud" was an early outline of the national scandal exposing the Justice Department's political influence on elections. Recently, he focused national attention on the illegal destruction of ballots from the 2004 Ohio presidential election.

Lance deHaven-Smith is a professor of Public Administration and Policy at Florida State University. He is the author of fifteen books on topics ranging from religion and political philosophy to Florida government and politics. His most recent book is *The Battle for Florida*, which analyzes the disputed 2000 presidential election.

Bob Fitrakis is the editor of the Free Press (www.freepress.org), and a political science professor in the Social and Behavioral Sciences Department at Columbus State Community College. He has a PhD in Political Science from Wayne State University in Detroit, Michigan and a J.D. from The Ohio State University Moritz College of Law. He co-authored *What Happened in Ohio? A Documentary Record of Theft and Fraud in the 2004 election*, and has authored or co-authored ten other books. Fitrakis has won eleven investigative journalism awards from the Cleveland Press Club, Project Censored, and the Ohio Society of Professional Journalists, among others.

Brad Friedman is an investigative citizen journalist/blogger, political commentator and broadcaster. He is the creator and managing editor of The BRAD BLOG (http://www.Bradblog. com) as well as a frequent contributor to *The Huffington Post*. He has also written articles and editorials for *Mother Jones*, *Editor & Publisher*, *Computer World*, the *Columbus Free Press*, Salon.com, TruthOut.org, Harvard's Nieman Foundation of Journalism and *Hustler*.

David L. Griscom completed his Ph.D. at Brown University in 1966 and after a brief post-doc headed for Washington, DC, where he became employed as a Research Physicist at the Naval Research Laboratory (NRL) until his retirement in 2001. Griscom's research ultimately garnered him Fellowship in the American Physical Society and several national and international awards. During the 2004-2005 academic year, he was appointed adjunct professor of Materials Science and Engineering at the University of Arizona. He now resides with his wife Catherine in San Carlos, Sonora, México.

James H. Gundlach is a professor emeritus of sociology at Auburn University. He earned his PhD from the University of Texas at Austin in 1976 and spent his full postgraduate career at Auburn. He has authored or co-authored more than twenty refereed publications. In retirement, he works on developing statistical procedures to detect manipulation of election returns and consults as an expert witness to identify and measure under-representation of minorities on juries.

Jean Kaczmarek has been an election reform activist since November 3, 2004. She has also worked in the fields of writing, communications and public affairs on in radio and TV. Jean has lived in DuPage County, Illinois for twenty years and is the mother of two teenagers.

Robert F. Kennedy, Jr. is president of The Waterkeeper Alliance. He is also a clinical professor and supervising attorney at Pace University School of Law's Environmental Litigation Clinic and is co-host of "Ring of Fire" on Air America Radio. Earlier in his career, he served as assistant district attorney in New York City. He has worked on several political campaigns, including the presidential campaigns of Edward M. Kennedy in 1980, Al Gore in 2000 and John Kerry in 2004. Among Mr. Kennedy's published books are the *New York Times*' bestseller *Crimes Against Nature (2004), St. Francis of Assisi: A Life of Joy (2005), The Riverkeepers* (1997), and *Judge Frank M. Johnson, Jr: A Biography* (1977). His articles have appeared in *The New York Times, The Washington Post, Los Angeles Times, The Wall Street Journal, Newsweek, Rolling Stone, Atlantic Monthly, Esquire, The Nation, Outside* Magazine, The *Village Voice*, and many other publications.

Paul Lehto practiced law in Washington State for twelve years, specializing in business law and consumer fraud, including, most recently, election law. He is now a clean elections advocate. His forthcoming book is tentatively titled *Defending Democracy*.

David W. Moore is a full-time writer and polling consultant. From 1993 until 2006, he worked for The Gallup Poll, first as managing editor and then senior editor. Prior to joining Gallup, he was a professor of Political Science at the University of New Hampshire, where he taught from 1972 to 1993. He was also Director of the University of New Hampshire Survey Center, which he founded in 1975. Moore recently completed his second two-year term on the governing council of the American Association for Public Opinion Research (AAPOR), the foremost organization of public opinion pollsters in the country. He is the author of *How to Steal an Election: The Inside Story of How George Bush's Brother and FOX Network Miscalled the 2000 Election and Changed the Course of History* and *The Superpollsters: How They Measure and Manipulate Public Opinion in America*. Moore has published numerous articles in academic journals, newspapers, books, and magazines, including *Public Opinion Quarterly*, the *New York Times*, *Foreign Policy*, the *American Political Science Review*, the *Journal of Politics*, *Public Perspective*, and the *Boston Globe*. He lives in New Hampshire.

Bruce O'Dell is an information technology consultant who applies his broad technical expertise to his work as an election integrity activist. In the aftermath of the 2004 election, O'Dell co-founded U.S. Count Votes, a volunteer scientific research project to investigate the integrity and accuracy of American elections. He is currently affiliated with the Election Defense Alliance, a non-profit organization working to achieve transparent, secure, and accurate elections. He lives just outside Minneapolis, Minnesota, and shares a love of good books with his wife and their talkative cat.

Michael Richardson lives in Boston, where he writes about voting rights, election law, law enforcement, voting machines, and music. He is a former disability rights advocate and has served on the Nebraska Commission on Aging and the Illinois Human Rights Authority. He is a senior writer for *OpEdNews.com* and a feature writer for *Big City Rhythm & Blues* magazine, and is currently researching and writing about COINTELPRO and the Black Panthers.

Steven Rosenfeld is a Senior Fellow at *Alternet*, where he reports on election and democracy issues. Previously, he was executive producer of "RadioNation" with Laura Flanders. Before that, he was senior editor at *TomPaine.com*, where he wrote and edited commentaries, and researched their *New York Times* op-ads. In the late 1990s, he was one of two "Money, Power and Influence" reporters at National Public Radio. He has written or co-authored several books, including *What Happened in Ohio: A Documentary Record of Theft and Fraud in the 2004 Election*. He lives in San Francisco.

Jonathan Simon is a graduate of Harvard College and New York University School of Law and a member of the Bar of Massachusetts. He was a former political survey research analyst for Peter D. Hart Research Associates in Washington. Dr. Simon is a co-founder of the Election Defense Alliance (www.election-defensealliance.org), a national coordinating body for citizen electoral integrity groups and individuals, and has also worked cooperatively with other major election integrity organizations.

Nancy Tobi is legislative coordinator for the Election Defense Alliance and co-founder and former chair and website editor for Democracy for New Hampshire (www.democracyfornewhampshire.com). She is also chair of the New Hampshire Fair Elections Committee.

ABOUT THE EDITOR

Mark Crispin Miller is a professor of Media, Culture and Communication at New York University and a well-known public intellectual. His writings on film, television, propaganda, advertising and the culture industries have appeared in numerous journals and newspapers the world over, and on his blog News from Underground (markcrispinmiller.com). His show *A Patriot Act* ran at the New York Theater Workshop in the summer of 2004, with a film version released a few months later. He is the author of *Boxed In: The Culture of TV* (1998), *The Bush Dyslexicon: Observations on a National Disorder* (2001), *Cruel and Unusual: Bush/Cheney's New World Order* (2004), and *Fooled Again: The Real Case for Electoral Reform* (2005). He is currently at work on a book about the Marlboro Man for American Icons, a series that he edits for Yale University Press. He lives in New York City.